USING COMMUNICATION THEORY

USING COMMUNICATION THEORY

An Introduction to Planned Communication

Sven Windahl and
Benno H. Signitzer
with Jean T. Olson

SAGE Publications
London • Newbury Park • New Delhi

First published 1992

SAGE Publications Ltd
6 Bonhill Street
London EC2A 4PU

SAGE Publications Inc
2455 Teller Road
Newbury Park, California 91320

SAGE Publications India Pvt Ltd
32, M-Block Market
Greater Kailash – I
New Delhi 110 048

British Library Cataloguing in Publication Data

Windahl, Sven
  Using communication theory: An introduction to
  planned communication.
  I. Title II. Signitzer, Benno III. Olson, Jean
  302.23

  ISBN 0–8039–8430–8
  ISBN 0–8039–8431–6 pbk

Library of Congress catalog card number 91–50651

Typeset by Mayhew Typesetting, Rhayader, Powys
Printed in Great Britain by Biddles Ltd, Guildford,
Surrey

Contents

Preface

The purpose of this book is to provide an overview of theories for communication planning. We pursue two goals. First, we aim to familiarize practitioners working in the field of communication planning with the many theories that both communication scientists and practitioners have developed over the last two decades or so and which, so we shall argue, can be quite helpful to planners in the design, implementation, and evaluation of their projects. Second, we offer to the student of communications a first exposure to the often bewildering world of communication theory. The particular approach of the book should facilitate access and overcome some of the psychological obstacles vis-à-vis "theory" often experienced by beginning students. Frankly, we also expect communication students other than beginners to find the book worth while.

What, then, is our approach? We will attempt to relate communication theories to situations of communication planning work. Thus, the practitioner is informed about theories in a way that is designed to be "close" to his or her everyday work situation and experience. The student of communication, correspondingly, will find that "theory" is something that can and does have a very practical use.

The book can be used both as a textbook for the (mass) communication student and as a thought-provoking book that can inform the practitioner's work. It covers a wide range of theories, (nearly) all of which are illustrated by practical examples from communication planning – thus bringing home the point that the study of theories is not *l'art pour l'art*, an end in itself, but can serve very useful purposes. This, we believe, makes it unique as a communication theory textbook. And we know both from our own personal teaching experiences and from other communication teachers that there is a need for such a text.

We wish to extend our thanks to Stephen Barr and Nicola Harris of Sage for being such kind and competent editors; to the anonymous reviewers whose critical evaluations were particularly helpful; to Professor Everett M. Rogers for his comments on an early draft and his very specific advice; to our students in Sweden, Austria, Germany, and the United States who were exposed to the content of the book as it evolved and provided us with invaluable critical insights, and, above all, with the very rationale and motivation to bring the work to completion. We are also grateful for the economic support given to us by the Växjö University, Sweden, which made several trips between our three countries possible.

S.W.
B.S.
J.T.O.

1 Introduction

Communication planning is a broad and multi-faceted concept; it is used every day by thousands and thousands of people – by public relations practitioners, technical writers, information campaigners, advertising professionals, organization consultants, educators, health communicators, and many, many others. The term "communication planning" is probably less common than the activity it describes. That may have to do with a hesitancy to connect the notion of communication, which is thought of as being spontaneous in nature, with the idea of planning, which is usually associated with such concepts as "management," "control," and "strategy." In this book we shall argue that in order to achieve good results (for good causes), the two – communication and planning – must go hand in hand.

Theory and Practice

All communication planners use theories to guide their work. Often these are their own theories, based on their own experiences and on common practice. Many are unaware that formal research, both academic and non-academic, has generated a continuously growing body of theories applicable to planned communication. To some extent, these theories have gained their impetus from practical communication work.

There are several kinds of theory. McQuail's (1987) typology clarifies what we, for our part, mean by theory; he distinguishes four main categories: social scientific, normative, working, and commonsense.

Social scientific theory, which may be regarded as the most sophisticated type of theory for communication planning, is derived from work done according to scientific rules and methods. Most development of social scientific theories occurs in the context of a scientific community; these theories are characterized by their reliance on abstract concepts.

Normative theory tells us, based on values and ideological positions, how communication should be formed and function in certain cases. Normative theories for information and communication in, say, Great Britain, the Ivory Coast, and the People's Republic of China differ greatly; the working environments for communication planners in each country will, thus, be very different as well. Normative theories appear at other levels as well. A planner working in an organization may find that the organization views communication in certain normative ways: for example, communication should be conceived so as to enhance participation.

Working theory is both practical and normative. It instructs the practitioner on how to do communication planning to achieve a particular communication goal, according to communication theory often formalized by the practitioners themselves. For example, theory about communication networks in organizations, which may have its roots in observations of everyday work patterns, may help the communication planner use informal channels of communication more efficiently. In the same vein, an audience segmentation theory about lifestyles that originates in social science research can alert planners to consider certain traits of their readers, listeners, or viewers in creating messages.

Commonsense theory originates in our own experiences and guides us through everyday life, including the professional part of it. Communication planners cannot, even if they are committed to relying on scientific theory, escape from using this type of non-formalized theory. A problem for communication planners is that their work often is criticized by people using their commonsense theories and believing them to be as valid as scientific or well-grounded working theories. The professional communication planner, who may find this extremely frustrating, must recognize that the very nature of the knowledge base in communications does not command the same respect from the lay person as occurs in, for example, engineering. (We all consider ourselves communicators; few of us would pass ourselves off as builders of bridges.) On the other hand, the pay-off for this reliance on commonsense theories by the lay public at the expense of more rigorous scientific theory is a broadening of discussion and participation in the field. In many cases, this has led to testing that has validated a commonsense theory and added it to the body of social scientific theories.

As can be seen, these levels of theory are highly interconnected. Social scientific theory has been enriched by cross-overs from commonsense theory. On the other hand, the existence of a normative information theory in a given country, community, or organization may constrain the use of certain working theories or make impossible the testing and acceptance of a social scientific theory that runs counter to accepted theoretical precepts.

In this book, we shall dwell in the realm of social scientific and working theories. It is an explicit aim of the book to bring theory and practice together. Too often, theories and the applications they suggest are presented without such ambitions, leaving it unclear to the reader just what the links between the two are. We want to strongly emphasize that, used in the right way, theories have great practical value. The old saying, "There is nothing as practical as a good theory," could be used as the *Leitmotif* for this discussion.

The idea is to connect in a very literal sense the various communication theories with the concrete situation of communication work. In many cases, the presentation of theories or elements of theories will be followed by a discussion, outlining the way that particular theory can be used by planners in their work. Thus, practitioners will be informed about theories in a way designed to relate directly to their work situations and experiences. The student of communication likewise should gain insights into the practical nature of different theories and how to use them in communication planning.

A word of caution is in order. This is not a book of checklists and not a how-to book. Because every communication situation is different, it would make little sense to present you with narrow, technical advice. Rather, you should get an understanding of the different types of situations you will encounter as a communication planner that will require hard-nosed analysis and decision making.

A Multiple Perspective Approach

This book strives to present an array of diverse perspectives and approaches, first, to demonstrate the richness of the field, and, second, to show that there always are several options for the communication planner. For communication planners to cling to one sole solution to communication problems, regardless of the different characteristics of different problems, ranks, in our opinion, up there in the category of mortal sin.

We do not, however, intend to present a complete and comprehensive picture of all the theories that comprise the field of communication; this would be far beyond the scope of this book. Also, we are not particularly interested, for the purposes of this book, in purely scholarly disputes over details. When elaborating different approaches or even philosophies, our purpose is to alert you, the reader, to the many junctures in the communication process where choices both can and must be made and to how theories can guide those choices.

In our attempts to be useful to the practitioner we, by and large, remain within the many mainstream approaches that have been discussed for some years in communication science. This is another way of saying that preference will be given to the presentation of the theories over their critiques. Our purpose is not to contribute to theory development by juxtaposing different viewpoints. Throughout the book, however, you will find references to authors and articles that deal in more depth with the topic we are discussing, introduce you to other theoretical approaches, or present critical commentaries on other scholars' approaches. We encourage you to explore these supplementary materials.

A multiple perspective also emerges through a multi-cultural approach. While largely writing against an Anglo-Saxon backdrop, we have deliberately attempted to discuss other research traditions as well, namely Scandinavian and German. Although some of those researchers are strongly entrenched in Anglo-American thinking, it is nevertheless telling to observe differing priorities and viewpoints. (See, for example, Rogers and Balle 1985.)

A Contingency Approach

Our approach is one of contingency (see, for example, Goldhaber 1986), which means that we consider each communication problem to be essentially unique and existing under certain conditions; solutions to the problems may be found in very different theories or combinations of theories. We consider the contingency approach to be normative – an approach that prevents communication planning from becoming an assembly line routine. Viewing the planning process in this way has definite advantages and is the only way to arrive at optimal decisions which will lead to the most effective goal-fulfillment. We will find that information and communication do not by themselves ensure achievement of one's aims; rather in striving for even modest goals, careful planning, based on analysis and specification of the conditions of the situation, is paramount.

New developments in organization theory have influenced our adherence to this contingency "philosophy." The notion that there is no "one best way to organize" has emerged as a reaction to the one-sidedness – real or perceived – of such schools of thought as scientific management and human relations. Based on empirical studies by the British researcher Woodward, among others, the contingency theory argues that organizations are "not independent entities but interdependent systems. Because of this, they must constantly adapt to the changes going on around them" (Duncan 1978). Culturally and philosophically, the contingency view is grounded in the theory that modern society operates with multiple value systems as opposed to the universal and authoritarian values that characterized earlier periods. For the communication planner, the implication of this line of thought must be that there is no "one best way" to communicate.

We will apply the theories and models that we present primarily to non-commercial use. The reader will note that we are particularly interested in certain fields of communication work, health communication among them. That does not mean that communication planners in the commercial sphere, for example, in public relations, cannot make use of this book. On the contrary, they will find much of the information applicable to their work as well.

A Changing Field

Theory-building within our field has developed and changed considerably during the past four to five decades. We have attempted to reflect these developments by presenting material that is as up-to-date as possible. For example, strategies of planned communication have become less rigid, less one-way, and less sender-oriented; we shall review these changes, but not at the expense of more traditional approaches, which we think are still rich in applicable material. For example, James Carey's (1975) distinction between the traditional transmission/mechanistic and the ritual/symbolic communication approaches is of great importance for understanding this shift in theory and practice. We will explore this distinction and its impact on communication planning in the next chapter.

Plan of the Book

The book is organized in three parts. Part I introduces communication planning in terms of a presentation of basic concepts and strategies as well as outlining the role of the communication planner. Part II elaborates some of the theoretical approaches among which a planner may choose. In Part III we present a number of mass communication theories and elements of theories to be used in designing strategies in communication planning.

PART I   THE BASICS

2   Conceptual Tools

A large part of this book will be devoted to the description of theories that can function as the basis for different communication strategies. Before studying the theories, however, we need to understand the concepts used in describing and analyzing communication problems. This chapter will present and define some of the concepts that commonly underlie communication strategies.

Both theorists and practitioners use concepts. Without concepts it is impossible to communicate thoughts and intentions to others; without them it is difficult to communicate clearly to yourself what you mean and want to do. Concepts are tools – and just as good tools are maintained so they are ready to use, so should concepts be maintained. Maintaining concepts demands that theorists and practitioners be conscious of them and their impact on communication. The more carefully we define our concepts before and when using them, the less problematic they will be when used to address a communication problem. We will see, however, that many of the concepts used in planned communication are not totally clear and problem-free. Let's look at some of the main concepts and the implications of the different meanings that may be assigned to them.

Communication and Information

The terms "communication" and "information" have been defined in many ways for many purposes.[1] The definitions of communication reflect at least two lines of thought. The first is preoccupied with the transmission aspect of the communication process, resulting in a Sender–Message–Channel–Receiver model, a type of linear model. Such models demonstrate how an idea, feeling, attitude, and so on is transferred from someone to someone else. In that vein, Theodorson and Theodorson define communication as "the transmission of information, ideas, attitudes, or emotion from one person or group to another (or others), primarily through symbols" (1969).

The other tradition stresses such elements as mutuality and shared perceptions. Representing this line of thought, Rogers and Kincaid define communication as "a process in which the participants create and share information with one another in order to reach a mutual understanding" (Rogers and Kincaid 1981: 63; see also Merten 1977: 57–8).

These different definitions of the concept mirror the historical development of an important division within communication theory and practice. In both the trend has been to move from the transmission/mechanistic linear type of definition toward the mutuality/shared perceptions type. One reason for this shift is the advent of interactive communication technology. As Rogers (1986) argues, it is becoming increasingly difficult to think in terms of "source" and "receiver"; instead, each person is a "participant."

A parallel to this distinction can also be found in the work of James Carey (1975). We already have mentioned his characterization of communication as "transmission" on the one hand, and as "a ritual" or "symbolic" on the other. The transmission holds as a central idea that communication is the "transmission of signals and messages over a distance for the purpose of control." The ritual approach sees communication not primarily as the "extension of messages in space, but the maintenance of society in time; not the act of imparting information, but the representation of shared beliefs."

As we will see, it is not without importance which of the two types of definitions one adheres to when working in communication planning. The communication planner often shapes a strategy by choosing among options that represent one or the other definition. For some purposes, transmission types of solution are preferable; for others, solutions that are more of a ritual and mutual type are more appropriate. In general, though, it is more common that transmission-based strategies are mistakenly used when ritual-based ones would be more effective.

The other concept we mentioned, information, has been defined as "a difference in matter-energy which affects uncertainty in a situation where a choice exists among a set of alternatives" (Rogers and Kincaid 1981: 48). Another receiver-oriented view defines information as the "reduction of uncertainty" (Wersig 1974: 73). Wiio looks at information from a general systems theory perspective: "Information is a change in the state of the control system" (1985: 216). Communication is here seen as "an interchange of information between systems . . . where output information from one . . . control system causes work processes in . . . other control systems" (1985: 217). Information, then, is exchanged in the communication process. Information is described sometimes as a one-way process, whereas the communication process is regarded as two-way, a dialogue. That distinction is not exactly correct, though – one-way communication is, of course, possible.

Power in Communication

The one-way, two-way distinction sometimes is seen as crucial in connection with power. In a one-way process, the sender is considered to have all the power and control over the communication process (which, of course, in most instances is a gross oversimplification). One-way processes, therefore, are seen as authoritarian. Two-way processes, in contrast, contain the promise of more balanced power relationships. Through dialogue and mutual understanding, the parties in the process potentially can influence each other. This may be misleading, however, as a two-way process may be designed in such a way as to give only the illusion of influence and power. An example:

The municipal council in Xbury has decided to rebuild a central area in town. The plans are drawn up and the project can begin. It occurs to the council members that opposition to the proposed project might emerge after it is actually launched. They decide to (a) arrange an open discussion at Town Hall, and (b) initiate a competition for suggestions allowing residents to propose their vision for the area in question.

During the Town Hall meeting, experts brought in by the council tell the public how many resources have been invested already in the project and point out the advantages of the existing plan. Criticism from the floor is unorganized; the experts subtly communicate, both verbally and non-verbally, that what they're hearing from the crowd is amateurish and not very feasible. In the closing remarks by a council member, however, the public is thanked for its "genuine interest," and the council's appreciation is "deeply expressed." As for the competition, most of the suggestions are characterized as "creative, but unrealistic." Some ideas that do not affect the form of the council's original plan are incorporated into it with a good deal of publicity.

The local media characterize the process as a good example of civic participation and governmental responsiveness.

This exercise of power through unbalanced two-way communication often is difficult to recognize. Many people would not even view it as an abuse of power. Such use or misuse of two-way communication occurs daily all over the world and points to the need for a further refinement of the definition of the communication process. Grunig and Hunt (1984) add the ideas of "asymmetric" and "symmetric" to their conceptualization of communication. Only in symmetric communication does the possibility of a true balance of power exist with regard to the effects of communication (see Chapter 8).

Sender and Communicator

In most of the earlier communication models, the communication process originates with a sender or a communicator (McQuail 1987), an expression of the assumption that the sender or communicator directs and controls the communication process. These models depict the receivers as wielding little power and usually regard them as objects or targets. In other models, especially circular ones such as the Rogers/Kincaid model (Chapter 7), communication roles are more diffuse because of their multi-functionality, often making it pointless to discuss the participants in the process in terms of senders and receivers. In most communication literature, the definition of "sender" is presented as unproblematic. If we look more closely at a specific communication situation, however, it becomes apparent how vague and unclear the concept can be. An example:

> A municipal traffic committee decides to produce a brochure about children and traffic safety; it will be distributed to parents of school-age children. In this communication situation, who is the sender? The traffic committee, based on its decision to produce the brochure and procure the funding? The National Traffic Safety Council, because it provided most of the text and is responsible for the facts and opinions expressed? The advertising agency that designed the brochure, selected the photos and text for the lay-out, and did the paste-up? Mr Bubbles, a well-known children's TV star, who appears throughout the text, saying wise and clever things about traffic safety?

Any one of these entities can be regarded as a sender. Indeed, they are *all* senders, each playing out a different aspect of the sender role.

There is in our example an initiating sender whose communication role is of an indirect nature only. There is one sender in charge of the strategic communication decisions in terms of content, both factual and persuasive. There is one sender performing the function of communication technician, a term that we discuss below. There is one sender whose name, voice, or face is used solely to make the text or the arguments more interesting, appealing, or trustworthy. A sender in this role often has little or nothing to do with the actual content of the message, as is the case when a sports star advertises a certain beer. Such an actor in the communication process is called a "pseudo-communicator."

As we shall see, the decision of who is to be regarded as sender may be crucial in communication planning. The planner usually is working for others, formulating their messages. In addition, a planner often is the one communicating the message and is thus regarded by the public as the real source of what is expressed. This confusion of communication roles bothers many communication planners. Conceptually at least, the problem of role definition can be resolved by using the term "sender" for the initiator of the message and "communicator" for the person who, in a more technical sense, designs the message strategy and produces the message content. The communicator is, then, the one who actually speaks to the audience, who writes the articles and designs the brochures. Thus, journalists are communicators, but the owners of the newspapers are not. Advertising personnel such as copy writers and editors are communicators, the marketing staff in the business being advertised are not. Of course, one can be both sender and communicator at the same time.

A further elaboration of the sender/communicator role arises from the distinction between "communication manager" and "communication technician" (Broom and Smith 1979). In terms of the internal organization of the communication planning process, it is useful to think along these lines. The two roles require different skills. The communication planner may aspire to carry out both the manager's role (which involves decision making about communication strategy) and the technician's role (which involves the implementation of the decisions made).

This discussion should make it obvious that one has to specify carefully who is or who should be regarded, for example, by the public, as the sender in a communication situation. The communication planning process may be more diffuse and less effective in the absence of a clear understanding of the different sender roles.

It is very important in many cases for the audience to know who is communicating with them. Too often communication is rejected because of an unclear perception of who is sending it; this can cause the audience to question the authenticity and legitimacy of the message. The complexity of today's communication industry, with its new roles and shifting combinations of different sender roles, will confuse audiences further and make them less willing to listen. Social psychologists refer to "the generalized other" to denote people's composite picture of significant people in their social environment; we might use the term "the generalized sender" to denote the vague picture the individual in today's information society constructs to represent "those out there trying to communicate with me." It is the task of the communication planner to make it clear to the audience who actually is communicating with them and in whose interests. This objective points out the danger of using pseudo-communicators: if they are not carefully chosen, the impact of the message pseudo-communicators convey may backfire, for example, if they are perceived as representing groups or interests other than those intended.

For example, a traffic safety campaign launched by several semi-private organizations under the umbrella of and partly financed by the Federal Ministry of Transportation may come under attack from some opposition parties who charge that the campaign is actually designed as an image-boosting device to enhance the minister's chances in the upcoming elections. The sincerity of the motives may be called into question.

Medium and Channel

"Medium" and "channel" often are used interchangeably, although several communication scientists distinguish between the two concepts.

"Channel" denotes "the physical means of carrying the signal" (O'Sullivan et al. 1983: 31–2). It has little to do with meaning, but rather refers to the capacity to carry information.

A "medium" is "an intermediate agency that enables communication to take place" (O'Sullivan et al. 1983: 134) through the use of one or more channels. Usually the term is used synonymously with "mass media" – reflecting, perhaps, a communication society that too often forgets that human beings also take on the role of medium.

There are communication situations where it is important for the communication planner to define the channels and media available. This enables planners to assess better what resources they have at their disposal. In a health campaign, for example, the channels at hand to convey a message in a hospital would include the loudspeaker system, staff meetings, employee newsletters, closed circuit television, and so on; the hospital itself would be regarded as the medium.

Message and Content

What is transmitted in the communication process is called the message. While this term has a number of different meanings, we will look at three dimensions that represent interesting and relevant concepts.

First, "message" describes a set of words or images expressed somewhere, somehow – words in a newspaper ad, lyrics of a song, or pictures in a comic strip. The focus is only on surface aspects of the message as such, not on underlying meanings attached to it. A second dimension is the meaning of communication content as perceived or intended by the individual who expresses it. Finally the message embodies meaning attributed to content by those receiving it.

That there often is some disparity between the meaning attributed to a message by communicators and receivers may seem obvious. This difference is not always considered by communication planners, however, and is the source of many problems in planned communication. It is a common flaw in sender-oriented communication theory and practice to embrace the sender's definition of the message and to disregard the interpretation by the receiving side. The result, of course, is ineffective communication. A criticism leveled at both researchers and practitioners is that they often completely ignore the intended meaning/received meaning gap, assuming naively that effective transmission of meanings is the rule.

Rather than viewing information as a thing, an alternative approach looks at information as a product of human observation at a given point in time and space. This approach holds that people are active creators of their own information (Pavlik 1987a), and the sense they make out of that information is crucial. This information-as-a-construction idea requires "that all information be understood as subjective and transmitted as subjective" (Dervin 1981: 75). Some scholars maintain that all messages are more or less open to diverse interpretations and will be understood differently by different receivers; nevertheless, a minimum of intersubjectivity, i.e. mutual understanding, between sender and receiver makes communication possible.

Receivers, Receiver Groups, Target Groups, and Target Populations

The terms used to describe the receiving end in the process also may be the source of confusion. For example, does "receiver" refer to the intended receiver, or to the actual receiver? As in the concepts discussed above, careful definition of this element is essential to a clear understanding of the communication process.

The use of the term "target groups" for groupings of intended receivers is very common in planned communication. Not surprisingly, there is ambiguity surrounding this concept. One health communicator refers to those individuals whose eating habits need to be changed as the target group, whether the communication goes to them directly or indirectly. A colleague, in contrast, defines the target group as those for whom the actual message is intended and who receive the message directly. People persuaded to comply but receiving the message indirectly do not, according to this definition, belong to this target group.

In order to resolve this confusion, we may use "target populations" for those individuals whose behavior, attitudes, or knowledge we want to influence, directly or indirectly. A group for which a certain message is intended is referred to as the "receiver group." (For a discussion of these terms, see Nowak and Wärneryd 1968.) This distinction offers several advantages that are illustrated by the following four examples. (Each example also represents a communication strategy.)

Target Population and Receiver Group are Identical
A municipal council wants to inform all households in the community that a city dump has been built; everyone will have to use the new facility after a certain date. All the residents in the community are required to comply with the new policy, which puts them in the target population. As everyone in the target population also is supposed to receive this information directly, they belong to the receiving group as well. Both groupings are identical, as seen in Figure 2.1.

This strategy is the one that most frequently comes to mind when people begin planning communication; seldom is it the most appropriate one. Target populations are often heterogeneous, making it difficult to reach and get attention and understanding from *all* people in the population. The communication planner may be required by law to use this strategy (everyone must be informed of a hearing about a governmental policy change, for example), or other reasons, such as economics, may dictate its use (there may, for example, simply not be enough money available to

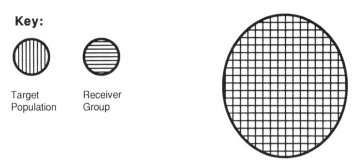

Figure 2.1 *Target population and receiver group identical*

produce several targeted information brochures). Its evident advantage is that, by ensuring that all members of a population are reached, the communication planner can exercise greater control over the front end of the communication process, i.e. everyone receives exactly the same message.

Receiver Group is Part of Target Population
The managers of a large hospital want to inform the employees about a planned expansion. It is impossible to gather everyone together in one place, so a representative from each ward is selected to attend an informational meeting. These people are instructed to pass on the information about the expansion to their colleagues. The receiving group, for whom the original message is formulated, is found within the confines of the target population, as shown in Figure 2.2.

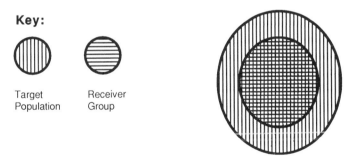

Figure 2.2 *Receiver group situated within the target population*

This second strategy rests on the assumption that communication can reach people indirectly, sometimes more effectively than if the communication were direct. The use of members of the receiver group as intermediaries enables selective transmission, that is, members of the receiver group choose the relevant parts of the message, reframe them in language understandable to the target population, and communicate them to the rest of the target population. Motivated intermediaries may facilitate more effective communication than is possible using the first strategy we discussed. Obviously it is difficult for the communication planner to control more than the first step of the process; effectiveness depends on the intermediaries' faithful forwarding of the message to the entire target population.

Receiver Group Lies Outside Target Population

A national athletic association wants to increase the number of students participating in high school basketball programs. Instead of trying to reach these students directly, the association communicates with high school gym teachers, passing out informational brochures and recruiting materials at regional educators' meetings. While the teachers are the receiver group, the association primarily is interested in influencing a target population to which the teachers do not belong, as shown in Figure 2.3.

Key:

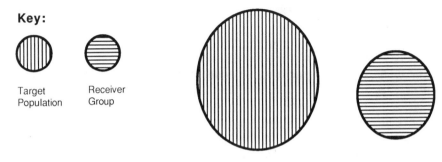

Target   Receiver
Population   Group

Figure 2.3 **Receiver group situated outside target population**

This strategy is similar to the last one, except that the receiving group is found outside the target population. It is likely in this situation that the intermediaries will be less informed about the target population because of their status as outsiders; this may lead to greater difficulties in communication between the two groups.

Target Population Lies Inside Receiver Group

High school teachers and staff are aware of a drug problem within the student body. The administration decides to launch an information campaign about the dangers of drug use. Certain that the problem is limited to a small number of students but unable to identify who the users are (the target population), it designs the campaign to reach all students. This strategy is illustrated in Figure 2.4.

The communication carried out in this strategy will be both direct and indirect – the whole receiving group may be regarded as potential communication intermediaries. Drawbacks of the strategy are that it wastes resources on the many to reach the few and could be dubbed overkill. Also, there is a possibility of alienating members of the receiving group who are subjected to messages that are of no use to them.

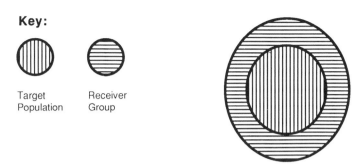

Key:

Target
Population

Receiver
Group

Figure 2.4 *Target population situated within receiver group*

Effects and Effectiveness

The use of communication to reach certain goals is often accompanied by a great deal of wishful thinking. Potentials are attributed to information and communication that simply are unrealistic, and expectations of effects are often exaggerated. Part of the illusion lies in a tendency to confuse "effects" with "effectiveness." It is commonly agreed that mass communication puts a clear stamp on society in many ways. Nor would anyone deny that mass communication content can change attitudes and behavior. The mass media undoubtedly produce "effects." A communication planner finding that a campaign has generated only meager results concludes that it has not been "effective." With mass communication effects in mind, he might have expected a better result.

Effectiveness is a product of goal fulfillment (Chapter 10). One communication campaign may not be very effective in and of itself, but combined with other efforts, it may bring about the long-term effects hoped for, and unintended effects as well. Throughout this book we argue that the communication planner must identify and analyze carefully the kinds of effects that are intended, unintended, long-term, and short-term.

Effects and Consequences

Sometimes it is fruitful to discriminate between outcomes resulting from the messages coming from a communication effort and outcomes resulting from other aspects of the campaigning activity or the situation it has created. Here is an example:

> In a remote Asian village, an international development team arrives. Its message to the local people is to boil their drinking water or dig a new well in order to avoid infection. Besides the results directly related to the message the team disseminates, some other effects occur. For many of the villagers, it is the first time they have stepped outside behaviors they have engaged in for centuries; it

piques their interest in how to improve their quality of life in other ways. For others, meeting people from the city and observing the material belongings that apparently accompany that lifestyle create a desire to move to an urban area.

Such reactions may be classified as unintended effects, but in this example, they are not results of the message *per se*, but only of the presence of the new people and interaction with them. In mass communication research, a similar distinction is made by some uses and gratifications theorists, where the results of the communication content itself are labeled "effects" and the outcomes caused by other aspects of media use are called "consequences" (Windahl 1981; see also Chapter 14).

Communication planners always should keep in mind this distinction between effects and consequences. Too often they are preoccupied with shaping their messages without regard for the consequences of the use of those messages. An example of the danger of such myopia would be a tendency of people receiving a certain campaign about, say, AIDS to become desensitized to messages about other sexually transmitted diseases.

Feedback and Feedforward

Almost every communication model includes some sort of feedback. Feedback is often equated with effect and, in some cases, can be regarded as such. On the other hand, all effects do not appear as feedback. Feedback is a reaction on the part of the receiver to a sender's communication. We usually regard as feedback only those reactions that are transmitted back to and actually reach the sender. We further differentiate between spontaneous feedback and inferred feedback. Spontaneous feedback in mass communication is rare; senders are often left to guess what the reactions are to what has been communicated. They may seek other indicators of how the communication has been received, such as sales figures or responses gathered in a survey. This provides them with inferred feedback.

To return to the different kinds of communication model, the view has been expressed that "adding a feedback loop to a linear process model does not make that model circular or dynamic – it is only there to increase the effectiveness of the linear process" (O'Sullivan et al. 1983: 90). That is, in planned communication feedback by itself does not assure the receiver of more power; in fact, it may result in just the opposite by providing the sender with a tool that permits more effective control of the receiver. For the planner, feedback often appears to be invaluable, giving him or her a good tool to better control the communication efforts.

The notion of feedforward sometimes is treated together with feedback. Feedforward is information about receivers and their possible reactions that is gathered by a sender prior to initiating communication with them (Rogers 1973). It is axiomatic in planned communication that the more one knows beforehand about the receivers and their needs, the greater the chances for effective communication. Hornik (1988) has pointed to the need for feedforward in Third World agriculture developmental work, where government agents are often insensitive to the needs of the farmers.[2] Feedforward may also encompass active communication by giving hints as to messages that will follow. For example, the flying of a trial balloon before an official announcement of a drastic reduction in the general speed limit would provide a measure of the strength of the opposition to such a measure.

A related concept, infusion, has been suggested by Fett:

> Change agencies expend great efforts in diffusion of information, but little effort in infusion. . . . By infusion we do not mean the same thing as feedback. Feedback, as generally conceptualized, is the response to a message received, while infusion is more of an elicited response of a felt need. It is information-seeking on the part of the diffusion or change agency. (1974, quoted in Kearl 1976: 171)

As you can see, infusion is the antithesis of diffusion. Like feedforward, it is an activity that enables the communication planner to formulate a comprehensive background upon which to design a communication strategy.

A Comment

This chapter has served to sharpen our understanding of the concepts that inform communication planning. Much as the carpenter's tasks are made easier by the right tools for the right job, so the communication planner's work is facilitated by the ability to analyze and apply the concepts of communication and information, one-way and two-way communication, sender and communicator, medium and channel, receiver groups and target populations, effects and consequences, feedback and feedforward, power, and effectiveness. Let us turn now to a survey of the practice of communication planning.

Notes

1 In his 1977 analysis of no fewer than 160 different definitions of communication, Merten arrives at a basic distinction between communication as a one-way process (75 definitions) and communication as a symmetric process (64 definitions); 21 definitions did not fall clearly into either category. Whatever the value of such quantitative inventories may be, they are illustrative of the fact that there are two basic approaches to communication that can be further broken down into nine categories of definitions:

Communication as a one-way process
- Communication as transmission
- Communication as a stimulus–response act
- Communication as interpretation

Communication as a symmetric process
- Communication as understanding
- Communication as exchange
- Communication as sharing
- Communication as a relationship
- Communication as a social behavior
- Communication as interaction

Communication science, of course, cannot claim any monopoly in research and theory development around the concepts of information and communication. In fact, harsh criticism recently has been leveled against an alleged "ethnocentrism" in communication science. Critics charge that it has failed to integrate relevant works from the humanities, semiotics, and the cognitive sciences (Beniger 1988; Paisley 1984).

2 Hornik (1988) distinguishes between three types of feedforward strategies in agricultural projects:

   1 an experimental strategy, which allows farmers to try out the innovation;
   2 a participation strategy, which brings farmers into the adoption process;
   3 a baseline investigation strategy, which conducts social scientific studies about how the innovation should be introduced, examining, for example, existing cultural, institutional, and agricultural structures.

3 The Nature of Communication Planning

From Communication Campaigns to Communication Planning

The original focus of this book was communication campaigns. It quickly became evident that the concept of communication campaigns was too narrow for what we wanted to present. But campaigns do constitute an important part of our discussion in that they provide, in many respects, good examples of putting theory into practice. Chapter 10 is devoted to communication campaigns.

The communication campaign is a planned effort on behalf of a sender to influence some or all groups in society with a certain message or set of messages. Campaigns play a leading role in the field of communication planning. Some of the best results of planned communication have been achieved from large health communication campaigns (e.g. McGuire 1984).

But a deeper understanding of what communication is and what different forms of communication can achieve, together with certain scientific and ideological shifts, have necessarily broadened our scope. Communication planning is a term suited to the 1990s. Communication planning, as we conceive it and will treat it throughout this book, includes the following characteristics in addition to those we have listed for communication campaigns:

- work done from a short- as well as a long-term perspective, but with an emphasis on long-term planning;
- communication efforts planned from the bottom up instead of from the top down;
- communication with more general and widespread goals, as opposed to the specific and fixed goals of a campaign;
- communication viewed from the receiver's perspective instead of from the sender's.

The Role of the Communication Planner

One of the consequences of this broader conceptualization is that the role of the planner becomes more varied. Planning may mean, for example, "planning" for unstructured, informal communication, that is, initiating communication among people for the sake of getting a communication process started. Also, the goals of planning may not always be as specific as those of a campaign. Emphasis on instrumental communication may give way to, for example, expressive communication.

Communication planners can appear in many forms. They may be full-time information and public relations practitioners in a large New York-based multinational corporation, or people who in their spare time produce and distribute recruiting leaflets for a small-town soccer club in Finland. They may even act as change agents[1] in an Indonesian family planning program, as described in Rogers and Shoemaker (1971) and Rogers (1983).

Communication planners operate at different levels. At a national level, they may work on health and safety information programs. Some of these efforts, such as family planning initiatives carried out in developing countries, are enormous in terms of complexity and resources involved. At a local level, community centers are organized to bring people together to engage in certain group activities. A community's keep-our-city-clean campaign is another example of local communication planning.

In organizations communication initiatives can begin at the bottom as well as at the top. For example, union officials try to increase enrollment through an information campaign, or a group of dissidents communicates its dissatisfaction with union leadership by distributing leaflets.

On the small-group level, immigrants form a discussion group to talk about politics in their home country in order to reach some kind of understanding. Or a neighborhood natural-food-buying group meets every other Tuesday night to place bulk orders and talk about trends in healthy eating.

All of these provide opportunities for communication planning. The goal of the person who acts as the communication planner should be the most effective use of the resources available to achieve the objectives of the participants in a communication situation.

Systematic and Creative Communication Planning

Communication planning always should include both systematic and creative elements. Both are essential to information/communication work, but different practitioners put different emphasis on one or the other.

Many communication planners perceive their work as predominantly creative. Finding new solutions to communication problems, formulating new messages, finding and combining new channels, defining and segmenting the public in an interesting (and perhaps fun) way offer opportunities to be creative.

The virtue of being systematic usually is acclaimed less enthusiastically by communication planners, but it, too, is extremely important in information/communication work. A systematic approach to communication planning includes seeing to it that all relevant receiver groups are reached, that messages are disseminated in the right order, that follow-ups and evaluations are done, that a thorough goal analysis is part of the initial stages of a project, and so on.

The two elements are presented separately here for reasons of clarity, but it is quite feasible to integrate the two into "creative systematics" or "systematic creativity." Creative systematics would encompass finding creative ways to structure systematic work; systematic creativity would denote striving in a systematic way for creative solutions to problems.

For the professional planner, systematics and creativity are inseparable. Depending on the phase of a communication program, one or the other may be in the foreground. Creativity usually dominates during the initiation and production phases, systematics during the implementation and evaluation phases.

The Importance of Perception

Among other qualities that are useful in communication planning, we want to draw attention to empathy, social perspective-taking, sensitivity to relationship standards, and understanding a situation.

Empathy

"Empathy" is defined here as the capacity to understand how other people perceive and interpret reality, including communication, without giving up one's own view of this reality. Empathy is more valuable to a communicator than sympathy, which is the capability to figure out what you would do yourself if put in another person's situation (Gudykunst and Kim 1984).

The importance of empathy among communication planners is recognized by Rogers (1983), who generalizes that the success of a change agent in the diffusion of innovation communication process is positively related to his or her level of empathy with the clients. Rogers and Bhowmik (1970) hypothesize that, in heterophilous situations – that is, when the sender and receiver are different in some important respect(s), such as social class – communication is more effective when the sender is more empathic than the receiver.

It is very common that communication planners have no direct contact with the people with whom they communicate. Communication and empathy are based on what is often very meager information about the receiver. In many cases, this is problematic for the sender since the audience is both distant and heterogeneous (Maletzke 1963). With an extremely heterogeneous audience, not even empathy will help very much. Responses to the problem of heterogeneity are varied; here are a few:

- targeting the message somewhere in the middle of what you perceive as the receiver group;
- letting an acquaintance, say your mother or your neighbor, represent the audience;
- seeking out people likely to offer sanctions, such as your colleagues or superiors, and have them serve as proxies for the real audience.

Obviously these last two suggestions are problematic. Use of a secondary audience is likely to lead to a misfit between the message and the primary public. Awareness of the problem will help somewhat in compensating for it; however, it won't substitute for first-hand knowledge of the real audience.

Social Perspective-Taking

Reardon (1987) differentiates between empathy, which she defines as a sensitivity to the thoughts and feelings of others, and social perspective-taking. This is the ability to understand the options available to others. This competency can influence positively the planner's selection of a communication strategy.

For example, a communication planner needs to be aware that receivers may accept a message, but lack the resources to behave in accordance with it. Or they may be hindered by religious or cultural norms. In Grunig's situational theory of publics, this phenomenon is called "constraint recognition," that is, the extent to which people perceive that there are constraints – or obstacles – in a situation that limit their freedom to plan their own behavior. When constraint recognition is high, people will not seek messages about themes related to the problematic area (Grunig and Hunt 1984). The chances for successful communication usually decrease as the gap (social, cultural, etc.) between sender and receiver widens. The wider the gap, the poorer the social perspective-taking.

Relationship Standards

Reardon also mentions the importance of sensitivity to the receiver's perception of the sender–receiver relationship and the receiver's expectations from it. An example from a health communication campaign illustrates this: The principal campaign communicator is a physician, who is presented in the messages as a good friend/good neighbor type of person. This confuses the public, who reject the message because they expect the more traditional doctor/patient image from the communicator.

Situational Knowledge

"Situational knowledge" refers to the ability to assess correctly what is appropriate and effective to communicate in a specific situation (Reardon 1987). A disturbance-free environment is necessary for communicating complex messages. The threat of an epidemic makes people more receptive to health messages.

Contexts

The contingency approach with its emphasis on analyzing the conditions surrounding communication events leads to an interest in more holistic kinds of theories and practices. Communication never takes place in isolation; there are always contexts to consider. This realization is invaluable for the communication planner.

Time

An understanding of and sensitivity to the concept of time is of considerable importance, both for the communication scientist (Kline 1977) and for the communication practitioner.[2] This is true not just for mass communication planning, but also for interpersonal communication (Miller and Knapp 1985; Capella 1987). The following examples illustrate the role of the time variable in the planning process:

Time-less or Time-bound Information
A piece of information can be characterized in terms of the time it will be valid for the user. In a brochure about a health care clinic, there is information that will be valid for several years to come, for example, the address, description of care offered, the clinic's mission, etc. It also contains time-bound information – names of staff members (who may quit their jobs in the near future), hours of operation for the different divisions (that soon may be changed). The communication planner must be able to identify information in terms of timeliness. A brochure containing enduring information is rendered obsolete by having time-bound information included. An obvious solution for the health care clinic is to include only the time-less information in the more costly brochure and to present the time-bound information on a single sheet that can be inserted into the brochure.

Time-bound information is dealt with better by some media than others. Radio is usually a better medium than television for presenting information with a short lifespan because it is less expensive in terms of both time and money. Desktop publishing on personal computers is proving to be a useful tool in the quest for the utmost flexibility time-wise for communication planning.

Process Time Requirements
In the case of distributing a simple message to a well-motivated audience, the planner can get by with allowing a minimum amount of time for the communication process. But a more complex message to a less motivated audience will require more time. Also, different phases of a communication operation will require different approaches to the time factor. In an anti-smoking campaign, for example, it takes little time to inform the audience that smoking is harmful – they've been hearing that message for years. But teaching them *how* to quit smoking and stay off cigarettes may be extremely time-consuming. Depending on the message and the audience, the planner must allow for longer sinking-in periods, or provide time for interpersonal communication to occur after a phase of mass communication.

Some strategies are designed to play out over a long period of time. This especially holds true for models that are characterized by a large amount of mutuality. Grunig's two-way symmetric model (presented in Chapter 8) is a case in point: the goal is to sustain communication over a long period in order to achieve mutual understanding.

Timing of Messages

Atkin (1981) notes that timing of messages may be decisive for the success of a communication campaign. There are two perspectives from which to consider this activity: completely within the communication campaign itself and in relation to external events. Thinking through the strategy of the most effective timing of the phases of the campaign is a necessary step. This intra-process strategy should strive for internal logic and consistency.

Events occurring outside the project, including other communication, can have a great impact on the timing of messages in a communication campaign. The inter-process perspective requires the communication planner to adjust the timing based on the impact of external factors. For example, whether an issue is already on the audience's agenda (see Chapter 15) has significant ramifications for message timing. AIDS information campaigns have undoubtedly profited from mass media attention to the issue, which put it on the public agenda. In the anti-smoking campaign we used as an earlier example, timing was influenced by the results of previous communication efforts about the dangers of smoking. Hornik (1988) writes that, in countries where there are several climate zones, agricultural communication planning must take into account how to ensure the content of messages directed to farmers is relevant in light of seasonal schedules.

The Intended Effects Time Span

A common time-related issue results from an inability to distinguish between long-term and short-term effects. Even when a goal for a communication effort is identified as long-term, the planning efforts may be done as if the goal were short-term. This is a problem in communication for the diffusion of innovations. If, in a Third World village, residents are taught only how to use an irrigation system, but not how to maintain it, the innovation is unlikely to provide enduring benefits for the population. Another common mistake is to measure communication success by assessing short-term effects when long-term effects are the objective. The following illustrates this problem:

In January of 1964 the "Report of the Surgeon General's Advisory Committee on Smoking and Health" was published amid unprecedented worldwide fanfare in the mass media. In the short term, smoking dropped dramatically – taxed sales decreased 15–20 percent in the month following the release of the report. "The curtailment was short-lived; what has been called 'the Great Forswearing' of January and February 1964 was followed by the 'Great Relapse' of March . . . Within a few months cigarette consumption was back almost to pre-1964 levels" (Wallack 1981: 226).

Changes over Time

Communication is a dynamic process; a common mistake is to treat it as static. Communication between sender and receiver develops over time. The communication "span" widens, i.e. the range of knowledge about the other party and potential communication themes increases. Dance (1970) illustrates this in his simple but suggestive spiral model of communication. The model suggests that in every stage of the communication process something is added in terms of knowledge, experiences, etc.

Scheduling

The technical aspect of timing is scheduling. This involves optimizing the dissemination potential so that messages receive adequate exposure among the target audience (VanLeuven 1986). Such aspects as time, placement, frequency, and reach have been explored widely in advertising literature. For the sake of illustration, we cite three of VanLeuven's recommendations to show how goals and scheduling strategy interrelate:

1 Reach is more important than frequency when awareness is the goal.
2 Frequency is more important than reach in holding already converted publics.
3 Frequency is necessary to place an issue on the public's agenda initially.

(Reach refers to how many people receive a message, frequency to the number of times a message is transmitted.)

Space

"The streets of Calcutta, the avenues of Brasilia, the Left Bank of Paris, the gardens of Kyoto, the slums of Chicago, and the canyons of lower Manhattan provide dramatically different backdrops for human interaction" (Barnlund 1968: 512).

The environment in which communication takes place is a factor usually overlooked in planning. Hall (1966) refers to space as a hidden dimension in communication; we view the ignoring of space as a potential inhibitor of effective and useful communication. Informal communication within an organization, for example, may be hampered by the lack of a space for people to meet – having no place to converse informally, employees are not likely to discuss and process the formal communication of the organization. Creativity, which thrives on interpersonal communication, also could be hampered in this situation.

Increasing recognition of the importance of space in the communication process is reflected in the planning of buildings and communities (Autischer and Maier-Rabler 1987). Increasing the possibilities for people to meet and removing obstacles to communication are the goals. A good example of spatial arrangements that encourage communication are science parks, built to give scientists, researchers, and practitioners a place to meet and communicate.

Obviously, communication planners do not frequently have the advantage of being in on the planning of new buildings and communities for a client. It may be within the planner's power, however, to elevate the establishment of meeting places to a priority item for a community or organization.

Another space issue is where information should be delivered. Is it wise, for example, to distribute the company newspaper in the workplace, where the employee may (should?) not have the time to read it carefully? Will offering drug treatment advice to addicts in locations that also are used by people with problems bearing less social stigma affect who uses a facility?

The Social Environment

While earlier models of communication have been criticized for ignoring the social environment of communication (e.g. Bentele 1984), others have analyzed thoroughly the importance of social contexts. (See, for example, our discussion of Maletzke's model in Chapter 11.) Different social groups communicate in different ways: for example, certain occupational groups (consider the channel – CB radios – and vernacular – "Put the pedal to the metal, ten-four" – of truck drivers) and social classes (cellular telephones and specialized argot of businesspeople). While group norms can function as an obstacle to communication with members of a group, they also can enhance the communication effects if the message fits within those norms.

During the last few decades, the importance of the social environment has been emphasized more and more. This development is mirrored in the theoretical underpinnings of a series of large health communication campaigns (Farquhar et al. 1985; Kim 1985, quoted in Rogers and Storey 1987). These campaigns view the individual receiver as part of a social and communication network; influence is a product of behavior and attitudes, which are acquired through social learning (McAlister 1987; Bandura 1977). The social environment here has a dual role – providing a good example as well as serving as a channel for influence.

The Cultural Context

"All communication is intercultural" is a thought-provoking quotation from Gudykunst and Kim (1984). It says to the communication planner, keep in mind that your publics often belong to cultures or subcultures in society different from yours.[3] A case in point is when middle-aged communication professionals try to communicate traffic safety to young automobile drivers, who belong to diverse youth cultures. The symbolic universes and mental maps of the sender's culture and the targeted youth group's culture are quite disparate; meaningful communication bonds may be difficult to establish. Culture is a decisive context to take into account.

Public Opinion

Communication is planned, sent, received, shared, and interpreted in yet another context, namely in certain climates of public opinion, or "Zeitgeist," which refers to "the (more or less specific) combination of ideas, opinions, beliefs, values, and evaluations embraced by (more or less specific groups within) a given society in a given period" (Rosengren 1981a: 719). Here, agenda-setting research, which deals with what people consider important, may help the communication planner to formulate the appropriate messages (McCombs 1981; Ehlers 1983). Among planners, there is a rising interest in "issues management" (Pavlik 1987a; Heath and Nelson 1986; Heath and Associates 1988),[4] one of whose tools is surveys of public opinion. Cultural indicator research (Rosengren 1981a) is another method used to reveal long-term trends in public opinion. In this type of research, one might study advice columns in order to find out what kinds of problems people tend to have in a given period.

Relationships

The relationships between communication planners and their employers on the one hand and clients on the other share some of the characteristics of a journalist/source relationship. (Bear in mind that, based on our definitions in the previous chapter, the employer is the sender, the communication planner is the communicator, and the client is the receiver. For purposes of this discussion, we will use the standard occupational terms.) There are several permutations of the relationship. Journalists may completely assimilate the views of the source, presenting them as their own (Gieber and Johnson 1961). The views of a source and the journalist may partially overlap (McQuail and Windahl 1983). Or the views of the source and the journalist may be completely different from each other.

Palm and Windahl (1989) have applied these observations to communication planning. The following figures represent the planner/message originator/receiver relationships. In Figure 3.1, the communication planner is more closely oriented to the message originator than to the client. Plans and goals are formulated by the employer. In Figure 3.2, the planner stands removed from the other two parties. We characterize this stance as a professional orientation – the communication planner uses experience, judgment, and education to identify the needs of both the

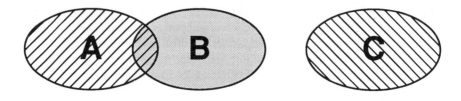

A=Message Originator; B=Communication Planner; C=Receiver/Client

Figure 3.1 *Communication planner oriented towards message originator*

A=Message Originator; B=Communication Planner; C=Receiver/Client

Figure 3.2 *Communication planner autonomous*

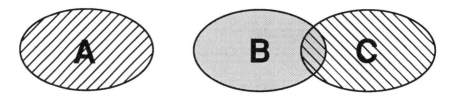

A=Message Originator; B=Communication Planner; C=Receiver/Client

Figure 3.3 *Communication planner receiver/client-oriented*

receiver and the message originator and to balance them. Figure 3.3 shows the communication planner oriented toward the receiver. The subjective needs of the receiver are the planner's point of departure.

Communication tends to be more effective when the communicating parties share common characteristics (Rogers 1983). If, as will occur with some frequency, communication planners perceive themselves to be so dissimilar to the receivers as to compromise the communication process, they may choose to use communication aides to serve an intermediary function. These should be people who are closer in respects important to the communication planning process to the members of the intended group. Opinion leaders (Chapter 6) from a group, for example, may serve as effective intermediaries in bridging the gap between planner and receivers.

Notes

1 Rogers and Shoemaker (1971: 227) define "change agent" as "a professional who influences innovation-decisions in a direction deemed desirable by a change agency. In most cases he seeks to secure the adoption of new ideas, but he may also attempt to slow the diffusion and prevent the adoption of certain innovations."

2 While this book adopts a pragmatic approach to time in communication planning, mention should, nevertheless, be made of the various attempts at its conceptualization in the social (and communication) sciences. Following Heirich (1964), F.G. Kline (1977) distinguishes the following dimensions:

1 time as a social factor
   (a) time as a resource
   (b) time as a social meaning
2 time as a causal link
   (a) time as setting
   (b) time as a sequence
3 time as a quantitative relationship
   (a) time as an interval level measurement
   (b) time as an ordinal level measurement
   (c) time as a nominal level measurement
4 time as a qualitative measure

3 It is not our purpose in this book to go into the numerous definitions of culture. As to the distinction between "society," "social systems," and "culture," we find Rohner's (1984: 132) view useful: ". . . an individual is a *member* of a society . . . individuals *participate* in social systems . . . and *share* cultures" (quoted in Gudykunst 1987: 848).

4 The steps usually associated with issues management are (1) issue identification, (2) analysis, (3) action plans, (4) implementation, and (5) evaluation of results (Pavlik 1987a; Shelby 1986).

4 Not All Problems are Communication Problems

A common reason why planned communication fails is that something that is not a *communication* problem is treated as though it were.

A politician explains a campaign loss by saying, "We did not reach the public with our message," or "People did not understand what we really meant," implying there was nothing wrong with the politics *per se* of the politician. A more truthful explanation would require statements such as, "I'm a weak politician with only limited contacts and intellectual capabilities," or "My policies were poorly conceived" – utterances unheard of in the political races we've observed. Similarly, a municipal official comments upon a series of accidents in a section of the city by calling for ads in the local newspaper to warn drivers; the real problem is that the road in question is poorly constructed and is dangerous to anyone under almost any condition.

Identifying Communication Problems

Calling something a communication problem indicates one of two things. First, the problem results from a lack of or the wrong type of communication; that is, communication, or lack thereof, causes the communication problem. The politician in the situation described above defined the problem as one of inadequate communication.

Second, a problem is a communication problem if it is possible to solve it with the help of communication. The municipal official's thinking exemplifies this: the accident rate is supposed to go down when information (ads in a newspaper) is given.

Another, more general, example is offered by Hornik, who discusses Third World aid in the form of information for the poor. In the 1970s the view of communication as a panacea changed. "Too often, information was being thrown at problems that were defined by lack of resources, not lack of knowledge. The assumption that if only people knew more they could readily better their situation was seen to be a cruel deception" (1988: xi). Poor farmers could not buy the recommended fertilizer because they could not get the credit to raise the money, Hornik concludes. The problem was *not* that they did not know that fertilizers would increase crop yields.

Blaming communication when other factors should be blamed is a common tendency of many communication professionals. Even more problematic, however, is seeking information/communication solutions when they are not adequate. That is the theme of this part of this chapter.

A natural question for a communication planner to ask is, How can the problem at hand be solved? The answer is one of the following:

1 By communication efforts alone.
2 By communication in conjunction with other measures.
3 By other measures only.

Depending on the answer, the planner has certain options. Only the problems that call for the first solution, however, can be labeled true communication problems.

An honest assessment of a problem occurs much too seldom, and communication solutions are suggested much too often, even when they are inappropriate. We already have hinted at one reason for that: communication solutions usually do not generate conflict to the degree many other solutions do; also, they often are less demanding in terms of economic, social, and psychological resources. Falling back on communication solutions also may be a sign of unwillingness to confront the real causes of problems (Ekecranz 1978).

Many communication planners have stories about a client or employer who defined a problem as a communication problem when the professional communicator realized that it wasn't. Arguing that other solutions are necessary in cases where it is so clear to the employer that he or she is faced with a communication problem may lead to a judgment that the communication planner is incompetent or – horror of horrors! – overly theoretical. But such misconceptions may originate with communication planners as well. They may be tempted to oversell the communication dimension of a problem, thus highlighting the planner's field of competence. Moreover, planners simply may have their blind spots, viewing the world only in terms familiar to them.

To a certain extent, of course, this is a problem of power and of professionalism. Strong communication planners will have less of a problem asserting their views and will, undoubtedly, be rewarded for their integrity in the long run. A less powerful and self-confident planner may regard compliance as the best solution. From a professional standpoint, such compliance will damage the reputation of the profession in the long term, since this will often result in the problem not being solved. Then it is too late for the practitioner to argue that the problem could not possibly have been solved by communication/information means alone.

Let's look at an example:

Complaints from patients about bad care in a hospital have increased considerably during the last couple of years. The real reason for this is that conflicts have arisen between several of the different employee groups as well as between management and the employees in general; this has led to a constant failure to cooperate with each other. Resolving these conflicts would mean a thorough investigation by hospital management, which would probably generate new problems to be solved. A communication campaign with the goals of increasing professionalism and building a sense of community is launched. The campaign fails, since the underlying cause – the lack of cooperation – is not addressed and remains unchanged. And the communication planner who unwisely agreed to the definition of the problem as one of communication assumes the role of scapegoat.

In many cases, communication solutions can be characterized as superficial. They are, of course, not always inadequate. They often are insufficient, however, and should be supplemented with other efforts. For example, in anti-drug campaigns, information is often accompanied or followed by other measures. Durell and Bukoski (1984) report that, in addition to media and school information programs, generic approaches have been used. These build on the fact that several behavioral, personality, and lifestyle characteristics, things that cannot be changed by communication alone, are associated with drug abuse. A program of this kind aims at increasing fundamental skills for handling stress, decision making, and developing good interpersonal relationships.

Another common way to make information more interesting and relevant is to activate the receivers somehow. Locketz (1976) reports, for example, about a national health campaign against schistosomiasis in Surinam; an art contest using the disease as its theme made the health message more interesting for the schoolchildren who participated in the competition.

Making a Goal/Means Inventory

A simple way for the communication planner to get an overview of potential solutions to a problem is to draw up a goal/means inventory. The first step is to state the main goal. Let's say our problem is a high accident rate among schoolchildren in our city. Our main goal may be phrased as "reduce accident rate for schoolchildren." To achieve this, we obviously have to fulfill some subgoals. After analyzing the problem, we find that we need to reach these subgoals:

- Make the parents aware of the problem
- Make the children aware of the problem
- Make drivers aware of the problem
- Make the routes to school safer

Our inventory now looks like this:

Main Goal: Getting the accident rate down
Subgoal 1: Make parents aware
Subgoal 2: Make children aware
Subgoal 3: Make drivers aware
Subgoal 4: Make routes to school safer

Of the four subgoals we want to achieve, three are communication goals; the fourth is of a technical nature and, while communication may be of some importance in addressing it, the principal means (changing the speed limits, requiring children to wear reflective clothing, etc.) are outside the realm of communication.

An inventory of this kind may turn out to be extremely detailed and complex when developed fully, but even in its simplest form it can be useful in sorting out when communication is an adequate means for addressing a problem and when it is not.

The picture is complicated further when you realize that a problem may be one of communication/information for some segments of the receiving group, while for other segments it will be of another kind. In other words, for some people communication is the main solution to a problem, for others it is not. Suppose that a campaign to introduce a new way of growing a certain crop is launched in a Third World country. One segment of the farming population responds in the manner projected by the planners; other farmers do not because they don't have the money required to change their farming habits. As long as the resource shortage exists, communication will not change their farming behavior.

Another illustration: for an alcoholic, anti-drinking information will have little effect on behavior; for potential alcoholics, however, it may prevent them from acquiring the habit. The alcoholic requires something more than communication solutions.

The Question of Blame

We have emphasized repeatedly the importance of recognizing the underlying causes of a problem, be it a communication problem or otherwise. If we go back one step further, we are faced with the question, who is to blame for the problem? Caplan and Nelson (1973) see two general possibilities: We can hold individuals responsible for the problems they have (individual blame), or we can blame the social system to which the individuals belong (system blame).

This analysis leads us into an ideological arena. The development of entire political systems has hinged on this distinction. The United States, for example, generally ascribes to the cult of the individual; this throws the burden on the shoulders of individuals to resolve their own problems. On the other hand, a number of European countries have adopted a more collective-based approach, in which the social system takes responsibility for its individual citizens. This ideology maintains that individuals are not always capable of solving their own problems and that the state should actively intervene to ensure the individual's welfare.

These ideologies are, of course, dynamic. Every system undergoes periods of decreasing and increasing adherence to the values on which it was founded. The Reagan years in the United States are considered to have been a reaffirmation of the value of individuality, reversing a trend toward heavier reliance on the system for dealing with social problems. Margaret Thatcher's tenure as Prime Minister in Great Britain saw a similar turn away from the system being responsible for the individual.

These shifts will influence the normative theory of communication accepted by a society. In a "system blame" environment, the social system is expected to assume greater responsibility for its "clients." Information and communication are used as intervention strategies to ensure the public's welfare. In an "individual blame" environment, on the other hand, communication is less prescriptive and guiding, leaving room for individual choice.

The question of who is blamed has great influence on a communication planner's choice of solutions to a problem. In our traffic example, the proposed solutions reflect a mixed assignment of blame. The parents are seen as responsible for their children, the children themselves are regarded as responsible for their behavior in traffic. If the accident rate is to be lowered, the community must help both parents and children to act responsibly. Communication is the tool that will be used to achieve that goal. At the same time, the school is charged with providing a safe environment, which is the community's responsibility. That is a "system blame" solution.

Because the issue of individual or system blame is so value-laden, the planner should be particularly careful not to depart from the contingency approach. Regardless of personal convictions, the planner must analyze objectively who is to blame while taking into account the subjective perceptions of his or her employer, the receiver and society at large as to who is responsible for the problem at hand. Common sense suggests that mixed approaches as formulated in the traffic example often are most appropriate and yield the best results. Unemployment, for example, can be viewed as mainly a structural or system problem but, at the same time, part of the responsibility for improving a situation is attributable to the individual who is out of work.

The Three Es: Education, Engineering, and Enforcement

The nature of communication solutions makes their consequences unpredictable. Under normal circumstances, the sender has no control over the receiving situation – the receiver is free to ignore the message completely. Furthermore, communication/information often can do little more than appeal to people and suggest alternatives, positive or negative, that may be quite indirect and removed from the receiver. At this stage of the process, the role of the communication planner is not a particularly powerful one; the sender usually will be the weaker partner in the sender/receiver dyad. This points to the fact that, as a means of bringing about changes, communication is not, in most cases, a very strong method of solving a problem or otherwise reaching a goal. Nonetheless, despite its weakness, communication is one of the most commonly used tools. The obvious can be added here, that well-planned communication solutions are always better than poorly planned ones.

In a discussion about the achievements of the US Forest Service in a campaign to prevent wildfires, Kurth (1981) talks about the "Three Es": education, engineering, and enforcement. These represent the efforts and measures required in order to reach certain goals.

Education activities include school programs, since children are responsible for a number of fires every year; person-to-person contact between fire prevention technicians and everyone in a high-risk area; and informational literature routinely given to visitors to national forests. The mass media also are viewed as channels: for example, local broadcasting stations can carry warnings during periods of high fire risk.

Engineering consists, in this program, of environmental modification of equipment design and inspections. For example, many fires originate with machinery being used in the forests. Through inspections of and modifications to these machines, the incidence of wildfires was reduced considerably.

Enforcement involves using legal remedies to prevent wildfires, for example, prosecuting people who do not extinguish campfires in the manner prescribed by law. As an extreme measure, whole areas may be closed to the public when the fire danger is very high. Enforcement also may entail incentives for behaving in accordance with the norms and rules.

Communication plays a role in all these measures, but only the first one is exclusively communication-centered. Ideally, while the most appropriate means are employed for each goal identified to solve a problem, interventions in each area should be planned to integrate into a coherent whole. The combination of approaches from the three areas may well prove synergetic, that is, the effects from the combined efforts will be greater than the sum of the effects of each separate effort (Rogers and Storey 1987). An educational program promoting condom use to prevent AIDS will be more effective if it is accompanied by an engineering effort ensuring that condoms are readily available for purchase. In some situations, measures of one type may be necessary to temper efforts from another area. For example, traffic campaigns to promote careful driving may be less effective if people believe that driving on newly built highways (engineering) is totally safe; education and enforcement programs may be needed to diminish the perceived effectiveness of the engineering effort.

Examples of engineering and enforcement in connection with communication are frequent in the literature. In a discussion about a hypertension information campaign, Schnoor and Tybjaerg-Hansen (1976) describe how the Danish heart foundation tested the blood pressure of some 24,000 people at supermarkets during a one-week period. At the same time, the foundation handed out information about the disease. Interest was great, with the number of customers in some supermarkets doubling during the period. The aim was to stress the importance of measuring blood pressure occasionally. The program enabled identification of a number of high-risk individuals, as well as motivating the public to learn more about its health condition.

The "Three Es" provide an additional framework for analyzing potential solutions and goals. Of course, this framework can be supplemented with other measures. Rewards, if not regarded as part of enforcement, would be one such addition. Another is negotiation, where the communication element is strong. Education is, from a communication point of view, usually more of a one-way solution, whereas negotiation is two-way.

What Communication Can Do

In much of this chapter we have stressed the limitations of communication and the importance of other factors such as resources and organizational and system structures. Lack of awareness of these factors accounts for many failures in planned communication – that is why we have emphasized them. Communicationism – that is, conceiving of and treating as a communication problem something that is not – is, we sense, a widespread tendency of employers and planners alike.

At this point, we would like to address the question of what communication *can* do in communication planning.

Hornik's (1988) conceptualization of the functions of communication planning based on his analysis of agriculture and nutrition programs in the Third World is, in our opinion, one of the best. Here are some of the roles, manifest or latent, intended or unintended, that Hornik ascribes to communication (and communication technology) in a planned communication context:

Low-cost Loudspeaker

(Mass) communication media are used to do things the individual communicator normally cannot do, for example, to reach large numbers of receivers at a higher level of quality than would be possible were the communication to occur in individual communication acts. Whatever its other qualities, a television ad about AIDS simply *is* the most inexpensive and efficient way to reach out to many, many people initially.

Institutional Catalyst

Regardless of various drawbacks, including its inefficiency as a catalyst, a mass communication-based program can mobilize sectors of society by its sheer existence. A campaign against drunk driving among young clubgoers may prompt bar managers to serve inexpensive soft drinks and advertise this fact as well; a taxi company capitalizes on the campaign by offering special fares to take people to the club and pick them up at a prearranged time. A local television station, hoping to improve its image as a caring member of the community, becomes the official sponsor of the campaign, running special reports on its evening newscasts about the costs of drunk driving and distributing at local clubs T-shirts printed with an anti-drunk driving slogan and its logo. According to Hornik, media-based projects have a "star" quality.

Political Lightning Rod

This is the cynical aspect of the role just described. Communication campaigns can be used by the power structure as an elaborate scheme to pretend to do something about a problem while really doing nothing substantive in terms of resources and conflict. Thus, the latent function of a hastily placed seat belt campaign after another weekend of widely publicized traffic accidents with a high death toll (involving some drivers not using seat belts) is to diffuse public outrage by "creat[ing] the image of public action" (Hornik 1988: 6). The campaign suggests political responsiveness while actually placing the blame for the problem (which is poorly designed highways) on the individual driver, who was told to drive carefully but didn't obey.

Organizer and Maintainer

If planners base their work on the assumption that media campaigns *can* change behavior, at least sometimes and in some fields, they still must tackle the problem of how to maintain and reinforce change over time. In this respect, communication can play a useful role through repeated messages over an extended period of time; however, the long-term approach must be planned (and budgeted) for from the very beginning. A case in point is the many heart-disease campaigns where long-term and sustained change in behavior (diet, exercise, smoking) is the goal and resources are allocated from the start with that goal in mind.

Equalizer

Hornik points cautiously to the equalizing potential of certain communication technologies. Satellites, for example, can reach both urban and rural areas at the same time and cost, provided, of course, there is receiving equipment available. Caution is prudent. Much evidence suggests that as far as innovations are concerned, "the better off do better" (Hornik 1988: 7). From seat belt use to dieting and exercise patterns, middle and upper classes innovate more readily and, therefore, benefit more and more quickly from the messages of planned communication. Hornik sums up the situation succinctly: "Only some people have anyone to call when satellite technology brings telephone service to rural villages" (1988: 8).

Accelerator of Interaction

Frequently it is imperative for receivers of messages to communicate with the sender and to do so quickly. In a blood donation campaign, for example, the success of the campaign depends on the receiver committing to donate blood. "So you don't forget, call 555-1212 now – operators are standing by," provides an immediate opportunity for a receiver to do that. Hotlines, suggestion and complaint boxes, postpaid surveys, telephone polling, computer bulletin boards, and similar devices have been used successfully as facilitators of interaction.

A Final Consideration for the Communication Planner

Let us underscore our message in this chapter by pointing out an interesting distinction between theory failures and program failures (Suchman 1967; Hornik 1988). Theory failures result from mistakenly applying a communication-based solution to a problem in the first place. (Recall our example of the unsuccessful politician.) Program failures, in contrast, result from poor design and implementation of efforts that were meant to solve communication problems, for example, overestimating the reach of a medium or using a crude segmentation technique.

Hornik (1988) adds another explanation of failure based on his study of development communication in the Third World. He calls the phenomenon political failure. This is not caused so much by the political system in a given context, but by the communication planner's failure to assess and account for the constraints (and opportunities) exercised by those in political power. A communication campaign must "fit" the general political climate and be useful to the politicians responsible for the realm it affects. Those politicians also may be the ones controlling the necessary financial and organizational backing. However frustrating it may be for the planner, avoidance of theory and program failures often is not enough to overcome the possibility of a political failure.

5 Categorization of Basic Strategies

In this chapter we will discuss some basic types of communication strategies. We rely on a contingency perspective, which in this case calls for the communication planner to consider the specific conditions and then choose among a number of different strategy options. And this is our point: there usually *are* several options available for every communication project. Rarely is there any excuse for falling back on routine solutions without considering alternatives.[1]

Historically, early strategic thinking built on linear and one-way processes, initiated and organized from outside the system (organization, group, etc.). Later, influenced by cybernetic theory, feedback devices were introduced into the strategies. The sender needed to know the reactions of the receivers so that communication could be modified, if necessary. Next, strategies incorporated the notion of mutuality – monologues transformed into dialogues. A recent development reflects a growing conviction that in many cases goals are better achieved not by talking to publics, or even with them, but rather by enabling them to communicate among themselves.

In an influential article in 1978, a leading scholar in the diffusion of innovation tradition, E.M. Rogers, noted the passing of the traditional paradigm of national development and communication. It was, he said, too heavily oriented toward change induced from outside and above.[2]

Paradigms of planned communication, then, change.[3] The reasons are varied. Theorists point to changes in overall social theory, causing changes in practices in the field of planned communication. Others hold ideological shifts responsible; still others believe changes stem from a maturing process within the field itself as planners develop and refine strategies of planned communication.

Strategies Defined from Outside or Inside

We will present four basic communication strategies in this chapter. This discussion assumes the existence of a problem that is to be solved by using communication. There are two principal means by which a situation is defined as a problem: it can be defined by people internal to the social system (group, organization, etc.) involved, or external to it. The definition of the problem implies as a goal that it should be solved.

A taxonomy of communication strategies could be based on several criteria. Ours has as its first variable *who* defines the problem and the goals necessary to solve it. The value reflected is that communication initiated, either fully or partly, from within a social system can be as effective as when an outside force assumes the communication initiative on behalf of a group.

The second variable deals with the identification of the (communication) *means* to address the problem. This may be done as well from inside the social system in question as from outside it.

A communication process designed to address a problem may, then, be initiated outside the social grouping involved, for example, in the shape of a centrally planned campaign. Or the process may arise, more or less spontaneously, from within the social system or grouping that wants to produce some result within or outside its system. (A similar classification for different types of social change is presented by Rogers and Shoemaker 1971.)

Traditionally, problems and the goals to solve them in communication campaigns have been defined outside the actual social grouping or system. In many cases, though, it may be difficult to determine whether a goal or a communication solution is defined and initiated from inside or outside a certain social system. Decisions that must be made in the planning process may be dependent on long processes difficult to picture clearly, making this sort of analysis instrumental to the planning. The combination of our two basic variables is seen in Figure 5.1.

Traditional Communication/Information Campaign Solutions
Rogers (1976) and others are critical of the fact that too many communication strategies, both past and present, fall into this category. While this

COMMUNICATION SOLUTION IS DEFINED

	Outside the System	Inside the System
DEFINITION OF PROBLEM AND GOAL ARISES — Outside the System	Traditional communication/ information campaign 1	External impetus requiring internal follow-through External initiative 2
DEFINITION OF PROBLEM AND GOAL ARISES — Inside the System	Internal impetus requiring external follow-through Communication support 3	Grass roots initiative 4

Figure 5.1 *Four communication strategies*

practice may seem undemocratic and authoritarian, in many cases it has been the only way to effect change. The most common example of this type of communication is commercial advertising. The major problem with this solution is that people are not easily motivated by communication coming from outside with goals set by others. For the sender, however, retaining control over message content and the formulation of goals may compensate for that problem.

External Initiative Solution

Cell 2 is illustrated by the government of a developing country suggesting that farmers cooperate more with each other, but doing nothing more to encourage or facilitate the effort. The sender hopes that groups of farmers will start discussing what can be done in their community to reach the goal. This is an inexpensive way for a centralized institution to get things done – perhaps. All resources can be focused on promoting the goal. Control of the subsequent process, however, is marginal. Again there is the problem of motivating people to strive for a goal defined elsewhere.

Communication Support Solution

Cell 3, like Cell 2, is a "mixed" strategy. Let's say that an association representing the owners of small business approaches the Small Business Administration, complaining about the amount of paperwork required to file taxes and asking for clearer guidelines; the Administration studies the problem and comes up with an information program that clarifies which forms must be filed in which cases. The advantage of this strategy is that the people with the problem define the problem and the goal; this can be a strong motivating factor. A problem arises from outsiders ascertaining what kind of communication support is acceptable and suitable for the group in question.

Grass Roots Initiative

The strategy of Cell 4 is the opposite of the traditional information/communication campaign solution. Both goal-setting and deciding on communication means to achieve them reside with the group of people involved or the actual social system. Every day, around the world, thousands of such communication groups and networks operate within this strategy. Sports clubs, study circles, trade unions, and cooperatives come into being every day as a result of initiatives coming from within the social system in question.

Put somewhat cynically, this is the optimal strategy because it allows goals to be reached and problems to be solved without cost to those outside the group involved. For example, if community volunteer groups maintain their own health programs, the result is inexpensive compared to a solution where the community is held responsible for health care. Alcoholics Anonymous is a good example of a grass roots effort that relieves the system of one of its functions, in this case, psychiatric units of hospitals with the function of controlling alcohol abuse.

These classifications suggest that there are several communication solutions to a problem. Let us see how the same problem might be approached from the four different perspectives just discussed – each representing a cell in our fourfold table. The goal in our example is persuading high school graduates to quit smoking and become non-smokers.

Case 1: The National Association Against Tobacco Use (NAATU) launches a major campaign against smoking. The campaign, directed toward high school students, consists of leaflets emphasizing the benefits of quitting. (Traditional information/communication campaign solution.)

Case 2: NAATU contacts student councils at the high schools across the country, announcing a competition for "The most successful high school quit-smoking program." Specific solutions to the problem will be locally defined and the communication will emerge in the form of small campaigns and local quit-smoking groups. (External Initiative, or Dumping the Problem on Your Doorstep solution.)

Case 3: The same association establishes and maintains a clearinghouse that offers informational materials to groups and individuals that want to initiate anti-smoking efforts. Materials tailored to different needs – small group self-help programs, audio-visual lecture materials, exhibit booth models, school curricular materials for all grade levels, scientific journal articles, statistical summaries – are available. Here, the problem and goal are defined by members of a group; they rely on an outside agency (in this case, NAATU) for the solution. (Communication Support, or Bring in the Heavy Artillery solution.)

Case 4: At several high schools, students form self-help groups to quit smoking. They know that the aim is sanctioned by society, but the actual initiative, both in terms of defining the problem and goals and coming up with a solution, is in the hands of the students themselves. (Grass Roots Initiative.)

The role of the communication planner changes in each different strategy. In the traditional information/communication strategy, the planner will be active in both defining the problem and goal and planning the communication. Most activities are within the sphere of the planner, that is, outside the target group or social system. The External Initiative Solution strategy, here also termed the Dumping the Problem on Your Doorstep strategy, calls for the communication planner to promote a goal and motivate the group or social system to find the means to solve the problem themselves. In the Bring in the Heavy Artillery strategy, the planner provides the communication wherewithal for the group to achieve the goals it deems necessary to solve the problem it has defined. And in the Grass Roots Initiative strategy, the planner acts as a facilitator, for example, in terms of logistics for the communication activities being used by the group. This function has not been common, but is one that we believe will be more usual in the future as this strategy becomes better accepted in communication planning.

The Content/Distribution and Processing Strategies

A similar distinction between different strategies in communication work has been presented by Palm and Windahl (1988), who suggest a dichotomy between a content/distribution type of communication strategy and a processing strategy. The former encompasses the production of certain content to be distributed among certain persons. The traditional information/communication campaign, as well as traditional communication models (sender, message, channel, and receivers), fall squarely into this category.

The processing strategy is less goal-directed, putting the emphasis more on immediate efficiency than does the content/distribution strategy. Instead, the process as such is valued and, in many cases, will stand out as an end in and of itself. Communication may be seen in this strategy as a means to reduce tension between people and groups in order to resolve conflicts or to initiate group processes. Another feature of the strategy is that typically it is dynamic and oriented to problem solving.

Obviously the two strategies fulfill different basic functions. The processing strategy is preferable in situations where the goal is long-range and acceptance by different parties is required. The content/distribution approach, in contrast, works better when the goals are uncomplicated, undisputed, and short-term.

Let us illustrate the distinction between the two approaches with an example.

Middlebury, a middle-class suburb of an industrial city, is suffering a rash of vandalism. Most acts are done by young boys, many of whom belong to ethnic minorities. The municipal council hires an advertising agency to produce a campaign against vandalism. Posters and leaflets that include statistics showing the costs of vandalism are distributed throughout Middlebury. The results are unimpressive. Why? This is not a one-way communication problem. People do not need to be informed that vandalism is bad and costly. Few of the vandals read the posters or leaflets; even fewer are influenced by the message. A better strategy would be to involve representatives from the groups affected by the problem (young minority members, homeowners, city officials, etc.) in small-group discussions aimed at finding a solution to the problem. This represents a processing type of strategy rather than the content/distribution one used by the council.

Conversely, the processing strategy is sometimes used when a content/ distribution strategy would be much cheaper and more effective. Many members of organizations recognize the situation where committees gather to discuss matters that have little salience for the people in the group and that will be dealt with the way the organization's leadership wants, regardless of committee recommendations. A five-line memo informing people of the disposition of the matter would save hours of working time.

The approach described in the last paragraph embodies the widespread and "folklore" notion that communication is inherently good. This thinking leads to what some have called communication fetishism (Ekecranz 1978). In some cases, communication may be detrimental to the actual goals of the sender. Increased communication efforts may have little chance for meaningful contribution to the goals of a project if they divert attention from the activities necessary to reach the project's aims. While it may appear paradoxical to question the value of communication in a book about planned communication, recognition of its dysfunctional nature as well as its functional aspects permits the communication planner to assess realistically the roles communication can play in systems and organizations.

The content/distribution–processing typology does not suggest an either/or situation. It would be logical for the planner to apply the content/distribution approach in the beginning phases of a project in order to set the agenda. In later phases, more processing-oriented procedures gradually can be adopted. In the vandalism example, the processing efforts could have been preceded very meaningfully by a content/distribution campaign aimed at generating interest in the issue.

Distribution vs. Supply Strategies

A somewhat more practical distinction is between a distribution strategy and a supply strategy. In the former, the communication planner sees to it that receivers get the information, whether wanted or not. That means that the communication planner defines the information needs of the receivers and chooses the time for the distribution of the information.

The supply strategy calls for the communication planner to store, retrieve, and/or seek stored information for the receivers. It is up to the receivers to define their needs and when they want the information. There are two kinds of supply strategies: passive and active. The passive strategy offers the receivers little personal assistance – the information is stored and made available. The active form is characterized more as a dialogue: information seekers inform someone of their information needs, and that person then helps locate the information sought. (A simple example is the difference between trying by yourself to find a piece of information in a library and asking a reference librarian for assistance with your search.)

Information/communication supply is becoming increasingly technology-bound. With computer databases, supply-type solutions will become more common in the future. The passive/active nature of the strategy will depend on the level of interaction possible with a given database system.

Each of these strategies has advantages and disadvantages. In a complex society, individuals lack a clear picture of their own information needs and do not know where to look for information, even in situations where they may have identified a topic as important. The distribution strategy offers the advantage that agencies and organizations that do know what people ought to be informed about can make people aware by disseminating the relevant information. Senders can send the same information to large groups of receivers, thereby ensuring that the cost per person reached will be low.

The disadvantages of the distribution strategy arise from the level of control a few agencies hold over receivers. The first exercise of control, and the most serious one, is the sender's decision as to what is important information. Second, very often, that information is distributed to the audience at the convenience of the sender, not when the audience needs it. That almost guarantees that the receiver will not react to it. Third, a distribution strategy typically uses mass communication, which is difficult to adapt to the individual. Further, even if the cost per receiver is low, the cost per *relevant* receiver may be high since a distribution strategy reaches people in an indiscriminate way. This also leads to information pollution, which occurs when so many messages clutter an individual's environment that information overload occurs (Rogers and Rogers 1976).

With the supply strategy, the sender can be reasonably sure that the information corresponds to a need and will be used. Costly and wasteful distribution to non-relevant receivers is avoided. The active form of this strategy often involves the use of interpersonal channels with the result that receivers can be more certain that the information given will suit their needs. Also, the risk of information overload decreases.

The down side of the supply strategy is that only the motivated will seek information (Abrahamsson 1972). How an individual becomes motivated is crucial. Hornik (1988) offers the example that when a child in the Third World contracts diarrhea, parents who recognize the danger of the situation will look actively for information. In this case, a passive communication system will be adequate, provided the parents know where to go for information. In less acute circumstances, more active systems will be required to generate an interest that will lead to information-seeking.

Failing to motivate large sectors of society may lead to widened information gaps (see Chapter 15). The burden in the process lies with the individual who seeks the information; as a rule only those with a high communication potential will seek information. According to knowledge-gap theory, those who are already well-informed will seek additional information, thereby widening the gap between the "information rich" and the "information poor" (Bonfadelli 1987b); Chaffee and Wilson

(1977) have coined the terms "media rich" and "media poor" to describe this phenomenon with regard to media use.

In many information areas, it seems, the trend is toward organizing supply-type systems at the expense of distribution ones. In their overview of Swedish civic information, Norberg et al. (1985) note that strategies have passed through the information campaign stage and the democratic stage (emphasis on citizen participation), and now are in the service approach stage (information offered in response to receiver demands). Active supply strategies fit neatly in this last stage. In the health communication field, many examples of active supply strategies can be found. Here is one:

> In Amsterdam, the Netherlands, two daily newspapers carry advertisements encouraging people who think they may have contracted a sexually transmitted disease to call a telephone number. A prerecorded tape (Schuurman and de Haes 1980) informs the caller of the importance of visiting a certain VD clinic. The results suggest that this strategy was successful in motivating readers to seek information: during a 15-week period, 70,000 calls were received. Results from a manned hotline in the United States suggest that an anonymous answering service of the type used in Amsterdam may be more effective (Bryant et al. 1976) when it comes to a subject as sensitive as venereal diseases.

McQuail's Four Communication Patterns

McQuail (1984) presents a comprehensive categorization of sender–receiver communication relationships that can be related to our distribution/supply dichotomy. Here, sender and receiver are characterized as active and passive (Figure 5.2).

The distribution strategy described above corresponds here to the address/dissemination communication pattern, a "one to many" structure

		SENDER	
		Active	Passive
RECEIVER	Active	Exchange/ interaction	Search
	Passive	Address/ dissemination	Time-filling, surveillance

Figure 5.2 *Four types of communication pattern (McQuail 1984)*

found in many types of communication situations – religion, education, and, of course, mass communication.

The supply strategy follows the search pattern most closely, but it also has characteristics of an exchange/interaction situation. Communication on the sender side then is activated by an information-seeking receiver. What is meant to be an active distribution strategy sometimes ends up in a "time-filling" type of situation. For example, in large organizations one often finds that the organization transmits messages, prints leaflets, etc. in a routine, fairly passive way. The audience may or may not take part in the communication process; people receive and read randomly what passes before their eyes.

In general, the shift towards the exchange/interaction cell mitigates some of the drawbacks of the supply strategy we discussed above. It is easier for those with low communication potential to describe their information needs when they engage in a dialogue with the sender.

McQuail predicts that new technologies will cause a shift from address/dissemination to search and exchange/interaction patterns. Increased storage potential of computer-based systems will facilitate information-seeking activity, while other technological developments will contribute to more exchange and interaction, McQuail maintains.

For communication planners, this may mean a change in the nature of their job. Less time will be needed to organize information dissemination via mass communication channels, more time will be spent in motivating the public to seek relevant information and in storing information in ways that ensure easy access. This will mean that providing information promotion or information about information will be a more essential part of the communication planner's work.

Communication for Conformity or Diversity

Communication planning usually views communication and information as means of control and conformity in terms of knowledge, attitudes, values, and behaviors. From a traditional viewpoint, the role of the public relations practitioner, for example, often is conceived of as ensuring that publics hold, if not positive, at least sympathetic attitudes about the company represented. This approach is based on a perception of communication as a unifying force.

Carey (1969), in a discussion of the roles and effects of mass communication, calls this unifying function "centripetal": communication is a force driving people's beliefs toward a center point. The reverse tendency, Carey says, is "centrifugal": (mass) communication functions to fragment, isolate, individualize, etc.

While this centrifugal function has been overlooked in communication planning, there are good reasons to consider its implications in some contexts.

A uniform stock of knowledge and values may be devastating for creativity within an organization. Granovetter's (1973) theory about "the strength of weak ties" is illuminating in this respect. It states that social systems characterized by great homogeneity and emphasizing communication among individuals with similar backgrounds and knowledge lead to less creative information-exchange than heterogeneous systems. A communication system whose aim is uniformity, therefore, may stagnate in terms of creativity.

Social systems will, in certain situations, benefit from encouraging the input of diverse or even contradictory information into the system, as well as from placing people and groups with different knowledge and ideas in contact with one another. Adaptive subsystems in certain generic types of organizational subsystems (e.g. research and development, planning) are designed to guarantee that the organization survives in a changing environment (Katz and Kahn 1978).

In more formal organizations, this need for fresh input has been institutionalized in the boundary-spanning function of the public relations role. This calls for public relations practitioners to function "on the edge of the organization, serving as a liaison between the organization and external groups and individuals. They have one foot in the organization and one outside" (Grunig and Hunt 1984: 9). The communication demands on people in this liaison role are quite taxing: while their loyalties and ties are with the organization that employs them, their communicative behavior must enable them not only to transport the views of their organization to the outside environments, but also to relay the attitudes and interests of the environments (publics) back into the organization.

An example of a situation where a centrifugal strategy would be preferred would be during the conceptualization phase of a research project. While encouraging participants to look for information from a number of different sources may result in conflict initially, the range of options will be greater and the basis for rational choices in the development of the research project strengthened as a result.

Let us turn from these fundamental and general bases for distinguishing different communication strategies to an analysis of different explanations of how communication occurs.

Notes

1 The theoretical foundations of the contingency approach were developed in management science. As early as the 1950s, researchers detected that some of the most cherished management principles worked only some of the time – depending on the type of the organization or the kind of environment. See, for example, Duncan 1978: 373–400; for an overview of German literature, see Staehle 1987: 92–105.

2 Not only the role of mass communication in national development, but the very notion of development, changed drastically from the 1960s to the 1970s. In 1978, Rogers defined development as "a widely participatory process of social change in a society, intended to bring about both social and material advancement (including greater equality, freedom, and other valued qualities) for the majority of the people through their gaining

greater control over their environment" (Rogers 1978: 68). In earlier definitions, only the modernization aspect was emphasized. As to the role of mass communication in development, its potential is viewed now as much more modest; its contribution to self-development is limited to two areas: (1) providing technical information about development problems in answer to local requests; and (2) circulating information about the self-development accomplishments of local groups so that other such groups may profit from their experience and perhaps be challenged to perform similarly (Rogers 1978).

3 A paradigm is a certain way of scientifically looking at a phenomenon, thus serving as a "guidebook" for a scientific community (Kuhn 1970).

PART II THEORETICAL APPROACHES TO COMMUNICATION PLANNING

In the second part of this book, we shall present several fairly well-known approaches to communication planning. "Approach", as we are using it, refers to ways of thinking about planning and not necessarily to specific techniques. We shall deal primarily with design and transmission issues in directed communication.

Some of these approaches, such as social marketing or communication campaigns, have been developed explicitly for communication planning; others (e.g. two-step flow, network analysis), in contrast, are tools for analyzing specific communication settings. They also can be treated as major building elements for strategies of planning.

6 Multi-Step Flow Approaches

The following discussion will deal first with the "classic" two-step model of communication formulated by Lazarsfeld and Katz, and its development over time. The two-step flow of information is a robust theory that has influenced the communication field for over 30 years. Recognizing that individuals receive information from each other within a communication environment as well as from mass media, the model structures the process by which messages move through mass media and interpersonal channels from source to receiver. The challenge for the communication planner is to take advantage of this structure; this involves as a fundamental step identifying and enlisting the support of opinion leaders, who perform the functions of receiving, processing, and disseminating information.

We shall also present the diffusion of innovations theory as developed by Rogers. Diffusion of innovations theory is partly informed by the two-step flow of information model. It combines and modifies aspects of that model and other theories to produce a model that provides communication planners with a body of knowledge directly relevant to their purposes.

Both approaches share two fundamental assumptions: more than one channel usually is necessary to effect successful planned communication, and communication results are not achieved through one step (or stage) alone, but often require two or more. Dating back to the 1950s and early 1960s, the two-step and diffusion theories have been subjected to a great deal of academic discussion and modification. From the situational perspective, they still provide useful guiding principles to the planner for choosing among options arising during the course of a communication effort.

The Two-Step Flow of Information Model

Few models in communication research have been as influential in describing the nature of mass communication and its effects as the one suggested by the two-step flow of information theory. The idea was first presented and described in 1955 by Katz and Lazarsfeld in their book, *Personal Influence*. (For a good summary, see Katz 1957.) Since then, it has, in the opinion of some researchers, become an essential part of the dominant paradigm of mass communication research (Gitlin 1978). Few theoretical models are considered by practitioners of planned communication to be as useful as this one. We shall see, however, that when transformed into a working theory, it is not without its practical problems.

The two-step model often is described as a portent of the decline of the so-called hypodermic view of mass media effects (see Chapter 15 and O'Sullivan et al. 1983), which maintains that the media tend to influence individuals directly and as isolated individuals. The two-step model also is viewed as an important contribution to the trend toward a more social-centered picture of the mass communication process (Delia 1987; Schenk 1987). Many point to it as evidence of the relative powerlessness of mass communication media; others, however, arrive at an opposite interpretation – that, in combination with interpersonal channels, mass communication can be very influential (Noelle-Neumann 1973; McQuail 1987).

The model grew out of empirical studies of how the public was influenced by media coverage of an electoral campaign (Lazarsfeld et al. 1944) and analysis of women's buying decisions (Katz and Lazarsfeld 1955). These studies suggested that individuals were more influential than the media in getting people to vote and purchase in certain ways.

Two Stages of Communication

Briefly stated, the theory suggests that information reaches the public indirectly via so-called opinion leaders. These are people who tend to consume more media output, discuss certain themes with others, and participate more in organizations than do others in their immediate environment. Opinion leaders function more or less as experts for others, mediating information gathered in the media. They then translate the perceptions they receive from the media and adapt them to the public, which sometimes is labeled "followers." Generally, these characteristics differentiate leaders from followers (Severin 1988: 201):

1 personification of values (who one is);
2 competence (what one knows);
3 strategic social location (whom one knows).

As we mentioned, this two-step flow process supplanted the hypodermic effects model, which had dominated mass communication theory for several decades. Figure 6.1 graphically contrasts the two theories.

One of the values of the two-step flow model is that it connects mass and interpersonal communication. This notion is of great importance for planned communication work, offering a point of departure for different strategies. Once it is understood that information spontaneously travels indirectly as described in the model, communication planners deliberately may try to design strategies that take advantage of this mass/interpersonal interplay.

The model also reminds us of the value of combining different channels in communication. This is acknowledged widely in theories of diffusion of innovations (see below) and in communication campaign designs (see, for example, Farquhar et al. 1984).

The two-step flow model suggests a more profound conclusion as well.

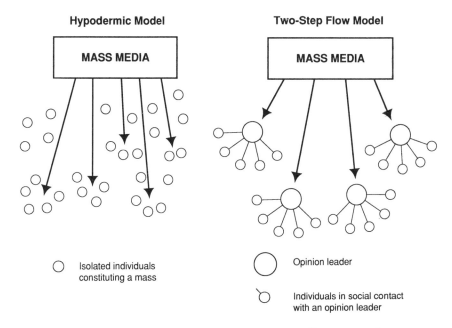

Figure 6.1 **Hypodermic effects approach and two-step flow approach**
to mass communication (after McQuail and Windahl 1983)

This model was one of the first to suggest that the audience is composed
of social beings who communicate among themselves, are more or less
influential, and are active in many contexts. Mass communication is not
just a matter of communication between media and the audience, period.
The mass communicator's message may travel in unforeseen ways. This
model takes an important step down the road toward the notion of the
(mass) communication process and its extensions as a ubiquitous phenomenon, permeating the social fabric in many ways. The implication for
the communication planner is to look outside routine mass communication boundaries for communication solutions.

The Relative Importance of Each Stage

Rogers (1983) points out that the two steps differ considerably in more
than just the fact that the channels employed are of different types. The
first step, he says, contains a transfer of *information*, while the second
provides a transfer of *influence* for *both* leaders and followers. This
supports the notion of supremacy of personal over mass communication
channels in terms of ability to influence and effect change. This conclusion characterizes Rogers' research, as well as that of others, about the
diffusion of innovations. In the process of innovation adoption, initial
information/knowledge about innovations, to a large degree, is conveyed
by the mass media; the subsequent decision of whether or not to adopt
is strongly influenced by interpersonal communication (see below).[1]

A common conclusion about the two-step flow model is, thus, that it demonstrates the superiority of interpersonal communication over mass communication in terms of capability to influence. Chaffee (1986) takes issue with that, pointing out that the influence of a communication channel depends very much on the specific conditions at hand. An important factor, for example, is how accessible either of the channels is; for some people, interpersonal communication is more influential because they are reached by more interpersonal channels. For some types of messages, people find the mass media more credible than interpersonal channels. A study of the dissemination of reports of the shooting of President Kennedy showed that of those hearing the news from another person, only 24 percent wholly believed it, compared to 44 percent of those receiving the news from television. A number of studies reviewed by Westley (1971) suggest that major news stories *generally* are more likely to be spread by the media than by opinion leaders. As you can see, stating that interpersonal communication is more effective than mass communication is a gross simplification.[2]

Not Simply Leaders and Followers

It is easy to get the impression from the two-step flow model that the mass communication influence process contains only two types of individuals: those who are active (opinion leaders) and those who are passive (opinion followers). This simplification, of course, does not reflect a complex reality. Large parts of the public do not belong to either of these groups. The notions of passivity and activity that are attached to the terms "follower" and "leader" are also misleading: followers are not in all cases passive, leaders are not always active. Followers may initiate interaction with the opinion leader; leaders may offer information in response to a request as well as on their own initiative (Bostian 1970; Troldahl 1966).

Two kinds of opinion leaders have been identified: those who actively attempt to influence others (talkers), and those who do not but, nevertheless, are asked about their opinions (passive leaders) (Kingdon 1970). Both types tend to be more knowledgeable than other people, with talkers being better informed than passive leaders.

Research through the years suggests that the original two-step flow model provides only a simplified picture of reality. It is apparent, for example, that opinion leaders may obtain their information other than through the mass media – through interaction with other opinion leaders (McQuail and Windahl 1983) is one possibility.

This suggests other versions of the model in which communication travels from a medium to one opinion leader, from the leader to another opinion leader, then to yet another who disseminates the information to followers. In a study of political opinion leaders in the Federal Republic of Germany, Schenk (1985) discovered they do not necessarily use media more extensively than the rest of the population, but they participate more actively in political organizations and groups. The two-step flow model becomes a multi-step, or N-step, model (McQuail 1987). McCombs and Becker (1979) view the relationship between interpersonal discussion and reception of mass-mediated messages as cyclical: people first learn about an event from newspapers or television; this stimulates them to discuss the event with other people. Attention to the media messages in the first place, however, may have stemmed from prior discussions. It is quite misleading to assume that only opinion leaders receive information through the media.

The very term opinion leader is misleading as it suggests that information originates with this individual, who, according to the model, merely reconstructs and mediates it. The concept of power, ignored in this characterization of the role, is evident in De Fleur's description of the social context in which the opinion leader functions: "An important information content or subject matter exists to which the opinion leader has greater access than the other members of the group. By controlling the transmission and interpretation of this information to the group he can influence decisions and consensus within the group regarding the content" (1962: 262).

"Using" Opinion Leaders

The communication planner tries to exploit the opinion leader's power over the group for the purposes of the planned communication. It is, however, a two-edged sword. Opinion leaders also may use this power to defeat planned communication efforts. Meyer et al. (1977) cite examples of campaigns to fluoridate city water that have been strongly opposed, sometimes successfully, by groups centered around strong opinion leaders. This phenomenon occurs in others areas as well, such as the environment, establishment of community-based mental health facilities, refugee resettlement, etc.

When, then, is the model practicable in directed communication work? What opportunities does it offer, and what obstacles should the planner anticipate? In principle, the model is applicable when the communication goals to be achieved require a reinforcement through personal trust. This, according to the model, is one of the things opinion leaders can supply. A fundamental prerequisite of the original model is the existence of both a mass communication and an interpersonal communication system. McQuail and Windahl (1983) point out that the model may be less applicable in developing countries where there are few mass media, and in developed countries in crisis situations where normal interpersonal and mass communication structures break down. In an organizational setting, "mass media" may include company newsletters, pamphlets, and so on. The organization's communication planner may use these media partly to inform opinion leaders and to motivate them to further these communications.

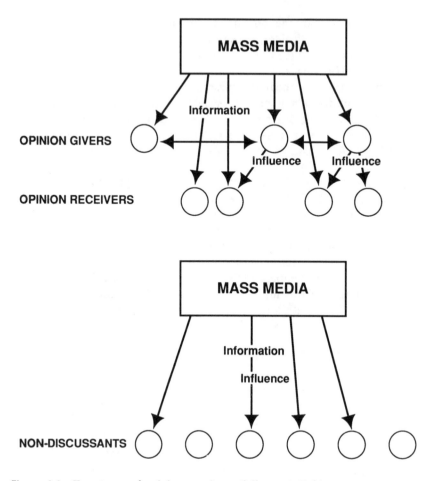

Figure 6.2 *Two types of opinion receivers (followers) (Robinson 1976)*

A serious problem for the communication planner in relying on this model is sometimes a lack of control over the process. The opinion leader/opinion follower relationship often is spontaneous and cannot be prescribed from outside. The opinion follower must be motivated to seek information from the opinion leader, and the opinion leader must find it worthwhile to inform others about the issue in question. Also, opinion leaders are selective about what information they receive.

The model's usefulness hinges on the ability to (a) identify and (b) reach opinion leaders. In some cases, we can assume that certain individuals or groups of individuals are opinion leaders because of their occupations or formal positions in the social structure. Players and fans consider a volleyball coach an opinion leader with regard to volleyball equipment; a doctor is an opinion leader in matters concerning health, even outside the context of the hospital. In less clearly defined cases, it is necessary to rely on surveys and other kinds of data to determine who is a probable opinion leader.

Variations on the Model: Opinion Leader to Opinion Leader

We can conceive of two-step influence processes other than the mass media/interpersonal channel one presented above. For example, both steps may be interpersonal. Say the communication planner of a company identifies and gathers together opinion leaders representing different sections of the organization; in a face-to-face setting, the planner gives them information and urges them to spread it to their colleagues. This approach may achieve greater effects in this situation than the mass media/interpersonal version because the communication planner has retained more control over the process.

The original two-step flow model also is limited in its characterization of followers. Robinson (1976), for example, distinguishes between people who are involved in social networks (they get some information from what he calls "opinion givers") and those who are not (they are more susceptible to a one-step influence emanating from the mass media). Hence, there are at least two types of opinion receiver, as presented in Figure 6.2.

Diffusion of Innovations Theory

For a communication planner, few approaches to the field of communication are as valuable as those suggested by the theories that surround the process of diffusion of innovations. The purpose of communication planning is often promotion of an innovation, be it a healthy lifestyle, a new way to save energy, or the introduction of personal computers to homes and workplaces (Dutton et al. 1987). Diffusion theory is founded largely on empirical observations of various forms of planned communication.

The diffusion process embodies several of the aspects discussed throughout this book, such as the two-step flow of information model, networking, information gaps, and attitude change. A planned diffusion process in many cases is a traditional communication campaign. As is the case in most communication campaigns, the outcome of the diffusion process is supposed to be change, very often behavioral change. Changes in terms of knowledge and attitudes are considered to be intermediary steps in a decision process. While some other approaches are interested primarily in how people receive information and then distribute it to others, diffusion theory's focus is whether and how people adopt or reject an innovation (Severin 1988).

As with many other models of communication, recent developments in the diffusion model have departed from a strictly one-way, downward directed communication approach. Traditionally the model emphasized, in McQuail's (1987: 273) words, "organization and planning, linearity of effect, hierarchy (of status and expertise), social structure (thus personal experience), reinforcement and feedback." In recent times, horizontal exchanges of communication as well as communication from below in social systems have become more important. An interplay between mass communication and interpersonal communication is characteristic of the approach.

The model is not without its weaknesses. Among them are a pro-innovation bias (assuming that innovations are good in and of themselves) and an individual blame bias (as opposed to system blame, see Chapter 4) (Rogers 1987). Sociologists criticize a lack of integration of diffusion and social change theory (Schenk 1987; Schmidt 1976; Lin and Zaltman 1973).

The most comprehensive and cogent presentation of the theory is found in E.M. Rogers' *Diffusion of Innovations* (1983). In 1986, 1987 and 1988, he published short versions of his theory of diffusion of innovations. Rogers is the principal figure in the development of this theory, and his work provides the basis for our discussion.

Two Definitions

Let us start by defining two basic concepts. *Diffusion* is the "process by which an innovation is communicated through certain channels over a period of time among the members of a social system" (Rogers 1987: 79). An *innovation* is "an idea, practice, or object that is perceived to be new by an individual or other unit of adoption" (1987: 79). Rogers' current views of the diffusion process are based on the convergence model of communication, which he and Kincaid developed in the context of their network approach to communication (Rogers and Kincaid 1981). We discuss the convergence model in Chapter 7 of this book; let us just quote here the basis of this model: "Communication is a process in which participants create and share information with one another to reach a mutual understanding" (Rogers 1987: 79).

The Adoption Process

For someone working in planned communication, probably the most relevant part of diffusion theory is the adoption process, in which an individual or groups of individuals are confronted with an innovation and react to it, one way or another. While communication occurs throughout the process – the individual receives unrequested information, seeks information, gives away and exchanges information – the interplay between mass and interpersonal communication is crucial at this stage.

The adoption process is divided into different stages, each with its own characteristics, for example, the media and channels involved. These stages are (in order of occurrence) the knowledge, persuasion, decision, implementation, and confirmation stages.

The Knowledge Stage

Acquisition of knowledge occurs when a person or some other unit of adoption is exposed to the innovation and its function. This stage may be characterized by activity as well as passivity. A person may actively seek a solution to a problem by turning to a variety of sources, from mass media to opinion leaders. Someone else, while not actively looking for a solution to a problem or need, may come across information about an innovation by chance or be the target of planned information about it. Or the actual innovation may be observed in use.

The different ways that information reaches these two types are of interest to the communication planner. To reach active seekers, information must be supplied to those media, institutions, and people the seekers are likely to contact. To reach members of the passive group, information should be transmitted through media and channels where those people habitually look for other kinds of information.

Rogers (1987) divides innovation knowledge into three types:

- *Software information*, or awareness-knowledge information, answers questions such as, What is the innovation? What does it do?
- *How-to knowledge* helps the individual obtain and use the innovation as it should be used. Information answers questions such as, Where can I find it? What does it cost? How do I hook it up?
- *Principles knowledge* includes the general ideas behind the innovation, for example, the scientific laws that apply to the functioning of the innovation. This information would answer questions such as, Is this really new, or does it essentially work the same way as its predecessors?

Of the types mentioned above, principles knowledge is in general the least called for by the public, although this varies with the type of innovation and public. The more expert the public, the more relevant principles knowledge information becomes.

How-to information often is overlooked by the communication planner. For example, if a campaign tries to convince people to accept the innovation of eating fiber-rich food, it is not enough just to say, "People should eat more fiber" if the public does not know which foods contain fiber and how to prepare them. In many cases, as Rogers points out, insufficient how-to information results in the innovation not being used or practiced properly which, in turn, may lead to its being abandoned.

(Another common mistake is the failure of a planner from one culture to account for factors that are inherent in the culture of the potential adopters. This can occur in any of the phases of the diffusion process.)

Many times, success in a diffusion campaign is measured in terms of knowledge of an innovation, which may mean only awareness of its existence. If the public is not informed properly about how to obtain the innovation, if members of the public believe they lack the resources to adopt it, or if it is not culturally acceptable, knowledge about the innovation, of itself, means very little. Diffusion of innovation theory points out that knowledge is not a one-dimensional concept.

Research shows, according to Rogers, that earlier "knowers" rank higher in the following dimensions than those who become informed about the innovation later: mass media use, status, education, and number of interpersonal contacts. In terms of channels, information in this stage typically is disseminated by mass communication media. Since knowledge about innovations often comes from outside, cosmopolites, e.g. people who travel extensively or who recently have moved into a community, are more influential than more provincial locals.

The Persuasion Stage

In the persuasion stage, individuals form an opinion or attitude, either positive or negative, about the innovation. Client-related information is important here since it is the individuals themselves who will experience the benefits as well as the drawbacks of the innovation, once it is accepted and put into practice. Our discussions of source and media credibility, expertise, etc. (see Chapter 10) are relevant for this phase.

In this stage, interpersonal channels are more crucial than they are in the knowledge stage. An interpersonal source may better formulate a message to be relevant for a potential adopter than can a mass communication channel. Much of persuasion will occur through peers who already have some experience with the innovation. Their behavior, then, is imitated.

The Decision Stage

The next stage in Rogers' scheme is that of decision. The two main options for the individual are either to adopt or to reject the innovation. Even if the two prior stages have convinced an individual to adopt, factors such as scarcity of resources and negative attitudes of others in the environment may prevent adoption. While most efforts of a communication planner are concentrated in the knowledge and persuasion stage, you can see the necessity of keeping in mind the whole process.

Providing practical assistance is one means by which the communication planner can influence decision making positively. Returning to our example of eating more fiber, suggesting a month's menus that suit the potential adopter's taste and resources is information that enables adoption. A free sample may encourage adoption, as would help to finance acquisition of the innovation. It is easier for potential adopters to decide to adopt if there are role models around, adopters with whom they can identify; the absence of such models may slow the spread of diffusion considerably.

The need for role models has proved problematic, however, in the case of AIDS campaigns. Persuading people to use condoms is problematic because adopters tend not to talk about it. That means that potential role models do not play a part in others' decisions. A positive example comes from the Stanford Heart Disease Prevention Program. Program organizers selected 500 people in two Californian communities. These people had taken steps toward lowering their heart-disease-related risk (through quitting smoking, changing their diets, etc.); otherwise, they were no different from the rest of the population. They became promoters of the health awareness program. Each was put in contact with ten high-risk followers, creating a pool of 5,000 people who would pass on preventive health information to the remaining 95 percent of the population (Rogers 1987).

The Implementation Stage

In this stage, individuals begin using the innovation. Here the client-related information becomes crucial. By this time adopters must know where to get the innovation and how to practice and use it. The how-to information given at this stage can determine whether or not the adoption will endure. For example, if villagers in a developing country drill a well and install a new pump, but install it improperly, it probably will break down and they will abandon the innovation.

For the innovation to be implemented and used, an adopter must be able to locate and obtain it. A Swedish AIDS campaign offers an example of a violation of this principle. In several ads and posters, Swedes were encouraged to take AIDS tests (a behavior that can be considered an innovation), and many were prepared to follow through. Hospitals, however, were not prepared to administer the number of tests being requested; instead they told the people requesting the test to call back some weeks later. Many probably reacted by never making the second contact.

The Confirmation Stage

It is well known from social psychological theory that people often seek reinforcing information after they make a decision (Schenk 1987). The last stage in the Rogers model, the confirmation stage, relates to this function of information. Negative post-implementation information from other sources about an innovation may cause frustration and discontinuation of the innovation. It is wise, therefore, for a communication planner to extend his communication efforts to the period after implementation, encouraging the continued use of the innovation and assuring the adopters that they were wise to implement the new practice. This is paralleled in what McGuire (1989) calls the "postbehavioral consolidation" phase of persuasion; in the consumer behavior literature, too, much emphasis is placed on communication after a purchasing decision (Kroeber-Riel 1984).

Stages and Channels

As indicated in our discussion of the adoption process, each stage has one or more preferred channels. Mass media on the whole are considered more effective in the first stages, while interpersonal channels are more important in the later stages. This is logical since the knowledge function has less personal significance for the individual than decision and implementation. Those activities involve higher personal stakes for the adopter. In the later stages of the process, individuals need information that (a) they can trust and (b) is relevant for people in their circumstances. As Hornik (1988) points out, however, it is premature to rule out altogether the importance of mass media in these phases. Radio in Third World agriculture campaigns, for example, may positively influence the adoption rate. (From a purely pragmatic standpoint, cost considerations alone, for example, may lead the planner to emphasize radio instead of interpersonal channels in all stages of the innovation process.) The situational approach, then, should be extended to channel choice as well (see also Chaffee 1986).

Degree of Innovativeness: From Innovators to Laggards

Based on when they embrace an innovation, Rogers (1983) categorizes adopters in the following way:

- innovators, making up about 2.5 percent of those accepting the innovation;
- early adopters, 13.5 percent;
- early majority, 34 percent;
- late majority, 34 percent;
- laggards, 16 percent.

The percentages are based on a normal statistical distribution, which puts 68 percent of the population within the limits of the standard deviation. The categories are ideal types and should be treated as such. The distribution is shown in Figure 6.3.

Innovators are described by Rogers as people who dare to take risks.

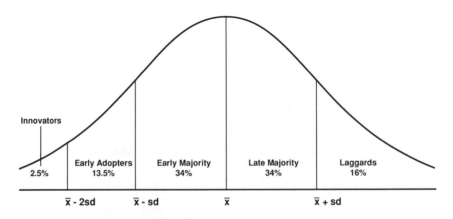

Figure 6.3 **The distribution of adopter categories (Rogers 1983)**

Their social environment includes more cosmopolitan relationships than those of members of the other categories. *Early adopters* are respected locals rather than cosmopolites. They tend to be the people to whom others turn for advice. The *early majority* tends to be deliberate in its decision making. It is an important link to the next category.

Members of the *late majority* are sceptical. They usually need peer pressure in order to adopt an innovation. To some extent, this caution may have its roots in scarce resources. The *laggards* are suspicious of new things. They are attached firmly to the traditions of their social system. They, too, as a rule are limited by scarce resources.

Like early knowers, innovators and early adopters are characterized by higher levels of the following: education, social status, upward mobility, ability to deal with abstractions, rational orientation, interconnectedness with their social network, and cosmopoliteness (Rogers 1987). Chaffee (1986) notes, however, that the most educated stratum often is not among the first to adopt, to some extent because its members tend to seek additional viewpoints, using more than one channel to seek information. In a health campaign, we would expect the more educated to initially seek information and discuss a new health practice at greater length than others. This takes some time, resulting in a delay in these individuals' adoption of the innovation.

Adopters, Channels and Arguments

As with the different stages of the adoption process, we assume one channel is more influential for each category of adopters. Chaffee (1986) notes that later adopters may rely more on interpersonally transmitted information, perhaps due to limited resources in terms of money, education, and literacy. These people typically do not use the media as extensively as the early adopters, making it likely that their awareness of the innovation occurs at a relatively late stage of the innovation-decision process when interpersonal sources are more readily available. This does not automatically mean this category *prefers* to learn about the innovation through interpersonal channels; rather, structural constraints make this form of acquisition more practical for the group (Chaffee 1986).

Some health communication campaigns have made use of early adopters to influence later ones. In the North Karelia project (see Chapter 10), early adopters of certain health practices such as quitting smoking were used to encourage others to follow suit. In such cases, early adopters may function as identifiable opinion leaders or role models for the communication planner.

We also suspect that different adopter categories are influenced by different types of messages and arguments. The innovators may be tempted by messages emphasizing the newness and actuality of the innovation, whereas the laggards react positively to arguments that the innovation is being used successfully by a great number of people, many of whom are similar to the laggards themselves. The automobile advertisement that urges the audience to "keep up with the Joneses" clearly is directed to laggards.

The Nature of the Innovation

While most of the attention in diffusion of innovations research has been devoted to the study of the individual, the nature of the innovation itself is not without importance. Rogers (1983) identifies the following qualities of an innovation:

- *Relative advantage.* To be adopted, something about the innovation must make it worthwhile to consider. For example, it may convey more status than the previous alternatives, or be easier to operate, or be cheaper.
- *Compatibility.* An innovation must fit into already existing arrangements, be they technical, logistical, or whatever. More important, it must fit into cultural norms and traditions.
- *Complexity.* The innovation cannot be perceived as too difficult to use or to understand.
- *Ability to be tried.* An innovation that can be tried on a limited basis, without total commitment to its adoption, is more likely to be accepted, all other aspects being equal.
- *Observability.* The consequences of some innovations are readily revealed to others; their uses, benefits, drawbacks, etc. are easy to grasp, making them more likely to be adopted earlier. The effects of other innovations are less easily appreciated.

The Course of Adoption

Different innovations are diffused and adopted at different rates. The process of diffusion generally follows an S-shaped curve: after slow initial development, the process takes off at about a 10 to 25 percent adoption rate (Rogers 1983: 11). As we have seen, many factors contribute to the rate of adoption, defined as "the relative speed with which an innovation is adopted by members of a social system" (1983: 252). Rogers summarizes these variables in the model shown in Figure 6.4.

The first bundle of variables represents the *perceived attributes* of an innovation. Remember that we are talking about subjective aspects of the nature of innovations; it is the potential adopter's own perception of the innovation that, in the end, will be decisive.

When it comes to the *type of innovation-decision*, clearly an innovation is adopted more quickly if the use or practice is prescribed by law rather than being at the individual's discretion. The use of car seat belts provides an example: purely informational efforts to convince people to adopt the practice have yielded only marginal results, but when a seat belt law is imposed, the adoption rate increases considerably. Other forms of collective pressure, too, may stimulate the rate of adoption.

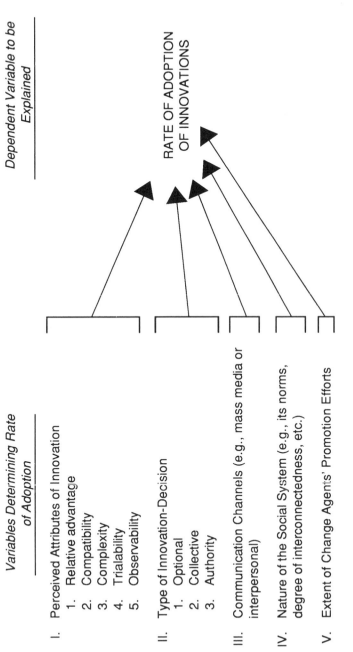

Figure 6.4 *The process of innovation adoption (Rogers 1983)*

As for communication channels, it is likely that adoption rates will be higher where a developed mass communication infrastructure exists; where this infrastructure is less developed, adoption, especially during the awareness phases, will lag.

The nature of the actual social system is of great importance. A traditional system makes acceptance of an innovation more difficult, especially if the innovation is not in line with cultural norms. A system characterized by disconnectedness and isolation also impedes diffusion.

Change agents are communication planners. Let us look more closely at the part they play.

Change Agents

A pivotal role in the diffusion of innovations process is played by the change agent, described by Rogers (1983: 312) as ". . . an individual who influences clients' innovation decisions in a direction deemed desirable by a change agency." Change agents may be found on different levels, from the grass roots up, in a diffusion program, and their role may be more or less explicit and visible to the clients and others in the environment.

The change agent has different functions at different stages of the innovation process. The agent often points out the need for change, establishes communication relationships, sees to it that adoption and change really take place, and, in the end, tries to transform adopters into change agents. Rogers (1983: 234) cites research showing "the greatest response to change agent effort occurs when opinion leaders are adopting, which usually occurs somewhere between 3 and 16 percent adoption in most systems." The stronger the change agent's orientation and the more extensive his or her client contacts, the more successful the promotion work becomes.

The change agent may be assisted by change aides, who perform the day-to-day communication work on the grass roots level. This approach has been employed in many areas of planned communication work. An often quoted example of the use of change aides is the barefoot doctor program in the People's Republic of China. People trained to take care of simple, everyday health problems in a community have the responsibility of enforcing and propagating good health practices.

The Principle of Homophily

The principle of homophily appears often in diffusion of innovations theory. It suggests that individuals are more prone to be influenced by people who are similar to them than by those who are different, for example, in terms of social status and cultural origin. This should guide the selection of communicators and change aides in diffusion work. Rogers (1983) argues that peers usually are perceived to be more trustworthy than professional experts, although the latter are seen as more knowledgeable and competent. With this in mind, the communication planner may choose to use lay change aides to influence their peers; this has been done in the North Karelia health program (see Chapter 10; see also Puska et al. 1985). In AIDS prevention work, peer education has become widely recommended as an effective way to inform and influence (see, for example, Reardon 1989).

While homophily is important in communication planning, it should not be followed blindly. The validity of the principle, in some cases, may stem from confusion between source and channel (Chaffee 1986). Clients/ receivers may regard professional expertise as less trustworthy because it generally reaches them through the mass media; the judgment regarding trustworthiness, then, would be a function of the channel's, not the source's, credibility. Peers typically exert influence through interpersonal communication; that channel's advantages include perceived trustworthiness. Expert *sources* using interpersonal *channels* might prove very persuasive.

Another reason for the effectiveness of homophilic communication is accessibility. Usually peers are more accessible to us than experts – where are the experts when you need them? When the receiver is open to communication about an issue, the usually present peer has a greater chance to influence than does the usually absent professional expert. Chaffee parallels this to the paradox of "the strength of weak ties": "contacts between dissimilar people are rare ('weak'), but when they occur they are more likely than other contacts to result in information transfer ('strength')" (1986: 67). Thus, an available expert may be what the clients are looking for in many cases. This means that the communication planner should not avoid a heterophilic communication relationship (i.e. expert–client) when the channel conditions are favorable.

A Special Case: The Diffusion of Preventive Innovations

Rogers (1987) applies his diffusion of innovations theory to the promotion of self-protective behavior, for example, the use of seat belts or precautions against crime or injuries. In these cases, an innovation is adopted in order to prevent something undesirable from happening. According to Rogers, a distinctive aspect of such innovations is that their benefits are "(a) delayed in time and (b) difficult to assess because, even without the precaution, harm might never have occurred" (1987: 80). Preventive innovations also are less profit-oriented (and prestigious) than other types of innovations – much more money can be made by selling cigarettes than by running an anti-smoking campaign; the medical professions continue to center on curing patients rather than preventing diseases.

The following are some lessons that can be learned from the diffusion of preventive innovations research (Rogers 1987: 93):

• Interpersonal communication through peer networks is particularly important.

- Patriotic appeals by government leaders are seldom effective.
- Perceived credibility of the communication source partly determines the success of a prevention campaign.
- Mass media should not be expected to change strongly held attitudes and behavior.

Another Special Case: The Innovation Process in Organizations

Many times the communication planner's goal is to get *organizations* rather than individuals to adopt an innovation, for example, a campaign for high schools to include more traffic safety education in their curricula. The unit of adoption is neither the pupils nor the teachers, but the high school system (assuming that curricular change is at the high school's discretion). Recent writings by Rogers (1986, 1988) propose a modification of the classical diffusion model in such cases. Figure 6.5 presents the modified model, consisting of five stages divided into two subprocesses, initiation and implementation.

This model alerts the communication planner to the fact that often organizations are entities that do not behave as individuals do. They can be very resistant to change induced from the outside, or they may cope with innovative approaches in ways that seem peculiar to the planner. These tendencies force the planner to design the innovation process in a way that can survive a retooling of the innovation by the organization. The innovation is not fixed or static, but a "flexible and adaptable idea that is consecutively defined and redefined as the innovation process gradually unfolds" (Rogers 1986: 138).

In our example of including traffic safety information in a high school curriculum, the planner (who, we assume, represents a municipal traffic safety board) would first see to it that the system is aware of the issue (perhaps by pointing out the school's responsibility to help address the day-to-day problems of students and parents).

Second, the planner would formulate the issue in a way that enables a new traffic safety component in the curriculum to be equated with responsiveness to the problem as it was framed in order to get it on the system's agenda.

Third, the planner helps the organization redefine the innovation (the proposed curriculum reform) in a way that fits it needs – for example, replacing the initial idea of introducing a new course with the notion of integrating traffic safety education with other subjects (thus enabling the organization to maintain its general policy of curricular "leanness").

In the fourth and fifth stages (clarifying and routinizing), the role of the planner becomes less prominent. The system may be monitored to determine whether the essentials of the original innovation are being practiced.

Planners must realize they do not act alone in the communication situation and, of course, do not have total control. While this holds for the

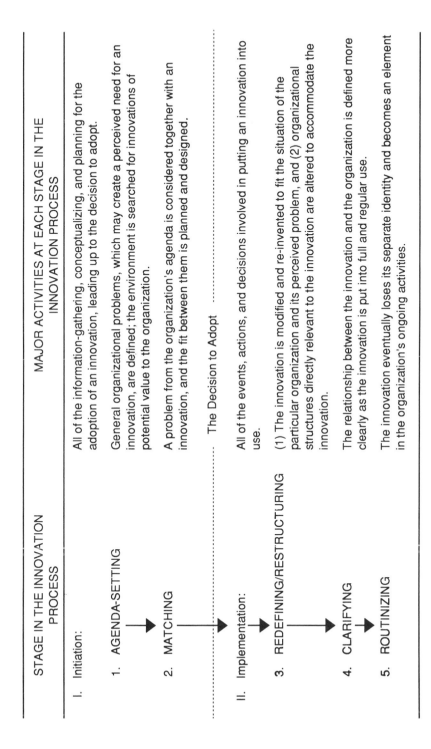

STAGE IN THE INNOVATION PROCESS	MAJOR ACTIVITIES AT EACH STAGE IN THE INNOVATION PROCESS
I. Initiation:	All of the information-gathering, conceptualizing, and planning for the adoption of an innovation, leading up to the decision to adopt.
1. AGENDA-SETTING	General organizational problems, which may create a perceived need for an innovation, are defined; the environment is searched for innovations of potential value to the organization.
2. MATCHING	A problem from the organization's agenda is considered together with an innovation, and the fit between them is planned and designed.
	--------- The Decision to Adopt ---------
II. Implementation:	All of the events, actions, and decisions involved in putting an innovation into use.
3. REDEFINING/RESTRUCTURING	(1) The innovation is modified and re-invented to fit the situation of the particular organization and its perceived problem, and (2) organizational structures directly relevant to the innovation are altered to accommodate the innovation.
4. CLARIFYING	The relationship between the innovation and the organization is defined more clearly as the innovation is put into full and regular use.
5. ROUTINIZING	The innovation eventually loses its separate identity and becomes an element in the organization's ongoing activities.

Figure 6.5 **Stages in the innovation process in organizations (Rogers 1988)**

innovation process in general, it is particularly true when the innovation occurs in an organization. A communication planner's cooperative skills as well as empathic skills will be put to the test.

Innovation Champions and Organizational Administrators

Two vital roles have been identified in the organizational innovation process: the innovation champion and the organizational administrator (Rogers 1988). The champion is usually one person who recognizes the usefulness of an innovation before others do and is instrumental in the introduction of information about the innovation into the organization. Later in the innovation process, only a small core of people actually carry through the process. If the communication planner does not act as the innovation champion (which rarely could or should happen), the planner must cooperate closely with, encourage, and, in some cases, create the champion.

The organizational administrator – usually the organization's top executive – is also a key person with whom the planner must cooperate. Studies of the introduction of computers into high schools show that the spread of the innovation occurs more quickly when the champion has the support of the top administrator, or if the top administrator is the actual champion. Rogers, however, cautions against assuming that the success of an innovation will be assured by an executive decision enforced from the top. Such an assumption contradicts the very nature of the process the theory of diffusion of innovations explains.

In our example of traffic safety education, the existence of an innovation champion and an organizational administrator's support of the champion's efforts would enhance the chances of modification to the curriculum. The planner's role includes identifying and convincing individuals to perform these two very critical functions.

Notes

1 Bostian (1970) has pointed out that one must separate the relay function from the influence function. Not all information relayed ends up influencing the receiver. To borrow a term from another communication theory, the opinion leader and gatekeeper functions are likely to be different. Schenk (1987: 259) concludes that as far as the relay function is concerned, the two-step flow model can "no longer claim any practical relevance."

2 For a German-language critique of the two-step flow of information model, see Silberman and Krüger (1973), Rencksdorf (1970), and Kreutz (1971); an English-language review of critiques is found in Severin (1988).

7 A Network Approach

The last few decades have seen a tendency to question and criticize traditional linear notions of communication. Linear models involve only the concepts of S–M–C–R (source–message–channel–receiver). While this may describe a simple communication *act*, it does not reflect the richness and dynamics of the *process* of human communication (Rogers 1986).[1] In planned communication as well, support for the previously dominant content/distribution model has shifted somewhat to the processing strategy (see Chapter 5); in Grunig's four-model set, the two-way symmetric approach with its mutual understanding view of communication represents newer public relations theory (Grunig and Hunt 1984).

Communication Networks

The communication network tradition is another line of thinking that reflects this same tendency and broadens our understanding of human communication. Rogers and Kincaid (1981) and Schenk (1984) offer comprehensive presentations of this approach. We rely to a large extent on their presentations.[2] Rogers characterizes a *communication network* as consisting of "interconnected individuals who are linked by patterned communication flows" (1986: 203). A *communication network analysis* studies "the interpersonal linkages created by the sharing of information in the interpersonal communication structure" (1986: 203), that is, the network. The analysis, then, also serves to identify communication networks in the first place. From this definition of a communication network, we can easily recognize the pervasive character of such networks, in the sense that virtually everyone in society belongs to one or several communication networks. This points out the importance of studying communication from a network perspective as part of the study of human communication in general.

Some Examples

Rogers and Kincaid maintain that the S–M–C–R picture of the communication process cannot describe what happens in dynamic and complicated communication situations. One of their examples stems from a study in Korea of how women in a small village organized themselves to improve the general living conditions for themselves and their families. This cooperative effort would have been impossible without communication, but how, using traditional communication models, can this communication process be described? Its very essence – its interaction, mutuality, and construction as an entire communication structure – is beyond the scope of a linear model.

The importance of thinking in terms of networks emerges in a description of a communication campaign about polio vaccination. While the campaign seemed to be functioning well, the response in many cases was not as good as hoped for. An analysis suggested that network support was lacking. Those people who had been vaccinated were supposed to influence others in their networks to be vaccinated by telling them about it. But the information was not fed into the network. Better communication in the social network would have helped to speed up the vaccination rate. AIDS information campaigns that rely on people who have been tested for HIV antibodies suffer a similar problem. Because of the stigma attached to the disease, those tested are reluctant to share that information with others in their communication networks. A factor that could contribute to the success of the campaign is effectively neutralized.

Important Network Factors

The idea of social networks is nothing new. The notions of sociometry and sociograms appeared over 50 years ago (Moreno 1934), and Barnes (1954) is credited with coining the notion of social networks, an outflow of his study of a Norwegian island parish in the early 1950s (Schenk 1984). Thinking in terms of networks and the method of network analysis have gained ground in many disciplines, including social psychology, anthropology, political science, and mathematics, as well as communications.

Scholars, very often sociologists, involved in basic research on networks stress the fact that communication is only one of three categories of content of the social relations in networks. The other two are (a) exchanges and transactions and (b) values and attitudes. While these three types of content often are interrelated, we may identify three basic types of networks (Schenk 1984):

- communication networks
- exchange networks
- normative networks.

The contributions of many communication scholars have expanded the knowledge base about the role of communication in networks. This knowledge clearly demonstrates the limitation of looking at communication as a simple sender–receiver, interpersonal relationship and ignoring communication as a property of groups. Group and network factors are often to blame when planned communication fails, but they may equally well explain why it succeeds.

The implications for the planner is that skill must be developed at another level of analysis. This may result in increased interest in communication climate (Glick 1985; Falcione et al. 1987) instead of, for example, formal communication methods. It should be noted that classical information theory, too, has been applied to the study of communication networks, providing such measures as:

- *traffic:* who does most of the talking and how much talking is done;
- *closure:* how open the group is to outsiders and ideas from the outside;
- *convergence:* whether members in group communication are on an equal footing or whether some are chiefly generators of communications while others are mainly passive receivers (Schramm 1955; Severin 1988).

The Convergence Model

Some central concepts of network analysis are found in a communication model by Kincaid (1979, also presented in Rogers and Kincaid 1981, and Rogers 1986).

The model, graphically illustrated in Figure 7.1, depicts two participants (A and B) sharing a piece of information in a communication situation or a series of such situations. A and B perceive, interpret, and understand the information, which may result in some sort of belief and action. This process, occurring over time, is a psychological one with an individual's background, personality, and so on playing a significant role. The accuracy of the perception, interpretation, understanding, and belief is irrelevant; the result could equally well be misconception, misinterpretation, misunderstanding, and disbelief.

Through the communication process, however, the participants may arrive at mutual understanding; that understanding may, but does not need to, lead to mutual agreement and possibly collective action. It is also possible that the participants will diverge from each other in their understanding of a topic. The interaction and communication takes place in a social reality, that is, an environment where certain social factors may be decisive.

While the act of sharing information is a natural starting point in the model, collective action could just as naturally be the origin of the process. The process does not always go full circle as the model suggests; sometimes only parts of it take place.

Mutual understanding, usually a product of ongoing interaction and communication, is a key element of the convergence model. The cyclical process of exchanging and giving meaning to each other's information is presented in Figure 7.2.

Mutual understanding does not have to be complete. In some cases the tolerance for misunderstanding is greater than in others. It also can happen that partial misunderstandings may function as a basis for creative action, e.g. misunderstood communication may trigger new ideas for the solution of a problem.

A New Perspective

In a model like this, concepts such as sender, receiver, and message become less relevant. Instead we talk about participants and shared

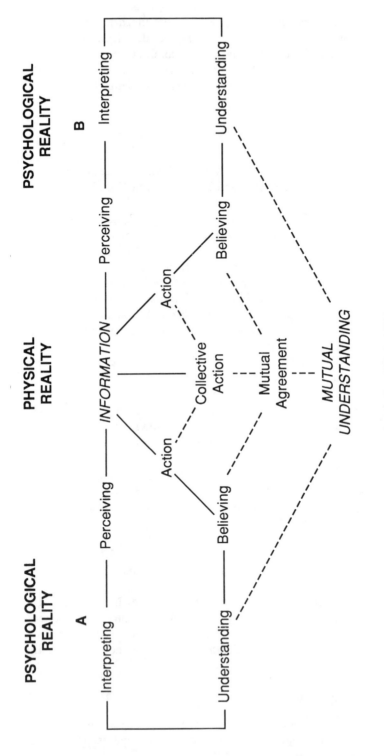

Figure 7.1 *Kincaid's model of convergence communication (Rogers and Kincaid 1981)*

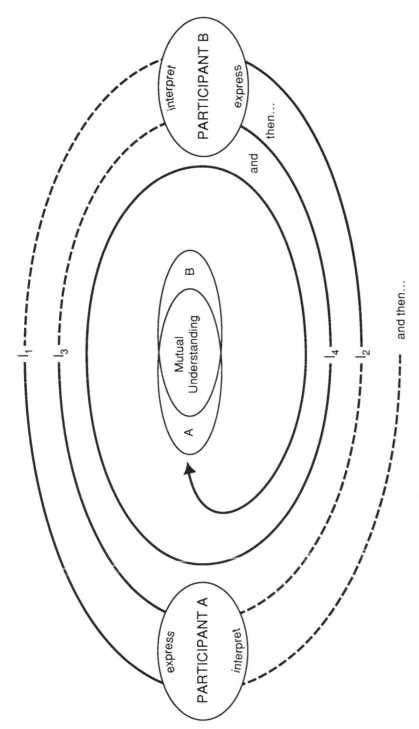

Figure 7.2 *Exchange and enhancement of meaning (Rogers and Kincaid 1981)*

information. In most communication models, the single individual is the unit of analysis; in the network model, the dyad, i.e. two elements – individuals, groups, etc. – linked together by communication, and the clique (groups within the group) are studied. One-way communication within these dyads or systems of dyads is usually less important than two-way communication.

Common definitions of effects do not apply in this model. Effects arise from a joint activity and affect all participants. In traditional models, influence is seen as traveling from source/sender to the receiver; the network perspective encompasses the notion that sometimes it may be the source that is affected by the communication, not the receiver.

The network model encourages communication planners and researchers to use new cause/effect variables in their analyses. For example, properties of the very communication network, such as connectedness, integration, diversity, and openness (Rogers and Kincaid 1981), may prove to be important to comprehending a communication situation.

The properties have direct application to communication planning. *Connectedness* measures to what extent the members of a certain network are linked to the network. A highly connected network offers greater potential than a loosely connected one for disseminating information to its members since there are fewer isolated individuals.

Integration measures the degree to which members of a network are linked to each other. For a communication planner, higher integration indicates more potential channels.

Knowledge about the degree of *diversity* may be especially important to a communication planner working with a creative network. Greater diversity indicates that ideas may enter the system relatively easily through weak ties (Granovetter 1973). (See Chapter 5.)

Openness affects decisions based on how well a certain group, system, or network communicates with its environment. A closed group will be harder for the planner to reach from outside.

As independent variables, these aspects of network structure may explain the results of planned communication; therefore, they should be taken into account in the planning process. The communication planner also may want to use these dimensions as dependent variables, trying to discover the causes of phenomena such as insufficient connectedness and integration. Within the scope of a communication effort, the planner may take steps to affect the structure in order to better control the effects produced by the informational efforts of the campaign.

Network Analyses

Network analysis is holistic, producing an overall image of how the whole network is structured. Let's look at an example.

In a health communication campaign, the planner focuses on relaying information about good eating habits to upper-level high school students.

As a follow-up, students in some classes are interviewed about what they think of the message, whom they talk to about it, what consequences talking with others has in terms of their own and joint behaviors, and so on.

The picture the planner forms includes information about the salience of the theme of good eating habits: Does this topic encourage discussions with others? If so, who are these others and did they also receive the initial campaign messages? Do those who hear the message from others in the network pass it on in some form? Do the students discuss the topic with their families, thereby helping the topic find its way into new networks? If so, does this lead to any kind of action by the family? And, do the families function as bridges into other networks? Is individual action more common than collective action? Are any cliques in the network more active than others in responding to the messages? Does influence travel through the network in only one direction or several?

Different Network Roles

Network analysis generates information about the following types of network roles (Monge 1987):

- the *membership* role in groups and clusters of the networks;
- the *liaison* role, that is, individuals who link clusters in the network together;
- the *star* role, held by individuals who are linked to a large number of other individuals;
- the *isolate* role – individuals to whom few are linked;
- the *boundary-spanning* role, which links the network to the environment.

In addition to these roles, we add the *bridge* role, which links two or more groups together (Goldhaber 1986), and the *non-participant* role, people who simply perform their job within a network without communication (Wilson et al. 1986).

Understanding these roles, together with the structural aspects of networks we have discussed, enables the communication planner to predict how and to what extent information will move within a network. For example, it may be necessary to identify the isolates, who probably will not receive as much information through informal communication as others do, and target them for additional communication efforts. It is a common finding that in organizations those working alone on night shifts are less well-informed. In health communication, it has been found that unhealthy people have smaller communication (and social support) networks than do healthy people (Albrecht et al. 1987). Other situations may be maximized by using network "stars" to spread information through the network.

Networking as a Strategy and a Means of Analysis

We need to distinguish between networking as a strategy and as a means of analysis. Although they are, of course, related, as a *strategy* or *guiding principle*, network models force the communication planner to think of communication efforts in holistic and dynamic terms. When relying on interpersonal communication, it may be useful for the planner to think in terms of networks, attempting to discover their existence and nature. Knowledge about a network's flow, stars, isolates, boundary spanners, bridges, and so on may prove invaluable. In some large communication programs, such as the Stanford Heart Disease Prevention Project, information has been analyzed in order to identify community leaders and establish support groups in attempts to inform and influence at both dyadic and clique levels (Kim 1985, cited by Rogers and Storey 1987). Recognition of networks' potential to change attitudes is valuable since individuals often are susceptible to social influence. The network may act as a change agent, offering support to individuals considering changing their attitudes and behavior. In the case of AIDS, a strategy among campaign leaders in San Francisco has been to create a normative support network promoting safe sex among homosexuals. The social network's message is clear: This is the way to do it (Windahl 1989). Knowledge about how communication networks function also can be instrumental in successfully forming groups like quality circles and social action groups.

Making information salient and transmittable within a network is important since messages that are processed and passed on are usually more effective than those that go no further than the first receiver. Sometimes the communication planner needs to find a "language" in which the network members can discuss a certain theme.

Networks are *analyzed* for many reasons. Communication about an innovation fails to change behavior in an organization, motivation is low, rumors of a take-over are damaging employee morale – all of these may be rooted in bad communication. Or a firm's chief executive may be curious about the cliques operating in the company's overall network structure. A larger task, but valuable to an organization in a changing business environment, is to do a multi-aspect analysis of the communication climate in which the company functions and to assess its position as a component of networks industry-wide.

Data for such analyses can be gathered in several ways. Trained observers can shadow respondents and record their communication activities. Members of a network can keep a communication journal, noting with whom and about what they communicate. A survey can ask respondents with whom and about what they generally communicate. The routes of specific messages through a network can be traced by trained observers.

The Spiral of Interaction

A fundamental characteristic of some network approaches is that communication and shared information may lead to collective action and attainment of goals that probably could not have been achieved otherwise. This theme – that communication is a means of empowerment – has been developed by a group of Swedish researchers in their book about the spiral of interaction (Thunberg et al. 1982).

Power in any society, Thunberg and her colleagues state, is unevenly distributed. Steps taken to achieve parity between the powerful and the powerless usually have only marginal success. To expect the powerful to relinquish some of their power is illogical in most cases; in the rare cases where this does occur, it smacks of paternalism. It has been suggested that the less privileged can improve their situation by improving their communication potential (Nowak 1977). Not only is this a means of making their voices heard, but it also brings about what Thunberg and her colleagues call an interaction spiral, which originates in communication between people. This is a rare example of discussion of planned communication used to achieve emancipatory aims.

The Functions of Communication

Communication traditionally has been assigned different functions. By mastering certain of these functions, individuals and groups of individuals may gain certain objectives like empowerment.

The functions mentioned by Thunberg et al. are:

- *The expressive function.* Individuals express themselves effectively in order to create an identity for themselves (and their group).
- *The social function.* By communicating together, people develop a sense of community.
- *The information function.* Through communication, individuals can share information and thereby increase their knowledge.
- *The control activation function.* Communication leads to joint action, modifying the environment and improving the situation of individuals and their groups.

These functions are related to each other. By using communication to fulfill one function, a group facilitates the use of communication to fulfill other functions as well. A process begins from which springs – provided conditions are favorable – a spiral of increased identity, community, knowledge, and action, enabling the group to reach its goals. This spiral is presented in Figure 7.3.

The conditions under which interaction spirals come into being vary. For example, in a working group, an interaction spiral may emerge when individuals share a common background and frames of reference, the work situation affords opportunities to communicate, members of the group have access to information about their concerns, and others who

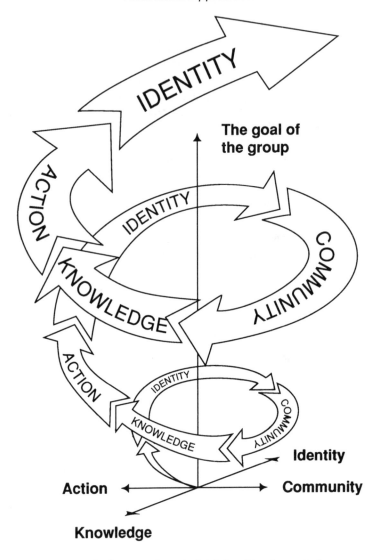

Figure 7.3 **The Spiral of Interaction Model (after Thunberg et al. 1982)**

are in a similar situation are identified. It is also advantageous when there are organized plans for action and influence that can be used by the group.

Threats to the Spiral

The interaction spiral may be threatened from above, below, and within a system. At the top, societies, communities, and organizations all have their own goals, their organizational lifestyles and their developed structures. They have little interest in making room for the activities of a small group, much less in ensuring that the group's voice is heard in a sea of competing voices.

The spiral is threatened from below by its own participants. Communication may not be strong enough to unite individuals with very different opinions and group affiliations, much less to coalesce them in collective action. In such a case, the communication planner may conclude that the problem cannot be dealt with through communication means.

The third threat mentioned by Thunberg et al. comes from within. Bureaucratization, professionalization, and institutionalization are dangerous for successfully growing interaction spirals; they develop due to the size and complexity of the spiral. They cause informal communication – the energizing factor in a good spiral – to give way to more formalized types of communication. A solution to this problem is to revitalize the group every now and then in order to recapture the dynamics that exist in smaller groups.

Communication Planning and the Spiral of Interaction

Thunberg et al. offer little advice about how to actually create spirals of interaction; they merely point to the need for them. It is possible that relatively small efforts will suffice to achieve results. On the community level, offering meeting space to minority groups may be an effective catalyst. In principle, the primary function of the communication planner is to increase the communication potential by using such methods as increasing education and encouraging communication.

The theory of interaction spirals makes at least four suggestions for communication planning:

- Communication is not uni-functional, but multi-functional. Communication offers not just one tool, but several.
- Mastering communication may mean increased power for groups that have very little of it.
- Helping a group increase its communication potential may enable the group to attain certain goals by itself, needing no further assistance from outside.
- The spiral is always threatened by both communication inadequacies and factors that lie outside the communication sphere.

Notes

1   Rogers (1986: 198) lists six biases that stem from the linear model of communication:

   1   to view communication as a linear, one-way (usually vertical or left-to-right), rather than cyclical, two-way process over time (a cybernetic view);
   2   to exhibit a source bias rather than focus on the interrelationship of those who communicate;
   3   to focus on the objects of communication as simple, isolated physical objects at the expense of the context in which they exist;

4 to consider the primary function of communication to be one-way persuasion, rather than mutual understanding, consensus, and collective action;

5 to concentrate on the psychological effects of communication on separate individuals, rather than on the social effects and the relationships among individuals within networks;

6 to assume one-way mechanistic causation, rather than mutual causation, which characterizes human communication systems that are fundamentally cybernetic.

In German-language communication science, the critique of the linear model often goes hand in hand with a rejection of a mass communication view of communication (Burkart 1983, 1985; Fabris 1985). For a critique of the linear view in the light of network thought, see Schenk (1984); also, German proponents of participatory views of media and communication have advanced at times harsh criticism of the linear model. (See, for example, Eurich 1980.)

2 While Rogers and Kincaid (1981) have concentrated their efforts on *communication* networks (based on a new model of communication, the convergence model), Schenk emphasizes the analysis of *social* networks in general, with communication networks being only a part of the former. Schenk's approach, then, is much more sociological than that of Rogers and Kincaid, which, in turn, seems to be more directly applicable to our purposes. It should also be mentioned that researchers in the field of organizational communication increasingly are using the network concept. (See, for example, Farace et al. 1977; Goldhaber 1986; Wilson et al. 1986; Daniels and Spiker 1987; Monge and Eisenberg 1987; Mucchielli 1974 offers a French perspective.)

8 Systems Theory Perspectives

Communication planning takes place so frequently in organizational contexts that it is useful for the planner to be familiar with the work of organizational theorists and its relation to communication. Organizational communication has developed into a subdiscipline of communication studies, offering the communication planner a growing body of knowledge about communication processes in organizations (see, for example, Goldhaber 1986; Goldhaber and Barnett 1988; Jablin et al. 1987).

What are the communication planner's ties to organizations? Very often, and almost by definition, the planning agency is an organization, and the planner is a communicator in its employ. It could also be that the receivers of the messages are organizations or individuals who work for an organization. Thus, an anti-smoking campaign may emanate from the Ministry of Health, to which the communication planner has organizational ties (either as an outside consultant or as an employee); the messages are aimed at directors of public schools, who are asked not only to put up anti-smoking posters but also to encourage teachers in their schools to participate in activities around "Non-Smokers Day," inaugurated several years earlier by another organization, the World Health Organization.

This scenario shows that communication planning can involve several aspects of organizational communication. One of the leading authors and practitioners in the field, Gerald M. Goldhaber, offers this definition: "Organizational communication is the process of creating and exchanging messages within a network of interdependent relationships to cope with environmental uncertainty" (1986: 17).

While the term "organizational communication" is frequently used to refer to internal communication activities, it has a strong external component as well, both in terms of public organizational communication (Goldhaber 1986: 319) and interorganizational relations (Evan 1976). Our discussion will center on open systems theory, which has been quite pervasive and influential in the field of organizational communication in the past decade.

General Systems Theory

The basic idea of *general systems theory* as developed by von Bertalanffy (1969) is that the whole equals more than the sum of its parts (also known as the synergistic effect). The theory, then, deals with "wholes made up of interdependent parts, the relationships between parts, and the relationships between the wholes and their environments" (Myers and Myers 1982: 47).

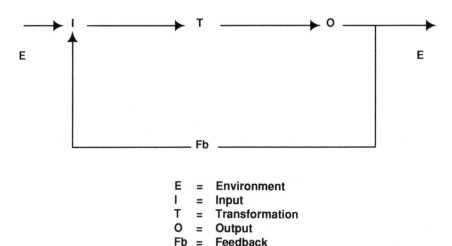

Figure 8.1 **The organization as an open system (Goldhaber 1986)**

Katz and Kahn (1978) introduced the view of organizations as *open* social systems characterized by permeable boundaries that permit interaction with their environments. Structures and functions of such open systems are continuously changing. *Closed* systems, in contrast, have fixed boundaries that do not allow for environmental interaction. Their structures and functions remain relatively stable. Figure 8.1 depicts the organization as an open system.

Some of the key concepts of open systems theory, according to Katz and Kahn (1978) and summarized by Goldhaber (1986), are:

- *Feedback.* Open systems are influenced by the environment and, in turn, exert influence on the environment through their output. Information from these influencing outputs is fed back into the system to provide orientation and control for the system's future operations.
- *Balance.* A system's survival depends on balance (a state of homeostasis) between energy input and product output. When more is exported than imported, the system dies. Static systems contain nothing of homeostasis; open systems, by their very nature, are dynamic as they constantly transform inputs into outputs.
- *Input.* Just as the human system needs oxygen, open systems need energy, people, materials and information to maintain themselves. These are the system inputs.
- *Transformation.* Also called throughput, this is the process that changes inputs into outputs. For example, a school system may transform students from children who know very little about mathematics into individuals who are knowledgeable about this subject.
- *Output.* Whatever the system exports, usually a product or a service,

is its output. In the long run, the nature of the output will secure or threaten the system's existence. The output of a university, for example, includes educated students and research activity.

- *Interdependence.* "The nuts and bolts of systems theory is interdependence . . . it means the interlocking relationships between the parts of a system and the whole system" (Goldhaber 1986: 54). A change in one part of the system leads to changes in other parts too.
- *Boundaries.* The organization is both separated from and linked to its environment through a boundary, which, according to Rogers and Rogers (1976), is defined by communication flows.

Finally, the roots of the *contingency approach*, on which we base our approach to communication planning (see Chapter 1), are found in systems theory. Here the principle is called *equifinality*, meaning that, in open systems, the same final state can be arrived at from different initial conditions and by different paths. Put more simply, "There are many ways to reach a given objective; there is no one single method that will be the best under all conditions" (Myers and Myers 1982: 42). The essence of equifiality, according to Myers and Myers, is expressed in the saying, "There is more than one way to skin a cat."

The Systems Theory View of Communication

How, then, does communication fit into systems theory? The process view of organizations comes close to some of the more recent ideas about communication (see, for example, our discussion of the convergence model of communication, Chapter 7). In systems terms, the unit of analysis is "not a thing, a person, an event in isolation, but a *relationship* – between people, and between people and environments" (Myers and Myers 1982: 50). These relationships can be approached, at least in part, in terms of communication. The assumption is that social structures are held together partly by meanings shared by the people who belong to the system.

General systems theory focuses on the *transaction* nature of communication, going beyond mere interaction between senders and receivers. Transaction implies mutual causality among the parts of the system, that is, interdependency. Constantly shifting roles of senders and receivers and their simultaneous reciprocal responses characterize this approach. Planners must picture themselves as both cause and effect, stimulus and response, sender and receiver. Using a transactional view of communication, the planner would *not* isolate communicative acts by imposing beginnings and endings in what is an unending process.

Some widely accepted communication principles have arisen from the application of general systems theory to the study of human communication. (See the work of the Palo Alto Mental Research Institute – Watzlawick et al. 1967 – as summarized by Myers and Myers 1982.)

- *You cannot not communicate.* Communication does not have an opposite. Body language, silence, tone of voice – all these elements do have some effects. For the planner, it is important to remember that communication does not only occur when it is planned, conscious, or successful. "You communicate many things you may not intend to communicate. You are not always aware of what indeed you communicate, and you may not always be understood. Yet, communicate you do, and in many behavioral modes" (Myers and Myers 1982: 71).

- *Communication occurs at two levels: content and relationship.* Content refers to what is said while relationship (between the communicators) defines how to interpret the content of communication. While the relationship may be expressed verbally ("I was only joking"), it is more often conveyed non-verbally and contextually. For example, in a classroom, it usually is quite clear who is the teacher and who are the students, i.e. the relationship level is understood and determines how students interpret the content of the teacher's communication, and vice versa.

- *Communication is like the chicken-and-egg dilemma.* It often is difficult for us to realize fully the flowing and dynamic nature of communication. It is tempting to look for beginnings and endings, actions and reactions, senders and receivers, particularly when we want to find someone to blame for a problem. For example, a communication planner looks for an imaginary "starting point" for an AIDS campaign, ignoring important communication events that preceded the planner's involvement.

- *Communication transactions are between either equals or non-equals.* Examples of communication between non-equals are between mother and child, teacher and student, boss and subordinate. One communicator is in the one-up position, the other in the one-down position. The one-up position usually defines the nature of the relationship and thus of the communication. Such non-equal relationships usually are rooted in social contexts, not in communicative ones. This implies a limitation of the planner's role in that equality or non-equality may lie beyond his or her sphere of influence. Thus, the above-described convergence model of communication – in theory ideally suited for the conveying of controversial contents – may simply not work in a situation where strong, traditional hierarchies dominate the communicative setting, such as in a conventional husband/wife context.

Applying the contingency view to open systems theory points to the necessity of awareness of internal and external factors; only then can the planner decide what is the best way of communicating in a certain situation. Farace et al. stress the need for "tailoring the communication aspects of organization to the particular people, tasks, environment, and uncertainty at hand" (1977: 92). It is essential that organizational practitioners and theorists alike develop a broad understanding of the many communication models suggested by a systems approach.

Organizational Subsystems

Organizational theorists Katz and Kahn (1978) found that, in general, organizations have the following subsystems which affect both each other and the whole system:

1 *production* subsystems: departments that produce goods or services;
2 *maintenance* subsystems: departments (or functions) that administrate the organization (e.g. the personnel office);
3 *disposal* subsystems: departments that distribute goods and services (e.g. marketing);
4 *adaptive* subsystems: departments that enable organizations to adapt to environmental change (e.g. research and development);
5 *management* subsystems: departments that coordinate and control individual subsystems, and manage conflicts and relations among the subsystems as well as between the organization and its environment.

Public relations is one of several areas of planned communication with a bias towards continuous, strategic, and institutionalized communication. Grunig and Hunt (1984) claim for public relations a place within the management subsystem: a public relations department controls the organization's communicative activities with its overall environment on the one hand, and among subsystems within their specific environment (for example, the disposal system's relationship with research and development or the maintenance system's relationship with other organization departments via an employee newsletter) on the other. This conceptualization of the role of public relations is shown in **Figure 8.2**.

Boundary Role of the Planner

Like network theory (see Chapter 7), general systems theory recognizes that members of an organization play various roles in the communication process. Public relations practitioners, organizational communicators, or communication planners – whatever their title may be – fill a boundary role: "They function at the edge of the organization, serving as a liaison between the organization and the external groups and individuals. They can have one foot in the organization and one outside" (Grunig and Hunt 1984: 9).

Assuming the identity of what used to be called an organization man can provide useful insights to communication planners, even if they are not tied to any one organization or are working on a campaign-type communication effort. The planners must balance what they need to communicate to the organization's environment with attention to the information coming from the environment. The objective is to be positioned in a way that permits effective performance of the boundary role

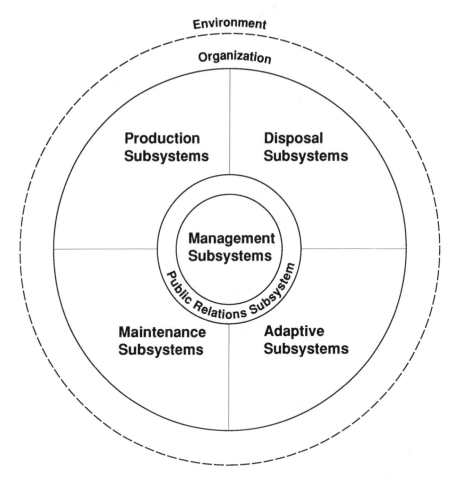

Figure 8.2 *The role of public relations in an organizational system (Grunig and Hunt 1984)*

which, of course, is quite sensitive; attaining the trust of both the organization and the environment is paramount. Current thinking is that a position near the top of the relevant organization or organizational unit can provide a certain measure of independence and autonomy necessary to function successfully in the boundary role.

Interdependence

Thinking in terms of the interdependence of the subsystems of an organization is useful for a communication planner. In our example about the anti-smoking campaign, that communication effort may be part of the overall strategy of the Ministry of Health (including tactical and political components with an eye to an upcoming election or the political ambitions of the minister in a quest for a higher-ranking cabinet post). The production subsystem may view it as a standard function – just one of the services offered by the Ministry, much like, in principle at least, the government's subsidization of health insurance. The campaign has an entirely different significance for the maintenance subsystem, where leading bureaucrats and other employees consider it a waste of money that is needed more critically for the purchase of scanners for lung cancer detection.

You can see how systems thinking can prevent the communication planner from falling into the trap of communicationism in still another way – not only are not all problems communication problems, but there are forces and powers at work in organizations that do not necessarily and automatically follow any kind of communication "logic." *Input, output, throughput* and *feedback* are important concepts to describe the behavior of systems that are open and in a state of moving equilibrium; they suggest that approaches to communication based in mutuality and two-way exchange of information receive strong theoretical support from open systems thinking.

Dominant Coalitions

An interesting facet of open systems theory is the concept of the dominant coalition – an organization's constituencies with the most power, both inside and outside the entity. These constituencies set the overall goals of the organization, as well as the goals of, say, communication programs it undertakes. This reinforces the point that the communication planner is not as autonomous in goal-setting as might be thought. The *real* (but hidden) goals of our anti-smoking campaign may be set by forces outside even the Ministry of Health and never be made explicit to the communication planner. For example, a government that has set a series of environmentally damaging pollution standards in the past may use an anti-smoking campaign as a propagandistic symbol to support its claim to care about the quality of the country's physical environment (Thompson 1967).

The Theory Applied: Public Relations

Public relations (PR) is an important field of planned communication. In theory, if not necessarily in practice, no other form of planned communication is more attuned to systems thinking than is PR.

Systems theory reasoning is found even in the more practical definitions of public relations, such as Harlow's, which is widely quoted and was adopted by the International Public Relations Association (IPRA):

> Public relations is a distinctive management function which helps establish and maintain mutual lines of communication, understanding, acceptance and cooperation between an organization and its publics; involves the management of problems or issues; helps management to keep informed on and responsive

to public opinion; defines and emphasizes the responsibility of management to serve the public interest; helps management keep abreast of and effectively utilize change, serving as an early warning system to help anticipate trends; and uses research and sound and ethical communication techniques as its principal tools. (Harlow 1976: 40)

This definition points out the importance of communication not only as an output, but also as an input to a system or an organization.

A much shorter definition that focuses explicitly on both management and systems dimensions was developed by James E. Grunig: "Public relations is the management of communication between an organization and its publics" (Grunig and Hunt 1984: 6).

The definition of public relations most obviously influenced by systems theory is from Long and Hazelton: "Public relations is a communication function of management through which organizations adapt to, alter, or maintain their environment for the purpose of achieving organizational goals" (1987: 6).

Publics

A public is a group of people who share some problem or project. Publics vary in the degree to which they are organized and are aware of the existence of the problem or project. For example, the media may view as a problem their need for information about an organization in order to inform their audiences about it. The project of a company's shareholders is to get a good return on the money they have invested. An environmental group views as its project the monitoring of the pollution policies of a certain industry.

Following the work of philosopher John Dewey (1927), Grunig and Hunt (1984: 145) define a public as a group of people who:

1 face a similar problem;
2 recognize that the problem exists;
3 organize to do something about the problem.

Again relying on Dewey, Grunig and Hunt (1984: 145) identify four types of publics:

- non-publics (none of the above characteristics apply);
- latent publics (characteristic 1 applies);
- aware publics (characteristics 1 and 2 apply);
- active publics (all three characteristics apply).

The planner should be aware of the status of different publics. Sometimes the planner may want to turn a latent public into an active one. For example, the personnel recruiter of a company suggests opening up a dialogue with students at an area high school in order to activate the adolescents (a latent public) to think about their future career plans (becoming an aware or active public). Or a public relations professional may want to deactivate publics (for example, publics concerned with environmental issues) by engaging them in communication, moving them from "active" to "aware."

Public Relations Models

PR has been criticized frequently for its lack of theory and for basing practice more on intuition than on scientific principles. This does not mean, however, that different principles or models in PR work cannot be identified.

Grunig and Hunt (1984) write specifically about theory and practice in this field. Their work is based to a large extent on four models, which they have constructed from the actual experience of PR practitioners in the United States. These models, which are simplified descriptions of information and communication strategies, are by no means unique; on the contrary, they describe many types of communication situations. Grunig and Hunt argue that it should be possible "to fit public relations people you meet into one of the models" (1984: 21).

The Press Agentry/Publicity Model

The models can be viewed chronologically, originating in different periods of public relations practice in the United States. The press agentry/publicity model dates as far back as the late nineteenth century. It is a one-way model where communication's main purpose is propaganda. The receiver is someone to be convinced of an idea, and, as Grunig and Hunt note, complete truth is not essential to the strategy. A great deal of the mistrust that continues to be directed toward public relations stems from the use of this model. It spawns PR that is performed to sell products or services. The research tool employed in the press agentry/publicity model consists of simple head-counting or the like.

The Public Information Model

The next model, which emerged in the United States around 1900, is the public information model. Its aim is the dissemination of information, not necessarily with any intent to persuade. In contrast to the first model, truth is an important criterion of the practice. The communication flow is one-way. A journalist employed by an organization to report objectively to the public about what happens within the organization is an example of PR practice following this model. When research is done, it studies whether messages really reach their destination and are understood (e.g. comprehension studies).

The Two-Way Asymmetric Model

Emerging in the 1920s, this model is more dynamic than the preceding ones. Information travels two ways, both to and from publics; the inclusion of feedback is new. But, as we noted earlier (Chapter 2), the mere

Table 8.1 *Characteristics of four models of public relations communication (Grunig and Hunt 1984)*

Characteristic	Model			
	Press Agentry/Publicity	Public Information	Two-Way Asymmetric	Two-Way Symmetric
Purpose	Propaganda	Dissemination of information	Scientific persuasion	Mutual understanding
Nature of Communication	One-way; complete truth not essential	One-way; truth important	Two-way; imbalanced effects	Two-way; balanced effects
Communication Model	Source → Rec.	Source → Rec.	Source ⇄ Rec. Feedback	Group ⇄ Group
Nature of Research	Little; "counting house"	Little; readability, readership	Formative; evaluative of attitudes	Formative; evaluative of understanding
Leading Historical Figures	P.T. Barnum	Ivy Lee	Edward L. Bernays	Bernays, educators, professional leaders
Where Practiced Today	Sports, theatre, product promotion	Government, nonprofit associations, business	Competitive business; agencies	Regulated business; agencies
Estimated Percentage of Organizations Practicing Today	15%	50%	20%	15%

presence of feedback does not mean that power and effects are equally distributed between sender and receiver; the relationship is asymmetric. The initiative still lies with the organization, and the aim of communication continues to be persuasion and attitude and behavior change. Communication theory and research are used to gain knowledge about the attitudes of the publics and to evaluate effects.

The Two-Way Symmetric Model
This model developed during the 1960s and 1970s. Practitioners cautiously are beginning to adopt it as a communication strategy. While the other models are characterized by monologue-type communication, the symmetric model involves the idea of dialogue. It would lead an organization's management to exchange views with other groups, possibly leading to both management and publics being influenced and adjusting their attitudes and behaviors. Communication in this model is fully reciprocal and power relationships are balanced. The terms "sender" and "receiver" are not applicable in a communication process like this, whose goal is mutual understanding, a concept we recognize from the Rogers and Kincaid convergence model described earlier. Research is used to find out how the organization is perceived by its publics and to evaluate to what extent the dialogue has fostered mutual understanding.

A summary of the four models can be seen in Table 8.1.

Grunig and Hunt present the two-way symmetric model as the one that best represents a truly professional approach to public relations. Power is more evenly distributed between the organization and its publics, with greater chances for mutual understanding. Pearson (1989) argues that symmetric strategies are a prerequisite for an ethical approach to planned communication.

Several years ago, Grunig and his colleagues initiated a research program designed to test the four PR models in various organizational settings. "We encountered much evidence that the organizations used more than one model in their public relations programs. We have come to realize that organizations may use different models as strategies for dealing with different publics or different public relations problems" (Grunig and Grunig 1989: 42). This confirms the applicability of the contingency view to these PR models as well. In this sense, the Grunig approach squares well with the overall philosophy of this book, which stresses the situationality of communication planning.

The basic argument of the contingency approach – "It all depends" – calls for a typology of the "upons." One approach to this issue is to ask which type of organization uses which type of public relations model. Grunig (1984) and Schneider (1985a, 1985b) have correlated four types of organizations suggested in organization theory by Hage and Hull (1981) with the hypothesized models of public relations practices by each.

Other aspects of what we present in this book appear in the presentation of these four models as well: the shift of communication from a one-way to a two-way process; and the content/distribution character of the press/agentry, public information, and two-way asymmetric models, while the two-way symmetric model neatly fits within the framework of the processing strategy.

A comment

To sum up, the communication planner has much to gain by developing both an understanding of and a feeling for systems theory. As a contributor to the achievement of larger, often organizational goals, a planner has only limited influence. In other words, whatever expertise in communication techniques a planner may have, it is essential to be aware that in many cases it will be necessary to adapt "ideal" practices to the complex requirements of the various systems the planner affects and is affected by. The conceptualization of communication planning work in terms of inputs, outputs, and throughputs can greatly enhance the objectivity and contextuality of the planner's strategic thinking.

9 Social Marketing Perspectives

Origins of Social Marketing

One of the mainstays of planned communication has been the social marketing model. Some of its concepts and perspectives are borrowed from commercial marketing and modified to serve in such settings as public communication campaigns.

The idea is that marketing can be regarded as an *exchange* process between two or more parties who view the process as meeting their individual needs (Kotler 1972). Communication obviously plays an important role: the client is made aware of the offer through communication, and communication about the client's needs, wants, and resources is important to the seller. This relationship is illustrated in the communication model in Figure 9.1.

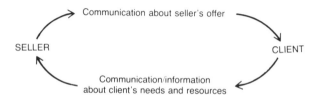

Figure 9.1 *Communication's role in marketing*

Wiebe's (1951) much quoted question "Why can't radio and television 'sell' the reduction of juvenile delinquency like they have sold the use of the home permanent wave?" triggered the development of *social* marketing. This concept gained momentum when one of the foremost marketing scholars, Philip Kotler (1972; also Kotler and Zaltman 1971), introduced the idea of a generic concept of marketing to be applied not only to commercial transactions but to non-commercial ones as well. According to Kotler, social marketing describes the

> use of marketing principles and techniques to advance a social cause, idea or behavior. More specifically: social marketing is the design, implementation, and control of programs seeking to increase the acceptability of a social idea or cause in target group(s). It utilizes concepts of market segmentation, consumer research, concept development, communication, facilitation, incentives and exchange theory to maximize target group response. (1982: 490)

Terms such as social cause marketing, idea marketing, and public issue marketing essentially refer to the same approach. Social advertising and social communication, in contrast, denote a much narrower view than that encompassed by social marketing (Kotler 1982; Solomon 1989).

Compared with commercial marketing, social marketing usually operates in less profitable markets and market segments. Where commercial marketing targets the most accessible part of the market, social marketing may aim at the hard-to-reach segments. Other differences in social marketing are that (a) there is less competition; (b) clients do not always have to pay in money for products and services; (c) powerful interest groups are often challenged (e.g. the tobacco industry); (d) the product or behavior being advanced often is not desired by the receiver (e.g. adhering to a low-fat diet); and (e) increased demand may be dysfunctional due to lack of resources (e.g. more readers in a local public library where books and personnel are in short supply). (See Solomon 1989; Webster 1975.)

The Four Ps

The Four Ps marketing model (McCarthy 1975, quoted in Solomon 1989) is a useful tool for communication planning. The Ps stand for *product, price, place,* and *promotion,* factors that the communication planner must define for the communication situation in question. For (social) marketing to be successful, all of the functions associated with the Four Ps must be performed by the marketer or other participants in the transaction process (Fine 1981).

The *product* may be a thing, an idea, a practice, or a service. The communication planner must clearly understand what the product is, or rather, how the public/audience/clients should perceive it. Solomon notes that it is sometimes wise to make an idea more tangible by attaching some physical product to it, as has been done with condoms and safe sex. Also, the practice in commercial marketing of distinguishing between a generic concept (such as mobility) and a specific physical product (an automobile) may be useful for the planner. In a seat belt campaign, the generic product would be safety; the specific product, the activity of using seat belts. Further, according to Solomon (1989), the commercial concept and practice of a product line is suggestive for the planner as well. Just as car manufacturers offer different types of cars for different customer segments, such product differentiation could be applied to marketing for social causes. "Imagine how health campaigns could be transformed if they provided a product line ranging from, in the case of physical exercise campaigns, for example, low cost information-only products, to one-shot activities, to higher cost lifestyle changes or ongoing daily participation programs" (Solomon 1989: 92).

The concept of *price* covers what is paid by the buyer in an exchange. For an Iranian housewife, taking a job outside the home poses a very high cultural price. For a small-town father, the social price of taking an AIDS test at the local hospital seems high. Farquhar et al. (1984) point out that people do not take part in health campaign activities, even when there is no charge. The price in terms of time and energy, not money, is too high.

Opportunity costs must be considered, that is, opportunities lost due to acquiring the product or service in question.

The communication planner may try to reduce the perceived costs either by actually lowering them or by increasing the perceived benefits from adopting the product. Manoff (1985) says finding points of resistance, be they public, economic, cultural, religious, or whatever, that add to the subjective price of a product is an important function of the communication planner. Fine (1981) proposes the term "social price" to denote such phenomena as ancillary price, collateral price, intangible price, intrinsic price, symbolic price, and so on. Fine suggests four types of social price (other than money) in terms of resources given up by the client in exchange for products: time, effort, lifestyle, and psyche.

Place is the channel through which the product, service, or idea is made available to the target group. The planner should ensure that the channel is easily accessible and identifiable. In a Swedish study on AIDS and adolescents (Jarlbro 1987), the burden of acquiring the product (in this case, condoms) was not considered. Some young men found the act of purchasing condoms so embarrassing that they stole them instead. It is also important to note that in addition to being motivated to offer the product, perhaps through incentives, the channel must also know the product well and support it over time (Solomon 1989).

A common practice in social marketing is using commercial channels for distributing non-commercial products. The non-commercial marketers gain a channel, and the commercial channels earn the goodwill that accompanies the product.

Promotion comprises the communicative/persuasive activities used to create awareness of the product among the target group. Choice of medium, selection of arguments, etc., have as their goal the achievement of desired results. Promotion goes far beyond mere publicity or advertising. In Solomon's words, it involves "actively reaching out to the right people with the right message at the right time in order to obtain the right effects" (1989: 93).

Promotion must be adapted to its target public. Manoff (1985) cites the example of an anti-diarrhea communication program in Nicaragua. The recipe for a homemade treatment called for bicarbonate, an ingredient that poor farmers did not have. Consequently, they could not make use of the campaign's message.

Solomon (1989) adds a fifth P, *positioning*, to McCarthy's model. This refers to how a receiver perceives a product relative to other products. A campaign to get people to donate to a Third World cause might be more effective if repositioned from the idea of doing something good for "them" to a more self-interested concept of maintaining world stability and avoiding being put in equally dire circumstances.

In marketing language, then, a rational interplay between the four (or five) Ps would be essential for the creation of the marketing strategy.

Market Segments

Marketing research traditionally has been interested in describing the market in terms of its segments. This is appropriate in social marketing work as well. As in public relations, segments are labeled publics (Kotler 1972). Identification of relevant publics has proved crucial to the success of health campaigns based on the social marketing model (Farquhar et al. 1984).

Manoff (1985) describes a breast-feeding promotion program in Brazil. The following eight audience groups/publics and their roles in the program were identified:

1 the doctors, who would be instrumental in persuading mothers to breast-feed;
2 the health services, to which mothers would turn for advice;
3 the hospitals, which would introduce new practices and revise old ones;
4 the infant food industry, which would ensure that breast-milk substitute was marketed properly;
5 industry (in general), which would have to comply with existing laws affecting mothers breast-feeding babies;
6 the community, which would offer psychological support and facilities for breast-feeding;
7 government officials, who would initiate new policies;
8 the mothers, who would be encouraged to breast-feed longer.

Often social marketing campaigns fail because the right publics have not been addressed. Before a campaign is launched, orienting key people in the system to the goals of the campaign and enlisting their support in identifying the publics to target can greatly facilitate communication efforts. Just as in other approaches to planned communication, goal-setting is crucial in social marketing. In its most general terms, the goal of social marketing would be social change. Kotler (1982) identifies four types of social change (and provides examples of each of them):

1 *Cognitive change*
   ● campaigns to increase recognition of high pollution levels in an area
   ● campaigns to inform people of what political refugees experience
2 *Action change*
   ● campaigns calling for people to demonstrate against pollution
   ● campaigns asking people to sign petitions on behalf of political refugees
3 *Behavioral change*
   ● efforts to make people routinely recycle paper and glass
   ● efforts to prevent prejudiced behavior against families of political refugees
4 *Value change*
   ● efforts to convince people of the value of clean air and water
   ● efforts to create values in favor of the actions of political refugees.

Relevant Marketing Principles

Some danger may exist in using marketing ideas uncritically in non-commercial areas of communication planning, or in blurring the differences between commercial and social marketing as outlined above. But even social marketing suggests that goals and communication are defined *outside* the target social system (see Chapter 5), thus rendering it less useful in certain situations. A social marketing campaign to achieve the environmental goals listed above may be less effective than a grass roots movement with the same goal.

Nevertheless, marketing research and practice have, over the years and in many fairly controlled contexts, produced insights into human communication. Some of the very ways of thinking in marketing terms – the marketing ideology, if you will – may prove useful for the communication planner. We are not suggesting in any way that this approach dominate the planner's thinking (that would run counter to our philosophy of contingency in planned communication), but we believe that some of the following marketing philosophies and principles may be fruitful as part of an approach to a problem (Solomon 1989).

The concept of *exchange* in marketing implies that the goal of the organization should be to meet the needs and wants of the consumer and that the participants in the communication process should interact roughly as equals. For example, is the goal of a cancer detection program the distribution of a certain number of leaflets, or is it to inform the people about the methods of cancer detection?

Profit-orientation and bottom-line thinking can be helpful, particularly when the question of profitability goes beyond monetary dimensions, e.g. happiness, decreased mortality, and so on. The point is that the planner should not shy away from (or should at least consider) setting measurable profit objectives.

The theory of the *hierarchy of communication effects*, developed by Ray (1973) from a marketing point of view, reminds us that the linear progression of effects – awareness, attitude change, behavioral change – does *not* always occur. An example is smokers, many of whom have been aware of the need to quit smoking for a long time. Many anti-smoking campaigns do not waste any time and money informing smokers about the danger of their habit; instead, they concentrate on learning skills to facilitate quitting.

Commercial marketers are acutely aware of the need for *rapid feedback* (e.g. sales figures) that enable them to quickly change the course of a campaign when results are not what they anticipated.

Finally, learning about the *competition* is common in commercial marketing; in social marketing, too, competition exists – for time, position, attention, as well as from other products, existing activities and so on. Understanding the competition can improve a campaign, even enabling it to establish a clear competitive advantage in the marketplace.

10 Communication Campaigns: A Meeting Place for Different Approaches

Our discussions of theory have built a foundation for understanding how the communication process develops and occurs. The next step is to link the theory with the practice. In communication planning, the communication campaign is where theory and practice meet. Let's look at the communication campaign itself, keeping in mind what we've learned to this point about communication.

Communication campaigns are the initial tangible product of the planning process. The term public communication (or information) campaign, which indicates a non-commercial problem, often is used. Sometimes, though, the distinction between commercial and non-commercial campaigns is hard to make; the theoretical foundations for the two types often are identical. The distinctions are further blurred by the concept of social or non-profit marketing (see Chapter 9).

There are a number of reasons why there is an increasing need for public communication campaigns (Bonfadelli 1987a):

- Governments and public administration units are suffering an erosion of legitimacy in the public's perception.
- The public increasingly is aware of the risks of modernization; these dangers led the German sociologist Beck (1986) to characterize modern Western society as a "risk society."
- In addition to acting as a means of social control and offering technical solutions to social problems, communication is becoming an ever more important means of implementing and enforcing public policy and social learning and education.

Additional reasons such as mobilization and modernization will be important motivations for campaigns in Third World countries.

When analyzed from a theoretical point of view, the communication campaign can take many forms. Some campaigns are built on a mechanistic stimulus–response model with expectations of immediate, direct effects. Others represent syntheses of several models, based on a long-term perspective toward effects (Schenk 1987).

An Overview

As the title of this chapter implies, there are different ways to think about communication campaigns. In the past, approaches to campaigns have been guided primarily by practical questions answered in very specific contexts; as a result, no theory of the communication campaign has been developed. In recent years, however, some researchers have tried to formulate such a theory – not necessarily a "grand" theory of campaigns, but a synthesis of empirical findings that offers some generalizations about the process. The merging of a very practically oriented field with the theoretician's efforts has led some authors to predict optimistically, "in certain respects, campaigns provide ideal situations for the study of human communication theory" (Rogers and Storey 1987: 817).

The results of these attempts at synthesis and integration are a fairly cogent definition of, and some generalizations about, public communication campaigns.

Public communication campaigns are purposive attempts to inform, persuade, or motivate behavior changes in a relatively well-defined and large audience, generally for non-commercial benefits to the individuals and/or society at large, typically within a given time period, by means of organized communication activities involving mass media and often complemented by interpersonal support. (Rice and Atkin 1989; adapted from Rogers and Storey 1987)

Campaigns may well deal with family planning, AIDS prevention, health behavior, preserving forests, conserving energy, voter registration and so on and so on; target audiences may be urban or rural, First World or Third World, men, women or the whole population, car drivers or motorcycle riders, and so on. The effects sought "range from creating literacy to getting votes, from preventing drug abuse to advertising cosmetics, from changing nutritional intake to transforming the social structure" (Rogers and Storey 1987: 818).

The above definition contains four basic elements (Rogers and Storey 1987):

1 A campaign is purposive. (Specific results are intended.)
2 A campaign is aimed at a large audience. (Large, of course, is a relative term, and distinguishes the campaign from interpersonal persuasion on a one-to-one or one-to-few level.)
3 A campaign occurs during a given time period, which may range from a few weeks (e.g. one involving traffic information concerning an upcoming holiday weekend) to many years (the Stanford Heart Disease Prevention Program, an intervention program designed to reduce cardiovascular risk behavior).
4 A campaign involves an organized set of communication activities. At a minimum, this involves message production and distribution.

One of the shortcomings of communication campaigns is that, in practice, campaigns generally unfold according to a linear model. Critics hold this characteristic responsible for the failure of some campaigns.

Let us now turn to some of the generalizations about communication campaigns. The following are factors contributing to campaign success

and have been drawn from literature reviews by Rice and Atkin (1989)
and Rogers and Storey (1987):

1 *The role of the mass media.* The mass media are important for creating
  awareness and knowledge and stimulating others to participate in the
  campaign process; more ambitious effects such as behavioral changes
  are unlikely.
2 *The role of interpersonal communication.* Interpersonal communication, particularly through peer groups and social networks, is instrumental for behavior change and maintenance of such change. (Social
  learning theory (Bandura 1977), which emphasizes learning through
  observing and modeling, is one source of theoretical support for this
  generalization.)
3 *Characteristics of source or medium.* Qualities such as credibility can
  influence the outcome of a campaign.
4 *Formative evaluation.* Both campaign objectives and messages need to
  be evaluated to make sure they fit media habits, audience predisposi-
  tions and sheer availability of resources. (For instance, if bicycle riding
  is promoted as a viable exercise possibility, is the supply of bicycles
  capable of handling increased demand?)
5 *Campaign appeals.* Campaigns must be specific rather than general in
  order to appeal to the values of individuals. For example, appeals in an
  AIDS campaign should stress the danger to the individual rather than
  referring to abstract national health standards.
6 *Preventive behavior.* Long-term prevention goals are difficult to achieve
  because rewards often are delayed and uncertain (e.g. using seat belts);
  delayed benefits must be related to immediate ones.
7 *Timeliness, compatibility, and accessibility.* Communication messages
  must be timely and culturally acceptable, and the channels over which
  they are transmitted must be available to the audience. Rogers (1983)
  refers to cues to action as critical events that may spur attitude or
  behavioral change; for instance, after a pregnancy scare, a woman may
  be disposed to adopting contraceptive practices.

A note of caution is offered by Rice and Atkin:

Campaign objectives and criteria for success should be reasonable; not only is
it difficult to pass through all the individual's information processing stages and
to overcome constraints on resources, beliefs, and behavior, but many public
communication campaigns have typically set higher standards for success than
the most successful commercial campaigns. (1989: 10)

Seeking Effectiveness

Effectiveness is a key objective in planned communication; it is measured
in relation to the goals for the campaign set by the communication planner. Those goals should be in line with established norms and values
(McQuail 1987). Those norms and values, however, may not be universally

accepted. If the norms on which a campaign is based reflect the planner/ sender's viewpoint rather than the public/receivers', the campaign is not likely to be very effective. A case in point is family planning, a positive value in most of the First World. In many Third World countries, however, considerable opposition to birth control campaigns has been presented by social and cultural groups.

The sender in a communication campaign is usually a collective, striving to appear as sympathetic, authoritative, and credible as possible to the receiver. The nature of the sender/receiver relationship is crucial in a campaign (McQuail 1987). If the sender ignores the needs, interests, values, and communication potential of the receiving group, or if the receivers do not trust, attend to, and understand the sender, it is likely that the campaign will fail.

O'Keefe (1985) notes that research about the effectiveness and effects of public information campaigns was common some 30 years ago, but has decreased in recent years. This is not to say that no research is being done into the effectiveness of campaigns, but several reasons for *not* evaluating the effectiveness of campaigning are notable: Evaluations are too demanding in terms of economic and time resources. The communication planner dares not find out the truth about the effectiveness or lack thereof. Or communication campaigns often come to be treated as ends in themselves, implying that only when the campaign is completed is the aim reached – a twist on the usual goal-oriented nature of campaigning. The area of public relations has been castigated by some researchers for avoiding evaluation or only paying lip service to the concept. Grunig says this about evaluation in public relations work:

> Lately I have begun to feel more and more like the fundamentalist minister rallying against sin; the difference being that I have rallied for evaluation. Just as anyone is against sin, so most public relations people I talk to are for evaluation. People keep on sinning, however, and public relations people continue not to do evaluation research. (Quoted in Pavlik 1987a: 68)

A Communication Campaign Model

A model of the communication campaign as presented by McQuail (1987) is shown in Figure 10.1. This model emphasizes the breadth of a campaign. The sender is not one person, but many, often an institution or an organization occupying a known position in society. The strategy is based on the use of more than a single channel, and the messages, too, are manifold in order to reach different parts of an often heterogeneous public.

A communication campaign has filter conditions no different from those of any other type of communication. They are, nonetheless, important as determinants of the success or failure of a campaign. The communication planner must consider the filtering factors that apply to the campaign under consideration. The McQuail model includes four

COLLECTIVE SOURCE	SEVERAL CHANNELS	MANY MESSAGES	FILTER CONDITIONS	VARIABLE PUBLIC REACH	EFFECTS
		Attention Perception Group situation Motivation			Cognitive Affective Behavioral

Figure 10.1 *A model of communication influence process (McQuail 1987)*

general types of filter – attention, perception, group situation and motivation – that may enhance the intended effect of the messages or mitigate against it.

Much has been written in communication and social psychology research about selective *attention*. The audience attends to a certain source or channel for a variety of reasons. Some researchers emphasize the role of routine (see, for example, Goodhardt et al. 1975), others point out the selecting activity that occurs prior to exposure to communication (Levy and Windahl 1985). Uses and gratifications theorists stress the needs of the receiver as a reason to attend to a certain type of information (Katz et al. 1974; see Chapter 14). In social psychology, consistency and dissonance research (Festinger 1957; see McQuail 1987) discuss the conditions under which an individual exposes himself to communication (Schenk 1987).

As with attention, *perception* tends to vary from individual to individual. Contemporary research strongly stresses that information usually is open to several interpretations (Dervin 1989). A sender can never quite be sure that the message will be interpreted in the way intended.

Their conceptualization of mass society led early communications theorists to regard the receiver as socially isolated, making communication effects an affair between the sender and the receiver. The two-step flow of information theory (Katz and Lazarsfeld 1955; see also Chapter 6) changed this conception drastically, and the *influence of the group* on the reception process became widely acknowledged by communication scholars (see, for example, Riley and Riley 1959). More recent approaches such as network theory have expanded and enlarged the group concept and its communication component. For example, operating from a social-cultural perspective, several scholars stress the crucial role played in communication by factors such as social class background. Group identity also may be a crucial factor. For example, the North Karelia health program (discussed below) played heavily on the concept of local identity (Puska et al. 1985).

Uses and gratifications theory (see Chapter 14) points out the importance of a *motivated* audience. Motives, according to the theory, stem from needs; the more strongly individuals perceive that communication, directly or indirectly, brings about need fulfillment, the more willing they are to use it. Grunig and Hunt (1984) use the terms "problem recognition," "constraint recognition," and "involvement" to describe differing degrees of constraints on the motivation to engage in communication behavior. Low problem recognition and low involvement combined with high constraint recognition result in information-processing at best, instead of the preferable active information-seeking.

Some of these factors have been presented earlier in this book, together with ways to counter them when they act as obstacles to the effectiveness of a communication campaign. Ignoring them will result in ineffective communication. These factors ensure that publics will be reached only to a certain degree, and in most cases the communication planner has little control over the receiving process: human communication takes place in open systems and is hard to predict and steer. The better the communication planner knows the intended audience and has adapted the campaign messages to it, the greater the chances that the filters will work advantageously, increasing the likelihood of reaching larger numbers of receivers.

Eventually, the campaign will either succeed or fail in producing the intended effects, and unintended effects may arise. While some effects are easier to obtain than others, it is especially difficult to effect changes in behavior and group-rooted norms. When the aim is to change or initiate a behavior, receivers of information may modify related attitudes but still resist changing the corresponding behaviors.

A Traditional Model

Nowak and Wärneryd's (1968) information campaign model is an example of traditional campaign thinking. Both the communication and goal-defining initiatives typically originate outside the social system in question. It is a systematic model – every factor in it is, in one way or another, related to other factors. It is practical in that it offers a crude checklist for the communication planner.

The process described by this model (see Figure 10.2) begins at the left with setting a goal (intended effect) and ends with an evaluation of the effectiveness of the campaign. This is, of course, an ideal type model and does not cover the contingency of the communication planner's having to change the campaign's initial goals midstream, perhaps in response to changes in campaigning conditions or to address a perceived ineffectiveness of the messages.

Intended Effect
Goal-setting is an important part of many campaigns. For example, in the Stanford Heart Disease Prevention Program, Farquhar et al. (1984) formulated highly specific objectives, including specific knowledge, specific attitudes, and specific behavioral intentions on the part of the audience members.

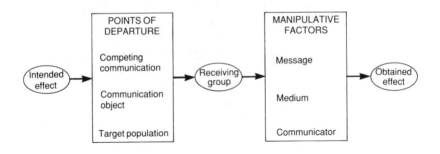

Figure 10.2 *Information campaign model (after Nowak and Wärneryd 1968)*

Bonfadelli (1987a), too, highlights the value of defining goals. He distinguishes different kinds of goals (cognitive, affective, conative); different levels at which goals are located (e.g. individual or group levels); and different time perspectives (e.g. short-term or long-term).

Other stages precede the formulation of the campaign's goals. A thorough problem analysis, including the question of whether the problem is a communication problem or not, is required. Also, an inventory of resources such as money, time, and staff should come prior to a final definition of goals and objectives.

Competing Communication
This includes communication and information that is more or less directly structured to counter the message of the actual campaign (e.g. an opponent's ads in a political campaign). The competing communication has a decisive impact on the campaign's messages. It has been suggested that pro-drug persuasion advertisements (Winick and Winick 1976) and pop music on the radio act as countermessages to anti-drug campaigns. Evans and Evans (1970) report that in the United States the public often was confused about water fluoridation because pro-fluoridation health professionals withheld their opinions, leaving the field open for arguments against fluoridation.

Another target for competition is the attention of the public. At times, major events and other information campaigns may steal all the public's attention. US charities noted a marked drop in response to their regular campaigns for contributions following the 1988 earthquake in Armenia, as people first focused on the news about the quake and then contributed to Armenian relief funds.

Also important is whether the public perceives the campaign's issue to be crucial among those on its *agenda* of issues. As Paisley (1989) points out, the marketplace of issues is overstocked; most of the time, more causes must be rejected than can be accepted. When public opinion research firms assess the public agenda, they usually find some universal gut issues (e.g. disease) and some pocketbook issues (e.g. inflation). Issues usually dealt with in campaigns cannot really claim universal appeal, so the struggle to land on the public agenda begins. The status of an issue can change, too. Many of today's mainstream issues were once special interest issues; the reverse also occurs. For example, not many years ago, acid rain was a fringe environmental issue; today it occupies a prominent place on the environmental agenda. On the other hand, with all the attention focused on the changes in Eastern European countries, Third World issues may have a difficult time garnering the public's attention in the early 1990s.

There is still another element that influences the position of an issue on the public agenda. The question of *entitlement* addresses who is entitled to advocate a certain view on a given issue. Usually the public would accept the entitlement of the aggrieved group to communicate in its own interest. In addition to, or instead of, this first-party entitlement, there may be a second-party entitlement as in the case of whales, future generations of children, white civil rights workers in the South of the United States during the 1960s, or men supporting feminist causes. In these cases, a credibility problem may arise for the public; this problem can be mitigated by a transfer of some of the entitlement to the second-party groups. "Putting oneself on the line" – witness some of the dramatic Greenpeace actions – may be quite helpful in achieving entitlement (Paisley 1989).

The Communication Object

A communication planner must decide how to define the object about which to construct messages. In an AIDS campaign whose aim is to prevent the spread of the disease to heterosexual groups, is the message going to treat the object, the disease, as primarily a moral issue or as a technical one that emphasizes the importance of using condoms during sexual intercourse? The role of the communication planner is to define the communication object clearly and to make other participants in the campaign aware of what that definition of the object really is.

The other elements of the campaign depend on this decision. The more specific this definition is, the less ambiguous the other elements of the campaign will be. It is also true that some objects are more easily communicated than others, regardless of all the filtering factors that may intervene. For example, the plausibility of an issue may strongly influence its communicability.

The Target Population

The target population is defined as those whose knowledge, attitudes, or behavior are to be modified by the campaign. It is not necessary that these individuals be reached directly by the message; the important thing is that they be affected in line with the goal defined by the communication planner. (See our discussion of the distinction between a target population and a receiving group, Chapter 2.)

The Receiving Group
This may be identical to the target population, or it may be a smaller group inside or outside the target population. Identifying a receiving group other than the target population may stem from scarce resources (one cannot afford to reach everyone in the target population) or the assumption that an indirect approach will prove more effective than a direct one.

The Message(s)
The message should have the following characteristics: it should fit within the values and norms of the receiving group; it should faithfully represent the communication object; and it should be capable of bringing about the change in the target population envisaged in the goal. If the strategy is to have the receiving group spread the message to others, the message should be constructed to (a) encourage further dissemination and discussion and (b) withstand negative reformulations and misunderstandings. The Stanford Heart Disease Prevention Program has included a tell-a-friend segment in its messages in order to stimulate further dissemination.

The Medium/Media
Channels and media differ in terms of credibility, physical and psychological accessibility, and other characteristics. Different messages may call for the use of different media, depending on characteristics of the various media or whom they may reach. Rock and pop music and the radio and television programs that carry it may be the best channel and media to pass on AIDS information to a young receiving group; small subsegments like prostitutes will be more effectively reached by interpersonal channels.

There is a great deal written about media and channel selection, but a major conclusion – painfully obvious, perhaps, but of crucial importance for the communication planner – is that all media have their strengths and their limitations. For example, media researchers commonly warn against using electronic media to disseminate large numbers of facts; television does function well, however, to create interest or transmit emotional content (Atkin 1981; Hawkins et al. 1988).

An interesting debate with great relevance to communication planning centers on the roles of big and little media, especially in the context of Third World campaigns. Rogers (1978) notes that the interest in big media, such as satellite broadcasting and instructional television, has decreased, while little media (interpersonal communication, booklets, etc.) and radio have gained in importance (Schramm 1977). Hornik (1988) maintains that mass media in communication campaigns suffer the disadvantage of not bringing communication planners in contact with receivers. Face-to-face channels have a better potential for feedback.

Hornik (1988: 130) also suggests that the advantages of multi-channel campaigns in comparison to one-channel campaigns are great:

- There will be fewer contradictory messages in the environment.
- The same message will be heard from more than one source.
- Each channel's characteristics can be maximized, for example, during different phases of a diffusion process.
- Each channel will have access to some members of the audience that other channels may not.

The Communicator(s)

Ideally there should be a fit between the communicator, the communication object, the receiving group, the message, and the medium. A certain communicator may function well technically on a certain channel, but have little credibility with the receiving group. Someone who is positively related to the communication object because of expertise or other relevant characteristics may be ineffective in a certain medium. Research finds three dimensions that influence the credibility of sources: (a) trustworthiness, (b) expertise/competence, and (c) dynamism/attractiveness. Which dimension is most important depends on the specific campaign setting (Atkin 1981). There are several theories about the effectiveness of different types of communicators. Rogers (1983) emphasizes the principle of homophily in the case of diffusion of innovations, meaning that the communicator ideally should be similar to the members of the audience. Heterophily is advantageous when the main goal is the opening up of close-tied networks and the introduction of innovations from the outside (see also Schenk 1987).

Thayer (1986) distinguishes between two types of communicators (or mediators): (a) *instrumental* mediators perform their function as anonymous communicators, and (b) *consummatory* mediators represent the worlds or realities they present. The famous heart specialist communicating about health is consummatory, where the newswriter who reports about the local health scene is instrumental. "A consummatory mediator is one in whom we see and vicariously experience those other worlds. The consummatory mediator is a celebrity; the instrumental mediator is a functionary" (Thayer 1986). The communication planner frequently must choose between these two types of communicators.

Effect Obtained

The final element in the model is closely related to the first, the definition of goals. It is the goal reached. At this stage, the planner compares what has been attained by the campaign with what was defined as the goal at the outset. The measurement should correspond to the goal; for example, if a campaign intends to bring about a long-term change in a behavior,

long-term behavior is what should be measured, not short-term manifesta-
tions of the behavior.

Evaluation is a demanding undertaking that may impose a burden on
the communication planner. It is important, nevertheless, not to shy away
from it. Both the quality of communication planning and the legitimacy
of the planner vis-à-vis the client benefit from careful evaluation. Evaluation research literature (e.g. Weiss 1972) distinguishes between summative
and formative research. Summative evaluation research explains whether
a campaign has reached its goals; it informs the decision of whether or
not to continue. Formative research goes beyond that. According to
Weiss, "formative evaluation produces information that is fed back
during development of curriculum to help improve it. It serves the needs
of the developers" (1972, quoted in Pavlik 1987a: 66).

Pfaff (1982) developed a matrix for measuring effects of a highway
traffic safety campaign. Designed as a checklist for carrying out effects
research, the matrix contains the variables: areas of effects (knowledge,
attitudes, behavior), indicators of effects (e.g. knowledge of traffic signs,
awareness of risks), and research setting (e.g. field study, laboratory
experiment).

Effectiveness and Effects

The Nowak and Wärneryd model focuses on intended effects, that is, on
effectiveness. Current thinking would call for the planner to assess all of
the effects – the latent and unintended as well as the manifest, intended,
and foreseen; the dysfunctional and negative as well as the functional and
positive. A latent effect may prove to be far more important than an
intended one. The simple fourfold table in Figure 10.3 illustrates our
reasoning.

The goal of an anti-smoking campaign directed at high school students
is to reduce smoking among those who already smoke and to convince
those who have not started not to. Following our table, the effects in

	Intended/ foreseen	Unintended/ unforeseen
Positive	"That's what we were hoping for" 1	"Now, isn't that nice?" 2
Negative	"The price we had to pay" 3	"Oh, my God!" 4

Figure 10.3 **Four types of effect**

relation to the campaign goal are of the following types:

- *Positive, intended effects.* The smoking rate among the students goes down and the intention among non-smokers not to start smoking is expressed frequently. "That's what we hoped for."
- *Positive, non-intended effects.* Quitting smoking is a topic of discussion both in school and at home. Awareness of the problem in the high school will continue after the campaign is over. The students may function as persuaders in their families as well. "Now, isn't that nice?"
- *Negative, intended effects.* If we stretch the effects far enough, we can come up with some negative, intended (or at least foreseen) effects, though they are difficult to conceive. The success of the campaign is so strong that cigarette sales nationally fall precipitously, leading to the lay-off of workers in the tobacco industry. "That's the price we have to pay."
- *Negative, unintended effects.* Reports surface of fights between smokers and non-smokers. "Oh, my God!" In other schools, the non-smoking message has a boomerang effect (see, for example, Vidmar and Rokeach 1974) – high schoolers regard the message as adults meddling and their reaction is to smoke more. Durell and Bukoski (1984) point out concern that anti-drug campaigns may have stimulated drug abuse and increased the gap between the establishment on the one hand and the youth and pro-drug culture on the other.

An overall assessment of campaign effects enables the communication planner to talk confidently about the campaign in terms of success or failure. The knowledge gained through such a procedure will also be helpful in designing the next campaign.

The Systematic Character

The Nowak and Wärneryd model demonstrates that we are dealing with a system of interrelated elements. A decision about one element of the model will affect decisions about the other elements as well. The most crucial element is the defined goal. As it changes, all the other elements need to be modified. Also, the more precise the goal, the fewer the options for defining the other elements. If a non-smoking campaign goal is defined vaguely as making young people smoke less, there is considerable latitude in the form the other elements take. Examples might be:

- A wide range of competing communication is possible.
- Smoking less can be interpreted in several ways.
- The planner can define the target population in many ways.
- The goal description does not offer much guidance for defining the receiving group.

If the campaign goal is to reduce by 10 percent the number of smokers aged 13 to 18 living in the community of Middlebury during a two-month campaign, ambiguity is reduced and the planner can more easily describe and plan the other elements of the campaign model.

Dimensions of Campaign Objectives and Effects

Another model useful in conceptualizing the dimensions of a communication campaign is presented in Figure 10.4. The authors, Rogers and Storey (1987), explain three dimensions:

1 *Level of objectives* refers to the many ways that goals and outcomes of campaigns can be ordered hierarchically:
   - to inform, persuade, and mobilize overt behavioral change;
   - cognitive, affective, and conative changes (Ray 1973);
   - attention, comprehension, yielding, and retention (McGuire 1969).
2 *Locus of change* refers to the level where change is supposed to occur: individual, group, organizational, or societal.

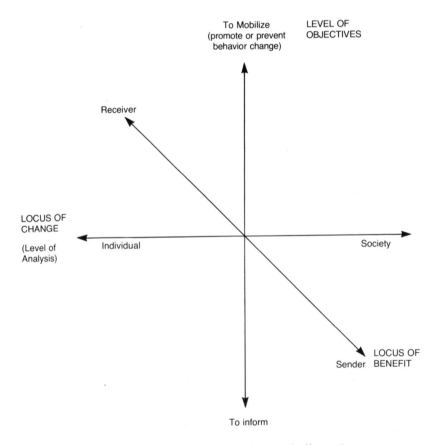

Figure 10.4 *Dimensions of campaign objectives and effects (Rogers and Storey 1987: 823)*

3 *Locus of benefit* refers to the question of who benefits from the successful campaign – the sender (e.g. in political campaigns), the receiver (e.g. in health campaigns), or both (e.g. in some commercial advertising campaigns).

Can Communication Campaigns Succeed?

Probably the two most cited articles about communication campaigns are Hyman and Sheatsley's "Some Reasons Why Information Campaigns Fail," which appeared in 1947, and Mendelsohn's "Some Reasons Why Information Campaigns Can Succeed," published in 1973.

Hyman and Sheatsley (1947) found a large, uninformed substratum of the American population that they labeled the chronic know-nothings. This category is almost impossible to reach with any information. They mention the three selective processes (selective exposure, selective perception, and selective retention) as common threats to the success of information campaigns. These filters, the authors believe, ensure that receivers will be immune to influence from campaigns.

Mendelsohn (1973) believes it is wrong to blame the public for not being influenced by information campaigns; rather, the campaigners are to blame. Planning for information campaigns often ignores communication research and theory, and evaluations involving both planners and researchers are frequently non-existent. Information campaigns can succeed, Mendelsohn maintains, if, among other things, the following conditions are met:

1 Campaigns should have realistic goals based on the assumption that the publics addressed are not overly interested, if at all, in the message.
2 The mere offering of information through a campaign is insufficient. The communication planner should use environmental support systems, i.e. interpersonal communication. Combining mass communication and interpersonal communication should be considered.
3 The planner must know the campaign's publics well enough to recognize them as different targets based on their mass media habits, lifestyles, values and belief systems, and demographic and psychological attributes. Receiving groups do not constitute a monolithic mass.

Mendelsohn's recommendations are as valid today as they were in 1973; we have developed similar themes throughout this book. But let us return to the question, can communication campaigns succeed? If they can, what makes them successful? The North Karelia Health Program is often mentioned as an example of a successful information campaign, and we shall now present the central elements of it. Similarly successful information campaigns include the Minnesota Heart Health Program (see, for example, Blackburn et al. 1984) and the Stanford Heart Disease Prevention Program (see, for example, Flora et al. 1989).

The North Karelia Health Program

In the 1970s and 1980s, large health communication programs in the United States and other countries were thoroughly analyzed from both a scientific and a practical point of view. The most notable non-US project probably is the North Karelia Project, a five-year heart health program that involved an entire county's residents and infrastructure in several ways (McAlister et al. 1982; Puska et al. 1985).

North Karelia is a province in the east of Finland. It has some 180,000 residents and is characterized by low population density, high unemployment, and an agriculture- and forestry-based economy. Cardiovascular diseases were widespread when the program started in 1972.

Two Publics

The project had two major publics. The entire population of North Karelia was targeted for a prevention program whose aim was to modify the general risk factor profile of all residents. This was the primary public. Further, a clinical project was launched to focus on a secondary public comprising high-risk groups, especially people with high blood pressure. The prevention program included:

- disseminating general information to the primary public through newspapers, radio, television, leaflets, lectures, etc.;
- cooperation with organizations interested in health-related problems;
- education of people working in health institutions;
- education of volunteer opinion mediators;
- influencing producers and consumers in the food industry;
- an elaborate system for project organization and evaluation.

In this project, heart health was seen not just as an information problem. It also encompassed clinical, administrative, and organizational dimensions.

Community Intervention

The prevention campaign used and activated the existing community structures to achieve its goals; this is referred to as community intervention.[1] Some system elements that may be utilized in a health information campaign include:

- schools (emphasizing health instruction in curricula);
- health institutions (e.g. offering free medical check-ups);
- volunteer organizations (e.g. lecturing at meetings, offering cooking demonstrations, etc.);
- local shops (e.g. promoting healthy food).

The design of the North Karelia program is presented in Figure 10.5.

CHANGES IN DISEASE RATES AND HEALTH

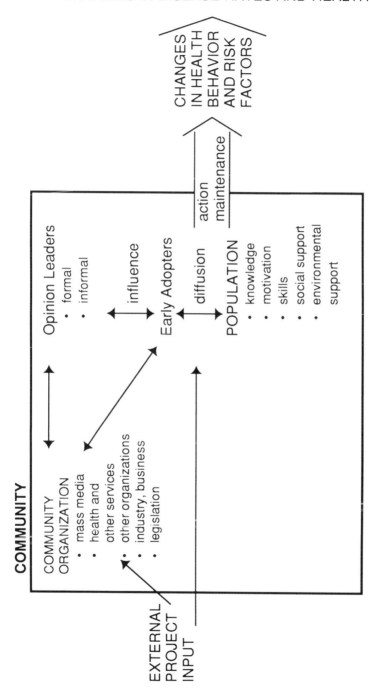

Figure 10.5 *The design of the North Karelia Project community intervention program (Puska et al. 1985)*

It is important to note that North Karelians are characterized by low mobility. Appeals could be made to a strong community identity, and communication efforts reached the same people over time. Both of these characteristics are present to a much lesser extent, if at all, in more mobile communities.

The theoretical underpinnings of this design include, according to Puska et al. (1985):

- *A behavioral change approach*, based to a large extent on social learning theory, especially Bandura's work on the learning process (Bandura 1977, see also Bandura 1986). Program objectives included helping people to identify risk factors, educating them about the relationship between behavior and their health, motivating people to adopt healthy behavior, increasing self-management skills, offering social support, and changing the environment in order to facilitate healthy behaviors.
- *A communication-behavior change approach* was based on social learning theory and some communication-persuasion models (e.g. McGuire 1969; Ajzen and Fishbein 1980). The project's persuasion model included the following steps: attention, motivation, comprehension, learning information, attitude change, health skills learning, health skills performance, and maintenance of performance.
- *The innovation-diffusion approach* led the project to focus on the importance of change agents (Rogers 1983, see Chapter 6 in this book) and opinion leaders. It used early adopters of health innovations to communicate with other residents about the benefits of the innovations.
- *The community organization approach* mobilized local institutions and organizations in order to create a multiple-channel communication campaign.

Encouraging Results

The results of the North Karelia project seem encouraging: cholesterol levels were reduced in the target population, a clear reduction in the incidence of heart attacks was noted, and both smoking rates and the overall risk score went down significantly. Also, people's subjective assessment of their health changed, that is, the proportion of people reporting that they felt good and very good increased significantly in comparison with a control group.

This project is a good example of a well-conducted intervention; it used a very mixed approach launched under some favorable conditions. The program was supported by several societal institutions, permitting encouragement of North Karelians to participate on nationalistic grounds in order to show other Finns what they could accomplish.

On the other hand, from an information point of view, the communication planners had to work with a very heterogeneous target population – the range of age, education, social status, occupation, etc. represented by

180,000 people is staggering. That points up a weakness of community interventions: the message is likely to be blander than it would be in more concentrated and focused campaigns.

The strength of the North Karelia program lies in its thorough use of communication, social psychological, sociological, epidemiological, and educational theory. It confirms what we have said throughout this book about the value of grounding communication planning practice in theory.

Concluding Remarks

Through the years effects theory has vacillated between the notions of strong and weak media in terms of producing effects. Assessments of the relative power of information campaigns have wavered likewise. A more balanced view of the power of campaigns now seems to be gaining ground, concentrating on intermediate and indirect effects of campaigns (Rogers and Storey 1987). For example, agenda-setting (see Chapter 15), although an intermediate effect, is considered worth pursuing in terms of goal-setting. Small but overt behavior changes are moving to center stage as the focus of information/communication efforts.

This more realistic view of the power of communication planning has caused some fundamental adjustments in how problems are defined. According to Rogers and Storey (1987: 831), "The shifting conceptualization of communication effects and communication process has led to recognition that communication operates within a complex social, political, and economic matrix, and that communication could not be expected to generate effects all by itself." This reinforces our earlier warning that not all problems are communication problems; it also ties in with Hornik's (1988) view that, at least in a development communication context, information or communication cannot resolve problems that are essentially caused by scarce resources, rather than a lack of knowledge.

Note

1 In addition to the concept of community intervention, recent theorizing has come up with the notion of community development. While the former implies a strategy based more on action from above, the latter focuses on the idea of activity from the bottom up and from the social system concerned. A community development project can take its energy from injustice and class conflict as seen from the perspective of an underdog. Community intervention is based more on a harmony vision of society and its energy emanates from interagency cooperation.

PART III   THE ELEMENTS OF MASS COMMUNICATION THEORIES

In the real world, communication planners often consider themselves mass communicators. At least two things explain this: (1) many of the media and channels used by communication planners are of a mass communication type, and (2) the tools, theories, concepts, and models that planners use spring from the study of mass communication.

The difference between a mass communication theory and other types of theories of communication is sometimes difficult to make; we have not found it necessary to develop clear-cut distinctions. Our aim rather is to present notions, models, and theories, more or less frequently used in mass communication research, that are applicable to planned communication. The main criterion for inclusion is, then, how useful and relevant the theories or models are for our understanding of planned communication.

Since the emphasis of this part of the book clearly is on mass communication, we neglect here important theories of intra- and interpersonal communication and organizational communication. In order to keep the book focused and manageable, this is necessary. You will find, however, that we do not have a mass-media-centered view of planned communication. On the contrary, in Parts I and II, as well as in Part III, we stress time and time again that in planned communication the very interplay between mass and other types of communication can be of crucial importance. Recent attempts at integration of the different levels of communication seem to be particularly promising (Berger and Chaffee 1987, 1988; Reardon and Rogers 1988; Hawkins et al. 1988). Also, developing communication technology suggests that clear-cut distinctions between mass and other types of communication will be less meaningful in the future (Rogers 1986; see also Dominick's 1987 category of "machine-assisted interpersonal communication").

Part III follows Harold Lasswell's (1948) formula: Who Says What in Which Channel to Whom with What Effect? We will, then, discuss theories dealing with:

- communicator and sender;
- the medium;
- the message;
- the receiver;
- the effects.

Of these themes, we will not deal extensively with the medium, but we will concentrate on the other elements of the formula.

As you will see, there are problems in following a traditional communication model like Lasswell's, even for the purpose of structuring a section of a book. The different parts of the communication process are not so distinct and the relations between them not so neatly ordered as the models with their arrows and boxes would indicate. Also, using a linear model as a point of departure ensures that certain notions about mass communication, e.g. what stems from cultural theory and a ritual approach (Carey 1975), receive less attention than they deserve. Nevertheless, we find it practical to use this fairly simple ordering principle.

11 The Sender/Communicator

The sender/communicator element of the communication process clearly has not attracted the attention of mass communication researchers that communication effects have. The research that does exist in this area, however, raises many exciting questions relevant to communication planning. Some very interesting answers to these questions can be suggested.

Theory teaches that the sender/communicator is part of both communicative and community/administrative/organizational structures; factors on these two levels, separately or jointly, will influence the sender's communicative work. The communication planner operates on these two levels as well. We will argue in this section that the communication planner often loses sight of the communicative function of his or her role, stressing instead its administration/organization aspects. We will illustrate the conditions under which senders work by using two communication models, the Westley and MacLean and the Maletzke models, as points of departure.

The Westley and MacLean Model: Co-orientation and System

We have chosen the Westley and MacLean (1957) model because it presents the communicator in a communication system setting. Three roles are present in the system:

- *The advocacy role*, A in Figure 11.1, strives to influence people in the environment, directly or indirectly. This role, thus, is clearly purposive. In mass communication the A role may be played by purposive sources such as political parties, the public relations department of a company, or someone in a media organization itself.
- *The channel role*, C, has a less purposive character. Its aim is to provide the public with information and to act as an intermediary between A and the public. This role is usually filled by a journalist who is a part of a mass media organization. The model depicts the C role, in relation to the A role, as non-purposive because individuals acting in the C role do not (theoretically) further their own personal interests in the communication process.
- *The behavioral role*, B, is held by members of the publics, that is, readers, viewers, and listeners.

The Xs in the model refer to extant events, phenomena, and objects that may be communicated about. These are picked up by those in the channel role, either directly or through individuals or organizations in the A role. The event X_3 is one that can be either mediated to C (and B) through A or perceived/experienced directly by C (X_{3C} and X_4).

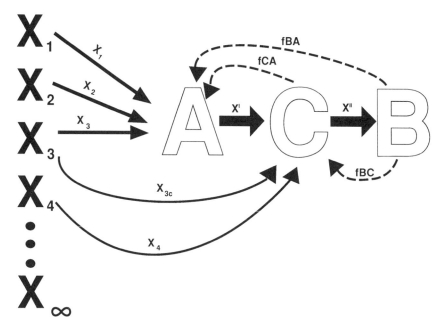

Figure 11.1 *The Westley and MacLean model (Westley and MacLean 1957)*

There are also different types of feedback in the model. One feedback route occurs between B and A (fBA), for example, the reduction of an individual's alcohol consumption in response to a mass media campaign initiated and supported by the Ministry of Health. Even a non-reaction would qualify as a kind of feedback. Other feedback occurs between B and C (fBC), for instance, a letter to the editor or the results of an audience research survey. A third feedback pattern is exemplified by the reaction of a journalist to a news release issued by the above-mentioned Ministry of Health (fCA).

Relevance for Planned Communication

Communication planners need to question not so much whether they take the A or C role in the model, but to what extent and in which situations they play the advocacy role, the channel role, or, in some rare instances, the behavioral role. All these roles can be functional. In many instances, planners will be purposive senders (A), trying to influence segments of the public by convincing the channel (C) to carry their messages. In just as many instances, planners may take the C role of intermediary between an A (e.g. their employers) and the Bs.

Consider this scenario. The Health Ministry launches another anti-smoking communication effort involving the media and other channels of communication. Clearly the Ministry is acting as an A, strongly advocating a position. Vis-à-vis the mass media (C), the Ministry's communication planner also assumes the A role. If direct contact is made with the target audience (the Bs), the planner then takes on some aspects of the channel role, becoming a sort of intermediary between the Ministry and the targeted groups of young people. In this role the planner still represents the interests of the Ministry, but at the same time relays back to the organization the interests of the potential non-smokers. Typically the planner would select from various informational materials and strategies provided by the employer those messages best suited for the campaign.

There are never any totally clear answers as to the exact role the planner is playing or should play. Even when adopting a strong advocacy role for the employer (both would then be As), the planner may be well-advised to consider elements of a C role that will enable understanding and dealing with Cs (for example, journalists) better. The delicate issue for the planner, then, is to be able to act as an intermediary even when serving as an advocate. This, in turn, becomes a problem of professionalism. Only if the planner can attain a degree of autonomy based on knowledge and respect will it be possible to straddle the advocate/channel line – something that is crucial to carrying out the requirements of the job effectively and professionally.

Some themes suggested by this model are, then, as relevant for the communication planner as for the journalist and the holders of advocacy roles, e.g. public relations practitioners or information officers.

The Locus of Power in the System

The model can be used to address the question of power distribution in a communication system. Power may lie with the As, that is, the sources who try to influence media coverage of their areas of concern. While this is certainly the case in authoritarian mass communication systems, this tendency is increasing in liberal systems as well. Researchers who have studied the degree to which public relations materials (e.g. news releases by As) actually are presented as news argue that there is a shift in the balance of power away from the media and the journalists toward the public relations systems that furnish the information. This diminishes the "autonomous researching" function of journalism (Baerns 1985, 1987; Grossenbacher 1986; Gandy 1982; Turk 1985). Not atypical of this trend is the title of the American book, *How The Public Relations Industry Writes the News* (Blyskol and Blyskol 1985). Its authors denounce the increasingly powerful role of As in the mass communication system.

This is not to suggest, however, that Cs (that is, journalists) have become altogether powerless. They may hold power in systems where the media themselves and the journalistic professional organizations control what is communicated and how. Also, the power to select continues to rest with Cs; this power may be viewed subjectively by As as stronger than it really is. That the power to select is less than the power to create is an abstraction that may be difficult to grasp.

Power also may be said to lie with the Bs, as when members of a mass communication audience with a variety of Cs from which to choose refuse to listen to and watch certain radio and TV stations or read newspapers because they do not like the medium, sender, or content. As some of the power struggles between different Cs and As are carried out in order to gain attention and responses from the audience, the Bs enjoy a fairly strong position. The media public *can* organize itself, as evidenced by parent and teacher groups who use their assembled strength to boycott advertised products and protest against violence on television.

Communication planners optimize power in the process when they are professionalized and legitimized as communication specialists and when they are not too strongly tied to the source/employer organization. The power relationship between the planner and the audience is highly conditional; many times when communicators/planners are ascribed power, it really resides with the true As in the system. Generally speaking, at an individual level, the communication planner's mission of communicating A's specific messages to specific publics affords less power than is held by the journalist counterpart in the model. Collectively, however, the power of journalists as an ensemble, a group whose members remain essentially constant, seems diminished in the face of ever-increasing numbers of well-qualified planners. Nevertheless, the mere fact that the communication system is an open one and typically has mutual co-orientational traits would suggest that power is seldom totally concentrated in one role.

A Communication Flow or a Marketplace for Communications?

The Westley and MacLean model portrays the mass communication process as a vehicle for certain sources in society who have something to say to certain audiences. The media and media workers serve to convey the messages that, in their opinion, the audiences need for information, orientation, relaxation, decision making, and so on. The image is one of a natural communication flow from As to Bs with the help of Cs, followed by a return flow via feedback devices. This idealistic picture also assumes self-regulation, mutual benefits, and balanced power relations. And it assumes that the actors share the same view of the process and actually have and carry out the intentions they are supposed to have, for example, the As really want to advocate and influence in a certain direction.

Critical observers of mass communication processes, such as Elliott (1972), maintain that mass communication is not communication in the true sense of the word and that mass communicators are not communicating. Elliott observes that mass communication is a contradiction in terms. While the mass communication system may be regarded as consisting of three different subsystems – sources, media, and audience – the relation between them is not primarily of a communication character. The media extract material from the sources for production of messages, as does any unit of production in society. And as in any market, Elliott (1972) argues, the clients – here the audience – are evaluated in terms of their preferences, etc. In this way, the audience also becomes a source for the media's production efforts.

Therefore, mass communication is not communication. The mass media tailor their content based on audience preferences. Media content, therefore, is merely content from a target audience, echoed back via the media. The audience is left to respond to the products produced by the media. We are left with the image of a market system where the needs and interests of each subsystem gain preference over the need to communicate. The audience, Elliott says, is not active, responsive, and demanding, but rather a group of spectators, looking at what the media present much as they would watch a tennis match on television or stroll through the aisles of a supermarket, seeing what products are on display.

Anderson and Meyer also underscore the distance between the world of mass communication production and that of the audience: "Mediated communication proceeds in two quasi-independent systems of production and reception. In the production system of interlinked media industries, a community of practitioners produces a commodity content for its own end" (1988: 47). In this situation, the nature of communication becomes something other than it is in interpersonal communication: "The shared meaning of interpersonal communication is the achievement of the joint performance of production and interpretation. Shared meanings do not develop between producer and receiver in mediated communication" (1988: 47).

This view is quite important to the communication planner. Many times, the communication planner may ask whether communication with an audience is really occurring or if just an offering of messages, pieces of content, is being made. The communication planner frequently is in a more or less isolated system, accepting material (orders, information, resources, etc.) from the employing system and from sources (A), and trying to distribute communication products to the audience/publics/clients (B). In many cases, a planner ends up producing messages for an employer; the production in and of itself becomes the end, rather than communication. The reasons for such a twisting of purpose are manifold – distance from the publics, holding a source/employer orientation instead of a client/public orientation, lack of empathy, disagreement with the message, and so on.

Elliott's conceptualization of mass communication content as an echo bouncing back to the audience is relevant for the communication planner. On the one hand, the planner is taught to find out about the audience and adapt the message to it. On the other, adapting too much may result in routine messages and, eventually, saturating the public with too much of the same. Another consequence is that the communication planner gives the audience more of what it wants to hear and less of what it, for one reason or another, needs to hear.

It is beneficial, then, to recognize first and foremost the planner's position as an integrated part of a communication system, not of a production or market system. Many planners lose sense of their communicative function by investing too much of their time and resources at the administrative/organizational level.

The Communicator and Communication Planner as Gatekeepers

The C role in the Westley and MacLean model is also a gatekeeper role. The term "gatekeeper" was coined by Lewin (1947), who used it to describe how food found its way into a household. It became a key concept in mass communication studies about news selection (White 1950). A gatekeeper in a social system decides which of a certain commodity – materials, goods, information, etc. – may enter the system. Media gatekeeping studies have shown how an editor's decision making may be based on a rich mixture of general principles of news values, organizational routines, input structure (e.g. a wire service's priorities) and, well, plain idiosyncrasy (Ettema and Whitney 1977).

Gatekeeping is vital in communication planning. Almost all communication planning roles include some aspect of gatekeeping:

- the agricultural consultant, who has to transform and reduce scientific news into practical advice intended for farmers;
- the leader of an environmental discussion group, who selects teaching materials to be used in the group;
- the planner of an anti-drug campaign, who must select among hundreds of arguments for quitting cocaine;
- the editor of a small monthly newsletter on the Soviet oil industry who chooses material coming from sources all over the world.

As a gatekeeper, the communication planner undoubtedly can exercise some power over the communication process by deciding what information to discard and what to let pass. Nevertheless, gatekeeping very often is a routine, guided by some set of standard questions, such as:

- What, from this material, do audience members need to know?
- What do they want to know?
- What do they know already?
- What will they understand?
- What will they refuse to accept?

Even though these questions are routine, they are important. There are reasons to think that all types of communication planning have their own sets of selection values, some of which are quite similar to those of mass communication gatekeeping. Journalism textbooks usually list news values such as timeliness, consequence, proximity, known human values, conflict,

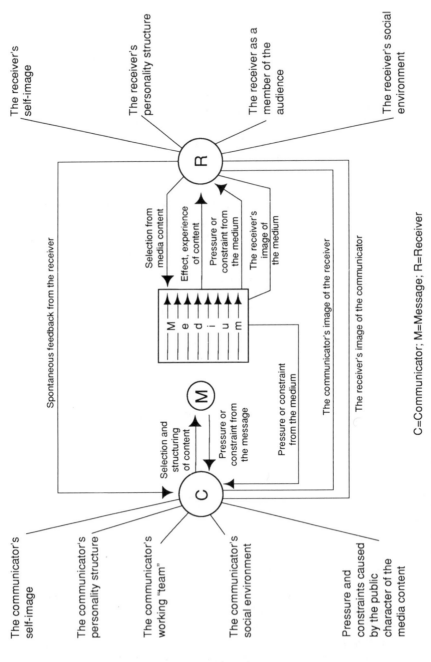

Figure 11.2 **The Maletzke model/Schema des Feldes der Massenkommunikation (Maletzke 1963)**

C=Communicator; M=Message; R=Receiver

and human interest (Ettema and Whitney 1987). In fact, planners may profit from more carefully studying mass media news values.

For the planner to act as a gatekeeper is not without its problems. Gatekeeping can become a way to reduce openness in a social system and may result in distrust and extra information-finding efforts on the part of people in the system (Rogers and Rogers 1976). The same people who in cases of information overload complain about too much communication may complain when dealing with gatekeeping about too little information or that they feel uneasy about what information is eliminated from the overall offering.

The Maletzke Model: A Social Psychological View

German mass communication researcher Gerhard Maletzke (1963) identified a number of important relationships and factors for describing and understanding the mass media communicator. These are relevant for other roles and functions of the sender as well. His model is presented in Figure 11.2. Some of the model's elements and relationships are very relevant for an analysis of the role of the communication planner.

The Communicator's Self-Image

The way communicators look at their own roles is essential to how they design and plan communication. Whether they define themselves as crusaders for their own ideas or as merely a megaphone for someone else makes a great difference. Many mass communicators take their function as a given and do not reflect on why they work, what motivates them, and the deeper nature of their work.

McQuail (1987: 159) describes different work orientations among journalists:

- the *pragmatics*, who measure their success in terms of ratings, which are also important for the organization;
- the *craft-oriented*, who are most interested in getting positive reinforcement from other professional journalists;
- the *organization-oriented*, who relate their work to the goals set by the organization;
- the *society/environment-oriented*, who assess their work in relation to relevant subgroups outside the organization.

This characterization of orientations would also apply to different types of communication planners.

- The health communicator could be a pragmatic, guided by the statistics about people reached and number of people reporting health-related behavioral changes.
- A traffic campaigner could be craft-oriented, holding as a goal to get the "campaign-of-the-year award" from professional colleagues.

- An organization orientation would be held by a public relations person for whom it is important to contribute to achieving organizational goals.
- A society-oriented planner could be a family planning change agent, who, for personal ideological reasons, may try to ensure the campaign message reaches those groups that are hardest to reach.

Every communication planner has a job orientation, and it is probably one of those just described or a combination of them. Whether or not a planner admits or even recognizes the orientation that guides him or her, its influence on his or her work should not be underestimated.

Professionalization of Communication Practitioners

In almost all communication-related occupations, potential conflict exists between the communication planner, the communicator, the journalist, etc., on the one side and the organization and employer on the other. Professionalization is a means by which communication practitioners may defend their interests in this confrontation. Professionalization offers a way of gaining power not only in relation to other occupations, but also in relation to employing organizations.

Professional status, however, is easier to claim than to achieve. Research has shown, for example, that journalists may attain only semi-professional status because, among other reasons, their knowledge base does not command the same respect as does that of occupational groups such as civil engineers (Windahl 1975; Etzioni 1969; Kepplinger and Vohl 1976).

To a greater or lesser extent, the characterization of semi-profession holds true for other communication occupations as well. For example, Grunig and Hunt (1984) conclude that US public relations practitioners cannot yet be considered fully professionalized. Commercial public relations obviously has a problem of both scientificity and plausibility of its knowledge base, two criteria of a profession.

This leads, however, to the more general question of whether the *kind* of knowledge the social sciences provide to "their" occupation supports professionalization; Wilensky, in his much-quoted article, "The professionalization of everyone?", is sceptical: "The lay public cannot recognize the need for special competence in an area where everyone is 'expert'" (1964: 145). This is a good example of the fact that knowledge about communication may never be as inaccessible to a lay audience as is, for example, medical, legal, or engineering knowledge. On the other hand, some degree of professionalization – and desirably a high one – is not only necessary and functional, but also a legitimate goal for a communication planner to hold in order to do a good job.

The Work Group Orientation

As was mentioned above, colleagues (the working "team") often serve as a reference group for communicators. In many cases this tendency will be intensified when communicators have little contact with their audiences. The resulting communication may be formed to satisfy colleagues and superiors instead of being targeted to the audience. Ryan and Peterson (1982) maintain that media workers learn a product image that is primarily that of superiors and colleagues rather than that of the audience. Surrounding workers, then, act as an important audience.

Colleague orientation is strengthened by professional organizations. For example, in Swedish advertising a "Golden Egg Award" is given to advertising professionals who have produced an ad especially appreciated by other members of the advertising industry. This has given rise to the term "golden egg philosophy," which denotes a colleague orientation. This orientation means that a client's needs are subordinate to the approval of advertising colleagues. No doubt communication planners, too, face the risk of becoming distanced from their actual clients.

The Social Environment of the Communicator

The choice of reference groups is not limited to individuals within the organization. Other people in the communicator's environment – spouses, neighbors, etc. – may serve as reference groups, thus functioning as audiences. Since most mass communicators belong to the middle class and associate with other middle-class people, you could assume that communication will have a middle-class bias (Windahl 1975; Fabris 1979; Prott 1976). This tendency may have negative consequences for the effectiveness of communication in situations where the communicator/receiver relationship is heterophilous (Rogers 1983; see Chapter 6), for example, when the audience is composed of working-class individuals. In a study of specialized British journalists, Tunstall (1971) found that journalists on the average underestimated the relative share of working-class readers by 20 percent.

The Communicator's Personality Structure

Little is said in mass communication literature about the importance of the personality structure of the mass communicator. Of course, some communicators have a stronger will to control others through communication, some have a need to talk *with* the audience rather than to talk *to* them. For some, it is of importance that communication is logically ordered, for others communication should be expressive, showing what the communicator really feels about an item.

Constraints from Message and Medium

Maletzke (1963) notes that communicators are restricted in their communication by limitations inherent in the message and the medium. In any branch of communication, rules emerge for how to communicate. In journalism, Tuchman (1973) reports that news journalists rely on typifications of news stories and that newsworkers tend to relate to different types of stories in certain ways.

In planned communication, this tendency to treat different types of messages in different but routine ways is obvious. There is usually a standard way to write health advice, a standard way to formulate press releases. For many communication planners, this is a means of playing it safe since standard solutions are usually appreciated by their superiors.

There are standard ways to use different media as well. An agreement exists between communication practitioners and the audience as to what constitutes television, what a newspaper should really look like, and what a local radio station should do. This agreement tends to be maintained by the routine way in which the audience uses the media.

This routinization poses a dilemma for the communication planner. On the one hand, new ways of presentation may be rejected because the audience does not accept the communication; the communication may be regarded as less credible because it violates the agreed-upon format as discussed above. On the other hand, new formats may increase attention and create interest in the audience. In a heart disease prevention campaign, for example, publishing another informational booklet may be the way of avoiding the risk of outright rejection by an audience that has become accustomed to and bored by this type of format. Trying out informational flyers meant to be affixed to refrigerators may appear risky, but also holds the promise of increased attention from the audience, the users. Formative research in a communication campaign (Maccoby and Solomon 1981) may help solve this dilemma. (For a further discussion of this routine/non-routine format choice, see our presentation of mediation theory, Chapter 13.)

There is also an international/intercultural angle to this problem. Often the very conception of what a certain medium is supposed to be like is shaped by the media and communication culture of another country. Thus, the "shape of the communication vehicle" (Boyd-Barrett 1977: 120–21) often does not correspond to the real communicative needs of a given situation. Such basic notions as, for example, what a weekly news magazine should be like or the principles of investigative journalism all originated in the United States and were subsequently adopted in other countries. While these notions make perfect sense in the country of origin, they often turn out to be dysfunctional in another.

This type of intercultural bias may be quite widespread in communication planning as well. One of the fundamental criticisms of the classic school of communication and development is that it transferred models and experiences from the US agricultural extension movement to the Third World. Here is another example: what works in an anti-smoking campaign in one country may not work in another where, for instance, the overall attitude toward health may be different, perhaps more cynical.

The Communicator's Image of the Audience

An important theme in communicator studies is that of the perception communicators have of their audiences. McQuail (1969: 82) says that "an examination of the communicator–audience relationship reveals a strongly felt need on the part of the communicator to know, and to be in a defined relationship with his intended audience." Ettema and Whitney (1987), however, report several communication studies in which researchers have expressed surprise over how little newsworkers know about their audiences. They cite Gans' observation about television journalists: they "filmed and wrote for their superiors and for themselves, assuming . . . that what interested them would interest the audience" (1979: 230).

It is often noted in the communication literature that communicators use audiences other than the primary, actual one. We mentioned above how communicators use superiors, colleagues, and friends as their secondary audiences. Several studies (Altheide 1974; Burns 1977) show that mass communicators tend to regard audiences as incompetent and stupid.

Anderson and Meyer's (1988) term "canonical audience" denotes the idealized image of the audience – an audience that is far from directly participating in the production process and that the communicator visualizes using wishful thinking or cynicism.

The use of secondary audiences is one of several consequences of insufficient audience contacts. McQuail (1969) mentions four others:

- *Paternalism.* Communicators regard it as their function to educate and inform the audience, whose subjective needs, interests, and likes are not of much concern.
- *Specialization.* This is the process of concentrating on parts of the audience whose needs and interests are known.
- *Professionalization.* This effect leads communicators to think they are competent to decide on media content, knowing better than audience members or clients what it should be.
- *Ritualism.* Communicators play it safe by not offering anything other than what has previously proved to be pleasing to the audience. McQuail notes that this effect tends to threaten creativity and freedom in mass communication.

The concept of a public being remote and anonymous is familiar to many communication planners; the consequences of this distance mentioned above are applicable. *Paternalism* is much debated in certain areas of public communication, especially in cases of information campaigns linked to developmental aid. In many countries, such intervention has been resented by parts of the actual public who accuse communication planners of not caring about social and cultural realities. This accusation has also been made in industrialized countries; for example, the slogan in a Swedish campaign to persuade people to eat more bread, "The Swedish social authorities want you to eat six to eight slices of bread each day," ignited discussion about paternalism in public campaigning.

Specialization, directing information to groups that are best known and easy to reach, has been discussed by Rogers (1983), who notes that change agents in family planning often would rather communicate with upscale people than with lower-class publics who have a greater need for family planning. The principle of homophily (see Chapter 6) tends to draw elite change agents and audience elites into a cozy togetherness which is, in many cases, dysfunctional.

Professionalization, according to McQuail, may result from a lack of audience contacts. It also could be the result of familiarity. Professionalized practitioners may build their work on professional skills and knowledge, believing there is no need to talk to people in the public because, based on other contacts, the public does not know what is going on. The communication planners take no action to find out more about the audience. (This effect may be more accurately called professional arrogance, rather than professionalization, which, in occupational sociology, refers to the process of upgrading an occupation on ideological and labor-market dimensions.)

Ritualism occurs in communication planning, especially in fields where, to a large extent, knowledge is built on anecdotes about and experiences with previous successes and where the planner's role is one of communication technician. It is also likely in situations where communication planners have scarce resources – time, money or analytical expertise – at their disposal.

Spontaneous Feedback from the Audience

We have noted that to a great extent mass communication lacks feedback. Studies of newspapers (Forsythe 1950; Vacin 1965) indicate that the feedback received does not accurately mirror the audience. People who write letters to the editor differ from the average reader in many respects and at different levels (Stockinger-Ehrnstorfer 1980). Given that communicators heed reactions rather than non-reactions, this finding is problematic for media organizations.

In non-mass communication planning settings, too, planners are well-advised to check the feedback they get against reactions from their general audiences. Communication planners also tend to overestimate the quality and relevance of the feedback obtained. If a communicator is guided by wishful thinking and pays attention only to positive feedback, that feedback will do more harm than good.

12 The Message

In mass communication models, the message typically occupies the central position between sender and receiver. The message is what the communicator and the audience have in common, what they share. In some models, the message is depicted as having an existence of its own, isolated from sender and receiver. This is somewhat misleading because the message is part of the sender, who produces it, as well as of the receiver, who, by receiving the message, internalizes and recontructs it to a greater or lesser degree. The message, thus, while existing on its own, may be the property of both sender and receiver more or less simultaneously.

Analyzing Message Content

Mass communication researchers studying messages rely on quantitative and qualitative content analysis (for a discussion of this methodology, see Rosengren 1981b; Stempel 1989). Such analyses may reveal a great deal about the actual communication (Hadenius and Weibull 1973).

- *The communicator's perception of reality.* The reality depicted in the media often differs considerably from the actual, quantifiable reality around us (Abrahamsson 1987; Gerbner et al. 1980; Gerbner et al. 1984). McQuail (1987) offers a long list of biases in mass communication content relative to the "real world," including the dominance of upper levels of society in the media; a media world map quite different from the geographical one – countries such as the United States being given much more prominence than others in the mass media; the stereotyping of minorities and outgroups; the overrepresentation of violent attacks against people as opposed to structural crime, etc. And while expectations of reality vary for, say, a news program, a situation comedy, or a science fiction program, all presentations are molded by these biases.
- *The intentions of the communicator.* An analysis might show whether communicators favor one party in a conflict over another or regard one political party as superior to another. Gans (1974) also notes that an analysis could reveal to what cultural level the communicator belongs.
- *The communicator's image of the receiver.* By analyzing language, symbols, pictures, and arguments, it often is possible to gain an understanding of how the communicator views the audience.
- *The receiver's possible reaction.* Analyzing the content of a message may enable prediction of its effects. This usually entails more

guesswork than science because so many other factors besides the message will influence the message's consequences. Nonetheless, this predicting, on a non-scientific basis, is an activity in which many communication planners engage regularly.

- *The cultural climate of society.* Scholars have analyzed content such as editorials, obituaries, and magazine ads in search of indicators of the cultural system (Rosengren 1981a).

Content analysis may also give information about non-mass media communication that may be useful to communication planners:

- Analysis of health communication from different communicators will reveal how perceptions of health and illness vary.
- Anti-drug information analysis reveals the different intentions of different senders in their campaign messages.
- Analysis of informational materials targeted to welfare recipients will show what tone communicators use to address this public – were members of that public communicated with as equals or were they talked down to?
- Family planning information content analysis may reveal what values and symbols are attached to that practice in different countries.
- In an interplay between planned communication and the media, content analyses of both news releases and actual coverage of a subject issue can reveal a great deal about how well communication planners assess news values and how effectively they deal with the media.

For the communication planner, the most practical use for content analysis is to identify weaknesses in campaign material. Content analysis may answer questions such as:

- Is the text readable? Readability tests exist to measure how difficult a text is for audience members to read (see Grunig and Hunt 1984: 193; Bosshart 1976).
- Is the text consistent or contradictory?
- Does the text contain too many themes?
- Does the text reflect the values and language of the target social category, e.g. does a message aimed at a predominantly working-class group use language, references, and metaphors of the middle class?
- Are too many different publics addressed at the same time?
- Is the appropriate style of argumentation being used, that is, one-sided vs. balanced (Schenk 1987)?

A Model

This section looks at the notion that a message can assume different shapes. Intended messages of the sender and the messages actually sent are usually identical, but need not be so. Likewise, the message received and how it is perceived by the receiver may differ. And, somewhere in

| Message | Message | | Message | Message |
| Intended | Sent | | Received | Perceived |

MESSAGE
per se

SENDER/COMMUNICATOR   RECEIVER

Figure 12.1 *Five meanings of message*

between, there is the message that may be seen in its own right, as an independent phenomenon, open to analysis without apparent connection to either sender or receiver. Figure 12.1 shows the different shapes a message can take.

These different versions of messages can prove problematic. Communicators might be criticized for attitudes and values in a message that they never intended – the receivers have put their own interpretation on the message. Likewise, the sender may misjudge the meaning of a message for the receivers. Senders and receivers talk about content as if there were an absolute interpretation of it (usually their own). Also, the senders and receivers themselves may not be entirely sure if their intention and perceptions actually match what they send and/or receive.

The *basic* structure of Figure 12.1, that is, a threefold representation of message intended/sent, message *per se*, and message received/perceived, will serve as the basis for the rest of this discussion about messages.

The failure to differentiate between messages sent and messages received and to recognize the message-as-text as an independent phenomenon can produce problems for the communication researcher and the communication planner alike. One such problem arises when communicators assume that their perceptions of the message will be identical to those of the receivers. Receivers may have quite a different image of the message due to factors relevant for them but not for the sender. Also, assessing the communication value of a message isolated from the originator and/or the audience is risky. To arrive at a clear picture of the message's effectiveness, knowing the intentions of the sender as well as the perceptions of the receiver is essential.

The Communicator–Message Relationship: Intentions and Functions

Prior to its delivery, the message belongs to the communicator, who shapes it by loading it with intentions and meanings. The intentions of the communicator may reflect functions of communication such as those listed below. (For a general discussion of communication functions, see McQuail 1987.)

- *The social function.* Communication serves to make people relate to each other. In mass communication, this function is fulfilled by, among other things, reporting social events and similar types of content in local media (Janowitz 1952; Jarren 1984). In planned communication, the social function is represented by the goal of producing a sense of "we" in an organization by means of internal newsletters and the staging of collective events. In such organizational settings, the shape of the communication effort frequently takes the form of conferences or small-group meetings. As is pointed out in the discussion of the spiral of interaction model (Chapter 7), the social function of communication may be useful for a group to initiate before proceeding to a higher level of relationship, e.g. an action.

- *The expressive function.* Discussions about journalism frequently center on whether journalists should express their own values and attitudes in the text (Nordenstreng 1977; Hemanus 1976). In planned communication, the need for expressive communication usually is beyond dispute since the very purpose of planned communication is to advocate and persuade. Also, in situations of conflict within a system, the planner may want to trigger expressive communication on the part of the receivers in order to make the conflict stand out more clearly and to use that as a step toward conflict resolution.

- *The control function.* Some communication content aims to get others to behave and think a particular way. This is a typical goal for most, but not all, kinds of planned communication, especially in communication campaigns.

- *The information function.* In this function, the motivation for communication is not so obvious. The aim is to bring about a transfer of knowledge (which, in turn, may change attitudes and behaviors). News fulfills this function in mass communication. The purpose of communication applied to this function may be to obtain a more knowledgeable public. This may enable the public to make better (from the sender's point of view) decisions.

The messages of planned communication may fulfill more than one function at a time. Messages aimed at telling the members of an organization that its goals have been achieved (information function) will, undoubtedly, fulfill a social function by creating a feeling of belonging. By letting people comment about their satisfaction with a healthy way of living (expressive function), planners of health campaigns can encourage others to comply with a campaign message (control function).

The intentions that communicators (and planners) pursue with the messages they produce are innumerable. A few suggested by Graber (1976) include mobilization, focusing attention, symbolical rewards for the audience, and making commitments. It is easy to find some or all of these intentions in planned communication messages – a good communication planner is able to effectively combine a number of these intentions.

Communication also may fulfill rather dubious functions. Hornik (1988) notes that communication programs sometimes are launched to create a sense of political responsiveness and an image of activity, not necessarily because they are particularly relevant or efficient. Planners need to recognize that the "sexy" communication solutions often garner the resources because they have high visibility. In an AIDS campaign, for example, a television advertising campaign may be launched instead of a face-to-face campaign oriented to minorities; while the face-to-face efforts in this case may better serve the needs of the public, the advertising campaign conveys to more people the impression that the government is active and goal-oriented as far as AIDS prevention.

The Message – A Meeting Place

In his theories about mass communication rhetoric, Nerman (1973) discusses how the communicator can use messages or media content to meet the audience member. One metaphor he uses is to compare the message to a stage, where different realities with different actors are shown, and where the receiver is a member of the theater audience. Mass communication becomes an act of invitation and sharing realities (or irrealities, depending on the medium). The more tempting the invitation, the more likely the reader or viewer is to accept it.

Television news, according to Nerman, stages a 20-minute visit to some distant, unfriendly, conflict-laden place from which there is always an escape for the viewer. Typically in TV news, the road back leads through a weather report, an anecdote, or the like. The viewer is taken by the hand by the communicator and safely led back home.

This is an interesting metaphor for communication planners to consider. Often their objective is to lead audience members into some reality and keep them there, at least until they have learned or promised to do something. A very practical example: If a communication planner wants to cut down on injuries in the workplace and shows a film about the dangers encountered, the audience should not be allowed the easy way out of just viewing the film and being allowed to leave. The audience members should, instead, be kept to discuss the issue until a real awareness about the problem emerges and they commit to taking steps to reduce injuries. In other instances of planned communication, however – namely, where the goal is not activity or behavior modification, but only awareness – the situation may be more akin to traditional mass media reception. The difference between mass media content and planned communication content varies according to the goals set by the planner.

Positioning in Messages

Nerman also discusses how a mass communicator, wittingly or unwittingly, explicitly or implicitly, often positions the communicator, receiver, and object (the subject of the message) in a social dimension. Journalists may report about the king and queen of their country in a "them/us" way. The reporters and the audience members are at one level, the king

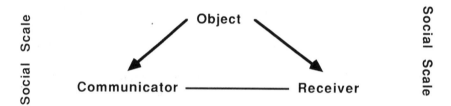

Figure 12.2 **Communicator and receiver as "common people"**

and queen at another, as shown in Figure 12.2. This figure also could illustrate positioning in an organizational newsletter, where communicators put top management high on the social scale and depict the reader and themselves as "common people."

In other situations (Figure 12.3), communicators want to position themselves as intermediaries. In a health program, a communicator may want to interview a known expert on health questions. At the same time, the communicator wants to show that he or she has expertise about the topic as well, albeit to a lesser degree. The receiver is treated as an interested amateur.

Figure 12.3 **Communicator as intermediary**

In a third case (Figure 12.4), journalists covering deviant groups, criminals, and minorities may choose to position themselves with the receivers and place the object much lower on the social scale. This may also occur in charity fund-raising campaigns. The communicator and the receivers are at the same level while helping, for example, Middle East refugees, who occupy a different position on the scale.

Communicators are to a large degree unconscious of this process, but

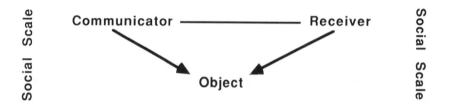

Figure 12.4 **Communicator and receiver looking down**

it is important that they be aware of it. Receivers may react to the object's or their own placement – either too high or too low. And communicators may lose credibility by positioning themselves too low or too high on this abstract social scale.

Messages as Messages

The study of messages as messages, suspending consideration of sender and receiver for the analysis, can be useful. Increased attention to semiotics and structuralism in mass communication research has created new and valuable tools for this inquiry. The underlying idea of this approach, according to Hall, is that "before a message can have an 'effect' (however defined), satisfy a 'need' or be put to a 'use', it must first be appropriated as a meaningful discourse and be meaningfully decoded" (1980, quoted by Fry and Fry 1986: 443). Thus, attention turns to the process by which messages become meaningful to audiences. For a more extended discussion of semiotics, we recommend Fiske (1982) and Fry and Fry (1986), who offer good introductions to the field.

News as Storytelling

In mass communication research, a large number of studies of content focus on news. Objectivity, bias, news values, and the like have been the topics of investigation for some time. In recent years, however, critical and structuralist approaches have become more common. "News as storytelling," part of this new tradition, offers a framework for looking at different forms of planned communication.

Looking at news as storytelling leads to the assumption that news stories do not just mirror reality, they give meaning to events and facts, often in a predictable form. We must understand these stories in the cultural and social contexts in which they originate, as well as take into account their rhetorical and narrative structures. Roeh and Ashley (1986) have listed some patterns and functions – characteristics of Western journalistic storytelling. Several of these have special relevance for the study of communication planning.

First, *concrete examples* are often used to represent abstract phenomena. A story about a traffic victim ignored by a metropolitan ambulance crew stands for the inhumanity of people in urban settings.

Second, *intertextuality* constitutes a central concept. We do not understand one story isolated from others told previously. Using the media's reporting on AIDS as an example, individual stories build on earlier stories, and the entire reporting adds up to the story of AIDS. According to Roeh and Ashley, "Today's newspaper story makes no sense unless yesterday's story is taken into account" (1986: 137).

Third, news stories possess *a surface and a deep meaning*. Elements may have manifest and latent meanings; deep mythological elements give surface facts new meanings. For example, the old David and Goliath myth, weak vs. strong, is found frequently in news reporting. The early reportage about the controversy over the cold fusion experiments by a University of Utah research team in 1989, for example, reflected the classic underdog theme.

Fourth, it is possible to identify several *types of stories* according to their motifs, patterns, and genres. Journalists do these categorizations themselves. "Hard" news vs. "soft" news is one of the distinctions in news reporting. A journalist's decision about which category an event falls into will shape the presentation of the information, both in terms of what facts are reported and the pattern the story follows.

Finally, metaphors are used to express *similarities and relations* between incidents, experiences, and objects that seem not to have much in common. For example, much of current reporting on ecological issues emphasizes the unity of mankind and its common destiny on the endangered planet Earth.

This is *not* to say, however, that news consists *only* of stories with no connection to reality; rather, news relates to reality in much the way that stories we recognize as conventional do. Undoubtedly, several of the storytelling characteristics make newsreading and newswatching more enjoyable for the public. They help the individual to make news subjectively more understandable and often help us to relate to other stories, either in the media or elsewhere.

Storytelling, then, may offer a way to analyze news stories, overcoming such conventional dimensions as bias or objectivity. It must be recognized, however, that the mass media communicator more or less deliberately uses storytelling devices to make the text easier to relate and to receive. The communicator may use metaphors, build stories on myth structures, etc., in order to communicate better.

This holds true for communication planning as well. By viewing information as storytelling, the planner can construct a way to relate to the receiver that will facilitate effective communication. For example, consider the characteristic of intertextuality. The planner must consider that the story being sent out is but one among many. An anti-drug campaigner cannot disregard the existence of other, pro-drug, stories. A health communicator in the Third World who ignores other health-related stories in that culture will fail. This points out the importance of recognizing that different messages within the same effort must fit together so there are no contradictions or communication inconsistencies.

Also, the storytelling device that uses concrete phenomena to represent more abstract ones can be useful. The story about a once high-risk heart patient who now jogs and feels good may, without comment, do a better job of telling the latent story that you can improve your health yourself than do descriptions of the relationship between physical exercise and health in a fact-laden campaign brochure.

Fragmentation of Reality

The mass media often are accused of presenting a fragmented picture of reality (Findahl and Höijer 1975). In radio news, for example, the audience typically hears short reports about events in a context shared with several other topics and themes. Most such events are reported as confined in time and space, and references to preceding and related events elsewhere are made in a way that often presupposes knowledge on the part of the audience. In these cases, an unintended intertextuality often emerges – not necessarily with reports on the same subject, but with other, often very different, types of story. Together, such groupings of news reports may convey the deeper and more general message that the world is chaotic and the common person is helpless. Fragmentation, which is especially problematic for the less knowledgeable, is one of the contributing factors to knowledge gaps (see Chapter 15).

Dervin (1981) points out that a sender may have a clear picture of how different messages form a pattern. But the receiver, who receives the messages without a key as to how they relate to each other, may create meanings quite different from those intended. Messages in a campaign ideally should contain a key as to the nature of their intertextuality.

On the other hand, as Wiio (1988) points out, clear understanding of a message between sender and receiver should not be overemphasized to the point of becoming an ideology. In certain situations, intentional obscurity on the part of the sender makes sense – especially when the goal is to keep things fluid, open to negotiation. A purpose that is too clearly stated may force the receiver into unexpected behavior. Intentional obscurity has been used advantageously by Japanese managers, who give everyone on a team a chance to say "yes" without the appearance of having given in.

Whenever communication planning uses elements of negotiation, this strategy may be well worth considering. The notion of intentional obscurity also points out that such Western (or North American) values as frankness and straightforwardness are not universally applicable. Following from this idea of accepting other values, messages with some ambiguity should not necessarily be considered flawed. If the goal is to foster creativity among the receivers, an ambiguous message may be more useful than a clear-cut one.

In general, however, the lesson for the communication planner is to facilitate the receiver's constructing patterns of messages that fit together meaningfully and not to fragment messages.

The Message/Receiver Relationship

During the last decades, mass communication theory has become increasingly interested in the message/receiver relationship. In his well-known general communication model, Gerbner (1956) distinguishes between two ways of perceiving the environment: psychophysical and transactional. The psychophysical perception holds that accurate perception is possible and results from favorable physical conditions. The transactional view, in contrast, emphasizes that perceptions of the environment depend to a large extent on the individuals who are doing the perceiving, their experiences, their own environments, habits, etc. According to this view, perception is as dependent on the individual as on the stimulus. The transactional view has come to dominate researchers' views of the message/receiver relationship, in theory if not in practice. Messages are no longer viewed as isolated phenomena that hit and influence the individual, but rather as something the receiver subjectively selects and processes.

The Information-as-Description Fallacy

During the last few decades, several communication scholars have further developed the transactional view. In an application to public communication campaigns, Dervin makes an important distinction between two ways of looking at messages and receivers, namely between "information-as-description" and "information-as-a-construction." The former approach assumes "information has truth value; has a known, testable description relationship with reality; and can be separated from observers" (1989: 72). The information-as-construction model, in contrast, assumes that "information is created by human observers; is inherently a product of human self-interest; and can never be separated from the observers who created it" (1989: 72).

In communication theory terms, the information-as-description approach is based on a *transmission* model of communication. Dervin defines this model as when "a source, assumed to be privy to specialized observations, is charged with the responsibility of transmitting that information to people who need it. The receiver is pictured as an empty bucket into which these information gems may be deposited" (1989: 72). The information-as-construction model conceptualizes communication as a process in which both sender and receiver are involved in creating meanings. "The sense people make of the media messages is never limited to what sources intend and is always enriched by the realities people bring to bear" (1989: 72).

The communication planner who designs messages according to the information-as-construction approach must use methods very different from those of a planner following the more traditional approach.

Communication campaigns using information-as-construction have yielded such results and insights as the following (Dervin 1989):

- The planners received information about the experiential realities of the receivers, information they did not have before.
- The planners learned how to change themselves rather than how to change the audience.
- The focus was on the audience's needs rather than on campaign or message elements.
- The campaign was directed at two targets: the publics and the planners themselves. This necessitated finding ways to empower the publics, who then served as advisers to the planners.

The Information-as-Construction Approach: Consequences

There are consequences of using the information-as-construction approach in communication planning (Dervin 1989). For example, objectivity may be indirectly detrimental to effective communication. In their quest for objectivity, communicators strive to give facts, ignoring personal feelings and subjective information that may assist the receiver in understanding and using the message. An overly factual, neutral, and depersonalized message offers receivers few keys as to how to use the information in the context in which they find themselves. This perspective, to a large extent, supports an information-as-storytelling approach in which examples, metaphors, personalization, etc., add subjective cues to what is being told.

Message Comprehension

One of the prerequisites for effective communication is that messages be understood by the audience. Research about message comprehension indicates a complex interplay between message and receiver factors. Let's look at these factors separately, beginning with receiver factors.

Receiver Factors

In their discussion about comprehension of mass media, especially television news content, Findahl and Höijer (1984) note that social characteristics such as gender, age, education, and occupation determine the conditions for knowledge about reality. This knowledge, in turn, is divided into general and specific knowledge. Specific knowledge concerns the actual topic – news about nuclear power is understood better by people who have previous knowledge than by those who do not. General knowledge is (a) the possession of schemes for events and texts, and (b) semantic conceptual networks. This type of knowledge would enable the receiver to comprehend the range of phenomena that relate to something like a nuclear power plant.

Höijer and Findahl (1984) point out that we understand events and stories about events that follow certain schemes we have learned to identify. For example, we recognize the procedure for getting a taxi: looking for a cab in traffic, signaling to one that is available, telling the driver where we want to go. When we see this happen on television, we understand what is happening. We also understand that something is wrong or special when the order of this scheme is somehow violated.

To these real-world "scripts" (Abelson 1976; Gudykunst and Kim 1984), we add those we get through the media. Television news has provided all of us with a scheme of what happens when high-ranking politicians from different countries meet: reception at the airport, flowers, two leaders sitting on a sofa to be photographed, etc. The media have familiarized us with this scheme, although we probably never have experienced it ourselves. In communication we expect what is communicated to follow either real world or story schemes. When this is the case, our understanding of what we see is reinforced.

Knowledge is also structured in semantic networks (Findahl and Höijer 1984), in which concepts are grouped together meaningfully. When the message's network fits that of the receiver, comprehension is easier. The schemes, of course, are not the only receiver-related factors that have an impact on understanding messages. Früh (1980) mentions some others: general skill in decoding, tolerance for processing new information, tolerance for complexity in texts, actual mental state, and interest and motivation.

Message-Related Factors

In a study of comprehension of newspaper content, Früh (1980) has found a number of textual factors that influence the understanding of written content:

- *the graphic structure:* paragraphing, use of different graphic characters (e.g. lower and upper case letters), underlinings, color, etc.;
- *word frequency:* the degree to which synonyms are used; if the same word comes up regularly and frequently in the text, it causes a sense of monotony;
- *the verb/noun relationship:* a text relying on verbs instead of nouns is understood better;
- *length of sentences:* sentences that are too short or too long negatively influence comprehension;
- *the number of clauses in a sentence;*
- *whether sentence structure is varied or not;*
- *the frequency of both common and uncommon words.*

Früh emphasizes that readers are prepared to put only a certain amount of energy into trying to understand a text. They may reach two types of thresholds. One has to do with complexity. Readers will reach a point beyond which they do not want to go; going further will exceed the energy "budgeted" for the message being attended to, or they stop because they cannot understand due to a lack of knowledge or skills. In both cases the text is too complex. Früh also talks about a banality threshold, which is reached when the text contains too little new information to hold the reader's interest, precluding the reader from reading and understanding the text.

Früh presents these two thresholds in a model (Figure 12.5) that demonstrates how the variables – understanding and motivation – vary under different circumstances. The horizontal axis represents information in terms of meaning (the farther to the right, the higher the amount of new information) and amount (the farther to the right, the higher the amount of complexity). When information is well-known beforehand and is not complex, it is viewed as unimportant and boring (threshold of banality). When information is new and complex, it will, to a certain degree, be viewed as important and exciting. This taps into the threshold of complexity, where decoding and understanding decrease. The vertical axis represents (a) the degree of understanding of the text and (b) the degree of motivation to read or listen to the text.

The model shows that text with a low informative value causes a reader to not decode it because of boredom. We also see that if text is gratifying in terms of new information, the individual may be willing to exceed the energy budgeted for that message.

Früh's reasoning contains a number of interesting points for the communication planner to consider:

● Messages have to be informative, i.e. contain content that was previously unknown; otherwise the receiver will react with boredom and apathy. Often it is wise to wait to issue communication until there is enough information to generate interest.
● Information that is understood is not guaranteed to be interesting.
● Knowing an audience well will help a communication planner identify the location of the two thresholds Früh has identified.
● It is possible to coax receivers into exceeding their attention "budget" by making messages more informative.

Other guidelines for creating more understandable messages exist, too. Bransford and McCarrell (1974, quoted in Höijer and Findahl 1984) emphasize that concrete details that activate the receiver's own experiences facilitate understanding. This is in line with Dervin's (1989) observations about information-as-construction perspective: elements of the text must help members of the audience to incorporate the message's meaning into their own contexts.

Cause and Consequence
In a series of experiments, Findahl and Höijer (1984) investigated the question of how television viewers understand and recollect televised news. Their conclusions include a strong criticism of TV news in that it seems to be designed for those who already have knowledge about a subject. Among other things, TV news is fragmented, which ensures those

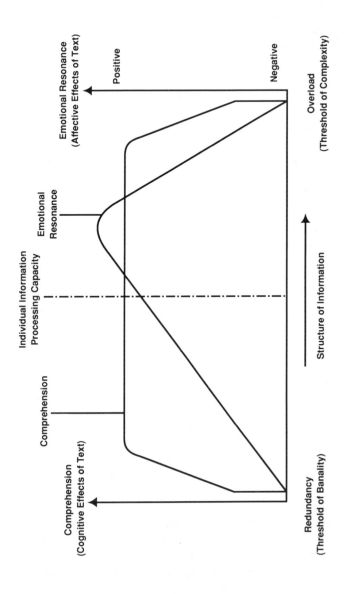

Figure 12.5 *Früh's model of comprehension (Früh 1980)*

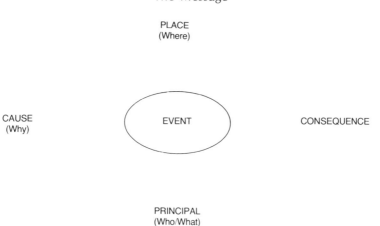

Figure 12.6 **Content categories in Findahl and Höijer's experiment (1984)**

who do not have adequate background cannot make use of the news.

In the experiments, people were shown fake TV news programs and asked to comment on them. The results were that people often had a distorted picture of what they had just viewed. Some of the misunderstandings stemmed from confusing participants and places in different news items; in some cases the subjects overgeneralized, for example, locating an event about Peru in Latin America. Some subjects gave their own explanations of events when they did not remember the real cause.

The news items in the experiment were divided into four parts: cause, place, principal (who or what was involved), and consequences, as shown in Figure 12.6. Versions where cause and consequence were repeated turned out to give the best results – all the elements of the news story were more memorable, and the subjects' ability to grasp the content of the news as a whole was facilitated.

The Findahl and Höijer experiments also show that individuals understand and recollect the more concrete parts of a message better. This points to the need to make abstract content more concrete by using illustrations and examples. It also reminds us of the importance of linking information, when possible, to the whole and to other events by emphasizing causes and consequences.

Information for the Initiated

Findahl and Höijer (1984) conclude from their studies of television news that, given the shortcomings in methods of telling and presentation, only a portion of the audience will understand TV news. They argue that TV news is for the initiated. News reports lack background, are fragmented, leave key concepts unexplained, etc. Only if you have enough prior knowledge about an issue can you put the pieces together and make sense of the messages.

The lesson from this research for the communication planner is the importance of pretesting messages and adhering to effective presentation in producing messages. Even if audience members attend to a message, they may not understand it. Television news is viewed by hundreds of millions of people around the world every day, and a large proportion of them do not really understand it. In Elliott's (1972) words, the audience members are just spectators, they are not communicated with. By not formulating messages in an understandable, motivating way, communication planners fail to communicate. Instead they just produce and display information.

"Framing" according to Media Format

The mass media communicator is – to borrow a term from Goffman (1959) – framing reality according to rules that apply to a medium's format (Altheide 1985). Every medium has its own mix of policy, view of reality, picture of the audience, and so on. These characteristics lead to news being presented in a certain way, sports programming in another.

This illustrates the thesis that media products are human products, constructs (Hall 1973; Altheide 1985) that the audience learns to take for granted. A part of the framing process is the communicator's decontextualizing the event or phenomenon so it can be recontextualized by the medium. Through this process of de- and re-contextualization, observations tend to change character. A familiar event presented in the media will change in character when perceived in its new context, and what used to be familiar may appear strange and unfamiliar.

The communication planner should be aware of the consequences of this process. Members of a communication campaign audience may find it very difficult to relate to a "framed" reality and to connect it with their own reality. For communication to be effective, receivers must perform the same process, i.e. decontextualizing the message from its media context and recontextualizing it into their everyday realities. It should not be surprising that the receiver may let the observation framed by the media remain so framed and not react further to it. Pretesting messages offers one method to reduce this problem.

Messages as Figure or Background

The mass media are frequently accused of mixing the important with the unimportant, of making news out of events that are insignificant. Content is presented so it is as though the receiver were in a stream of information – and always at risk of drowning.

This reproach is also applicable to planned communication. Information very often is produced in quantities that prevent receivers from assessing what is important to them and what is not. Using a perceptual or gestalt psychological approach, we might say that the figure does not stand out from the background. Communication thus becomes useless to the audience member as information. This problem has been noted in therapy work – patients who have too much access to a therapist are sometimes unable to determine what part of the therapist's communication is relevant for their well-being.

Obviously, this is a problem that is closely related to information overload. The solutions to the two problems are very much the same: cutting down on the amount of messages and creating gatekeeper functions in the process. A third solution may be to format important messages so they stand out as important. This last solution is exemplified by the practice of identifying as important any information that emanates from high-rank communicators in an organization.

Frontstage and Backstage Communication

In his book about the consequences of mass communication, Meyrowitz (1985) maintains that the mass media have given the public access to places and situations that used to be screened off. Meyrowitz, using the language of sociologist Erwin Goffman, describes this as the presentation of "backstage areas." For people who have only experienced the "frontstage areas" of, for example, political life and the entertainment industry, having access to backstage areas extends their perceptual range. At the same time, people may find it confusing when, via the mass media, they encounter situations they have never experienced before.

In communication planning, distinguishing between backstage and frontstage communication may be useful. But what is backstage and frontstage communication in a planned setting? First, we have to distinguish between communication mode and presented setting. Backstage communication may be "communication among those who normally inhabit the backstage of a given situation." In the example given above, however, backstage communication refers to "communicating a backstage setting to outsiders," thereby making it public.

In an organization, a backstage communication mode typically will be directed to internal publics, such as employees, and often will be effectively screened off from other, external publics. This is important since backstage communication discourse may be partly unintelligible to outsiders and may be characterized by, for example, cynicism. Physicians discussing patients among themselves is an example of backstage communication that an external public would find inappropriate. The doctors joke to relieve tension, and while this is functional within the system, harm is done when such a communication is presented outside the system.

Sometimes, however, it may be quite effective to draw people into backstage settings. A health care union may successfully present real life images of the everyday routines of nurses in order to gain support for their demands for higher pay. Or a Third World development agency may show employees working hard on the agency's projects, thereby justifying to their supporters the donations they have contributed.

The mixing of internal and external publics and backstage and frontstage communication frequently results in communication problems. It is sometimes tempting, for example, for an AIDS-prevention communicator to save money by using the same material produced for experts to communicate with the general public. Using backstage, expert language will confuse and frustrate the general public, while using language appropriate for them will bore the experts. In another example, an organization's public relations and marketing departments decide to create a presentation about a new factory for publics from both inside and outside the organization; the risk is great that neither of the intended publics will be served by the presentation.

13 The Medium

"The media as media" or "the media *per se*" have been the focus of interest in mass communication research during recent years. Altheide and Snow (1988), for example, emphasize media "format" as a key concept of what they call "mediated communication."

Mediation Theory

Mediation (or, as we could also call it, mediatization) refers to "the impact of the logic and form of any medium involved in the communication process" (Altheide and Snow 1988: 195). Media logic and form, so the argument goes, mediate, define, and direct social interaction. *How* something is communicated is studied as well as *what*. Patterns and styles of media communication are of prime interest.

"Format" refers to the way the media appear, to their essential form. The format also includes the "rules and logic that transform and mold information (content) into the recognizable shape and form of a specific medium" (1988: 199).

Although the mediation approach is employed largely with a view to a cultural-type media critique, it is useful for communication planners as well. The approach suggests that, although they work with existing formats, planners do not need to regard them as givens over which they have no influence.

For example, thinking in terms of formats and mediation leads the planner to ask, when is a particular phenomenon considered to be sports, news, entertainment, politics, or art? While journalists have defined criteria for deciding what is news, the planner, by using the mediation approach, may decide that "almost *any* event or item can appear as legitimate news when it is presented in a news format" (Altheide and Snow 1988: 199). Sports, entertainment, and so forth are also subject to this redefinition.

Once planners realize that different formats are not static but subject to negotiation, their creativity and imagination are called upon. One strategy may be, for example, to format as "news" what actually is a much more long-term phenomenon; or the entertainment format may be used for a so-called serious item. Planners may be successful in their dealings with the professional media or their peers precisely *because* they violate the rules and depart from well-worn modes of presentation.

On the other hand, mediation theory informs the planner that media format rules can also force changes in the events that appear in the media. Altheide and Snow (1988) mention the example of American professional football, which, since it started appearing in prime time, has been characterized by higher scoring, less violence, and more theatrics.

Mediation theory provides a good example of the usefulness of theories for the planner and illustrates why we concentrate on theory and principles throughout this book. Theoretical sophistication on the part of the planner can open up choices of strategy which otherwise might be overlooked. A better understanding of the communication process than that held by professional counterparts can give the planner a competitive advantage. Our example using mediation theory would lead the planner to study how best to use the available formats. This sometimes may mean manipulating them, but it also calls for awareness of and reaction to how the formats influence contents and strategies.

Communication planners have to know about the many features of the different formats available in order to use them in their strategies. Using the television news format as an example, a planner would consider factors such as accessibility, visual quality, drama and action, audience relevance, and thematic encapsulation, which refers to the ability to briefly present and tie an event to other events. This quality is desirable for television news, in terms of both a single news program and a series of broadcasts (Meyer 1988). The "packaging" of the event involves its transformation into a story of a specified maximum length (on US television, usually 90 seconds), with a tie-in to the reporter, the photographer's footage, and voice-over segments.

The planner, however, should not accept format characteristics uncritically. Mediation theorists offer information about audience perception of formats in a mediated communication context. And while this cultural critique does not really assist in concrete communication planning tasks, it does inform the planner as to when and to what extent certain formats can be used advantageously. It also points out when those formats can compromise the goals of a particular communication project.

Channel Selection

While mediation theory is a philosophical approach to a medium and offers strong practical implications, channel selection represents the economic and political side of this issue. Choosing which channel or medium to transport a message *and* to bring about behavioral change is one of the most complex and controversial issues in communication planning.

The critical issue is, according to Hornik (1989a), channel effectiveness as the "combined measure of reach (exposure) and effects (changes in behavior and knowledge)." This key criterion for choosing a channel, however, requires supplementation by three other criteria (Hornik 1989a):

1 *Cost.* If a network of field agents were three times as effective as a mass media campaign, but ten times as costly, the planner might opt for the mass media campaign.

2 *Managerial feasibility.* A planner for a governmental agency may find it easier to use the interpersonal channel of field agents already in place than a radio campaign, even though, considered objectively, the radio campaign would be more effective. The interpersonal channels are more practical administratively.

3 *Sustainability.* Which of the channels available can be best sustained over time in terms of recurring costs, motivation of talent and/or volunteers, and enthusiasm?

Thinking in terms of *several* criteria for channel selection is crucial. Planners also should free themselves from what Hornik (1989a) describes as the conventional wisdom that mass media channels are more appropriate for the distribution of knowledge and information, and interpersonal channels contribute to decision making and behavior change. While this conventional wisdom appeals to common sense and very well may be true in many cases, it falls apart in the face of the eminently practical criteria mentioned above. Each case must be analyzed situationally. If, for example, there is no funding to support field agents, the planner must think in terms of how to shape the mass media channels to influence decision making and generate change – or else have no campaign at all.

Here again, we see how the situational approach to communication planning may challenge the usefulness of theories which, as such, are quite convincing and powerful. On an academic level, too, arguments have been advanced against the idea that interpersonal channels are always needed to effect behavior change, but this is not our main point here. The point is that the planner must always look for, and think in terms of, alternative hypotheses. Hornik (1989a) offers five such hypotheses. The first two place great importance on the interpersonal channels (i.e. field agents) in achieving behavioral changes; the other three place less emphasis on interpersonal channels and allow for effects emanating from the media:

1 *Agent-Effects-Only Hypothesis.* Effects are produced interpersonally, the media are irrelevant.
2 *Agent-Necessary-for-Media-Effects Hypothesis.* Mass media have an effect, but only in the presence of a field agent.
3 *Additive Hypothesis.* Both media and interpersonal channels can bring about change, but independently of each other.
4 *Substitution Hypothesis.* Both channels are effective and may be substituted for each other.
5 *Reinforcement Hypothesis.* Both channels have independent effects, but with a positive interaction.

Fast Media vs. Slow Media

The political science/international relations literature dealing with public diplomacy offers the notion of fast media and slow media. In contrast to traditional diplomacy, which refers to negotiations between governments (Deutsch 1966), public diplomacy refers to the various ways, especially communications, by which governments and/or individuals attempt to influence the behavior of foreign governments by influencing the attitudes of their citizens (Malone 1988). In a way, public diplomacy could be regarded as planned communication by a nation state or a national society.

Fast media, according to this view, are radio, television, newspapers, and news magazines. Slow media are films, exhibitions, language instruction, and academic/artistic exchanges. This distinction is not technical, but strategic. Fast media are favored by the so-called tough-minded school of public diplomacy, which holds that the purpose of public diplomacy is to influence attitudes of foreign audiences through persuasion and propaganda. Hard, political information is considered more important than cultural programs. Objectivity and truth are considered important tools of persuasion, but not extolled as virtues in and of themselves. The overriding justification for public diplomacy is the good of the country as defined in terms of fairly short-term policy goals.

Slow media are preferred by the tender-minded school, which argues that "information and cultural programs must bypass current foreign goals to concentrate on the highest long-range national objectives" (Deibel and Roberts 1976). The goal is to create a climate of mutual understanding. This school sees public diplomacy as a predominantly cultural function. Its purpose is to transmit messages about lifestyles, political and economic systems, artistic achievements, and the like. Truth and veracity are essentials, not merely persuasive tactics (Signitzer 1988a).

This approach can alert the planner to possible connections between communication strategy and style on the one hand, and choice of medium on the other. In other areas of planned communication, too, we have found a preference to employ mass media when an asymmetric communication model is used, while non-mass media channels serve more symmetric approaches (see, for example, the four models of public relations by Grunig and Hunt 1984, Table 8.1 in this book). The distinction between short- and long-term goals also may have implications for channel choice. Certainly Hornik's (1989a) stress on channel effectiveness is relevant here, too, and should caution planners against too quickly selecting a slow media strategy just because they find it more sympathetic and more "human."

The Use of Entertainment Media in Communication Planning

Entertainment media have been used to attract audiences to educational messages for quite some time. Only fairly recently, however, have practitioners and communication researchers alike begun to look systematically at the manifold issues and problems involved in this strategy. There is no common terminology yet. Terms such as "pro-development," "enter-educate" and "edutainment" have been proposed. Rogers et al. (1989), in the proceedings of a conference on this topic, employed the terms "entertainment–education" and "entertainment–education strategy" to denote this interesting phenomenon.

The basic approach of this strategy is quite simple: take advantage of the broad appeal of entertainment media to include – "sneak in," if you will – in the entertainment programs educational content on such themes as health, family planning, sexual behavior, and so on. This requires a fairly close collaboration between those working in the entertainment industry and, for example, health planners and communicators. Recent thinking about the possibility of such cooperative efforts is quite optimistic: it *can* be successful and productive if media entertainment people such as talent, directors, writers, and executives believe that educational messages not only do not reduce their programs' audience appeal, but can even enhance their commercial value. Likewise, health and family planners should recognize that mass entertainment content can play a very functional role in the transmission of their messages. The idea, of course, is one of mutual benefit; both groups involved will be convinced of the benefits only if supporting evidence is presented.

The media of entertainment available are manifold: radio and television soap operas, prime time television programs, motion pictures, comics, cartoons, books, and, last but not least, popular music. Here are some well-known and fairly widely reported examples of entertainment-education.

On television there have been the Latin American "telenovelas" (soap operas), such as *Simplemente Maria* (broadcast in Peru in 1969, this was the first telenovela) and six entertainment–education soap operas produced by Miguel Sabido from 1976 to 1983. The Indian *Hum Log* TV soap promoted the equal status of women and a smaller family size. Normal Lear's CBS series *All in the Family* (based on the British series *Till Death Us Do Part*) can also be viewed as entertainment–education in that it presented Archie Bunker as a negative example of bigotry and often dealt with issues on the public agenda, such as premarital sex, the environment, etc.

The popular song "Cuando estemos juntos" ("When We Are Together"), by Tatiana Palacios (Mexico) and Johnny Lozada Correa (Puerto Rico), promoted sexual abstinence and responsible parenthood; it was a great commercial success in 1986.

While there are only a few empirical studies about the effectiveness of the entertainment–education communication strategy (one of them being Arvind Singhal's (1990) investigation of the Indian *Hum Log* ("We People") TV series), some preliminary lessons can be drawn from the many practical experiences in the field. Singhal and Rogers (1989) and

Rogers et al. (1989) have put together a summary that includes the following points:

1 The mixture of entertainment and educational messages can attract large media audiences, which means high advertising and/or sales profits.
2 The educational message should not be too hard-sell or blatant; this leads the audience to reject the content.
3 The strategy is better at creating knowledge than changing overt behavior.
4 With this strategy, one can appeal to the audience's emotions as well as intellects.
5 The effects of this strategy increase when supplemented by messages from an integrated campaign.
6 Repetition of the educational message in the entertainment–educational content is important for achieving effects.
7 There must be an adequate infrastructure to provide services that complement the mass media messages.
8 Formative evaluation of the message is essential.
9 The strategy is most successful when as broad-based support as possible is achieved, involving such groups as public health officials, broadcast media officials, development planners, religious organizations, commercial sponsors, etc.

14 The Audience

We will see in this chapter that the term "audience" carries several connotations. This ambiguity has caused considerable confusion among theorists and practitioners alike, bringing about an unnecessary misfit between theory and practice. Also, during the short span of communication research, the view of the audience has changed. In mass communication research as well as in practice, characterizations of audiences vary considerably. Taking mass communication theory as a point of departure, we will try to impose some order on the concept.

The Mass Society View of the Audience

Mass communication is often defined by descriptions of its audience. For example, mass communication typically has an audience that is heterogeneous and geographically dispersed, has an anonymous relationship to the senders, and lacks social cohesion and organization.

This definition is based partly on a view of the audience as a loosely aggregated mass. This notion also is found in what are generally described as mass society theories. Modern society, according to those theories, is characterized by specialization and the weakening of traditional bonds, etc. leading to psychological and social isolation. This type of theory was dominant during the first half of this century and strongly influenced early mass communication research.

Since individuals were not seen as socially active, psychological and biological factors became more important than social ones in explaining the behavior of people in mass society. For example, characteristics such as instincts and psychological drives become crucial when describing audience members. (See De Fleur and Ball-Rokeach 1982.) The consequences of this conceptualization of the audience are most evident in theories of mass communication effects, which became variants of the stimulus–response model (see Chapter 15).

For the communication planner, adoption and acceptance of a mass society perspective of the audience will mean at least three things:

1 Messages are sent to the receiver directly; as a rule, they will not be mediated by other people. That necessitates careful selection of mass communication channels to ensure that messages reach the target audience.
2 The message typically will not be spread from those who receive it to others; the planner should not count on any spill-over. It also means that the message will not, for good or bad, be modified by intermediaries.

3 Audience members are considered in terms of the individual, not in terms of social or cultural groups.

A great deal of planned communication still is produced along mass society lines of thinking. When a receiver is not encouraged to disseminate the message or when no references are made to group affiliations, a planner may be said to be using mass society thinking. In many respects, such communication works well since the audience member very often receives and reacts to messages as a fairly isolated individual; psychological and biological aspects *are* important. The problem lies in the planner's tendency to ignore social and cultural aspects, which may be stronger and more decisive than other factors for the outcome of communication.

The Obstinate Audience

Bauer (1964) originated the concept of the obstinate audience to denote an active mass communication audience that is sometimes reluctant to accept what the media offer. His view reflects thinking that built up during the 1940s, 1950s, and 1960s, marking a slow retreat from the mass society view of mass communication. During the period of limited effects (see Chapter 15), researchers and practitioners started to question which factors, internal and external to the audience, hampered effects.

Communication research eventually found new ways to describe the audience and the conditions under which it functioned. Bauer stressed *selectivity* as a key trait of audience members. Others pointed to social aspects, such as the use of reference groups (Riley and Riley 1959). Yet others emphasized intervening social processes, such as interpersonal uses of media contents. The two-step flow of information model (Katz and Lazarsfeld 1955, see Chapter 6) was a result of this approach. Its picture of social interplay among people became part of the accepted view of the mass communication process. A new concept entered the research rhetoric: audience activity.

These developments in mass media research offered new tools and insights to communication planners. It was now possible for their mass communicated messages to be further disseminated in conversations between initial receivers and other people. The amount of dissemination that took place depended on the level of audience activity. Also, planners had to recognize in their strategies that a certain part of the audience would, more or less actively, decide not to receive the message offered.

This expanded theoretical background necessitated much more complex descriptions of an audience, which led to some pessimism about the possibility of reaching audience members. One important lesson from this approach is that the planner should not expect too much from communication efforts directed at large publics.

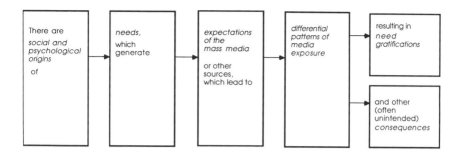

Figure 14.1 *A model of the uses and gratifications approach (after Blumler and Katz 1974)*

The Uses and Gratifications Approach

A fairly decisive change in how to regard a mass communication audience resulted from uses and gratifications theory. Because of its importance for planned communication, we will deal with it extensively.

The basic assumption of the uses and gratifications model is that audience members more or less actively seek the content that seems to be the most gratifying. The degree of perceived gratification depends on the needs (and interests) of the individual. The more individuals perceive that the actual content is need-fulfilling, the greater the chance that they will choose it. Based on a presentation of the approach by Blumler and Katz (1974), the model is presented in Figure 14.1.

It is noteworthy that most uses and gratifications models exclude the sender element of the mass communication process. Typically they start with the factors that contribute to the selection of media content by audience members.

Elements of the Model

Needs and Motives

Discussion of the uses and gratifications process usually begins with the individual's *needs*. The original formulations of the model more or less equated needs with *basic* needs. More recent developments in the theory suggest that relevant needs can be found at other levels as well (Windahl 1981), which leads us to include more superficial interests (which may be based on more fundamental needs), too. Relevant needs include the need for orientation, security, interaction, and tension-release.

Motives derive from needs and constitute their actional aspects. Several typologies have been suggested; one of the most commonly cited is that of McQuail et al. (1972), which includes the following dimensions:

1 *Information:* seeking advice, getting oriented about events in different parts of the environment, learning;

2 *Personal identity:* gaining self-knowledge, finding models of behavior, reinforcing personal values;
3 *Integration and social interaction:* finding out about the conditions of others, making it possible to relate to others, finding out how to play one's roles, establishing a basis for social interaction;
4 *Entertainment:* relaxing, escaping from everyday problems, filling time, satisfying sexual needs.

One conclusion to draw from these typologies is that there is a variety of motives for using the media. There is a widespread but often mistaken assumption among communication planners that people in the audience attend to messages for the reasons the sender intends. However, a reader may read a local health promotion brochure, not because of an interest in the health message, but because of a curiosity about the identities of the doctors and nurses whose pictures appear in the pamphlet. This points out the risk of measuring communication success in terms of exposure alone, since idiosyncratic motives may prompt the attending individual to pick up aspects and meanings other than those assigned by the sender.

Gratifications

Receivers are guided by their perception of what may be the outcome of consuming a certain message. Ideally the act of receiving should be gratifying. The gratification – the need-fulfillment – may be immediate or delayed.

The value-expectancy theory of media use (Palmgreen and Rayburn 1984, 1985) is an interesting approach to finding out what content will be sought in order to obtain a gratification. It is based on a social psychological theory by Fishbein and Ajzen (1975) that depicts behavior and behavioral intentions and/or attitudes as a function of two factors: expectancy and evaluation.

Expectancy is the belief or perception that an object possesses a certain attribute or that a behavior will have a certain consequence. When receiving a booklet on AIDS, for example, a person may question whether reading it will provide certain information about health issues related to the disease.

Evaluation is the negative or positive value attached to the expected attribute or consequence. The receiver of the AIDS brochure may ask how important it is to be well informed.

The communication planner must, therefore, be able to answer two questions concerning the audience:

1 Will the receiver believe that the communication leads to a certain outcome?
2 Will the outcome gratification be positively valued by the receiver?

An example: A health agency targets young people with a brochure headlined, "Read This – Live Longer." Interest is minimal. An analysis shows that the readers believe that the text actually will teach them how to live longer, but they do not regard longer life as especially important at that stage of their life cycle.

Uses and gratifications theory has been concerned mostly with gratifications that are consequences of use; to a lesser extent, it has been preoccupied with use as an aim in itself. Some researchers, however, distinguish between "content gratifications" and "process gratifications." The former refer to outcomes of media use where the messages themselves are gratifying. Process gratifications, in contrast, are outcomes of the process, rather than of the content. Here, the user values participating in the process of using media rather than receiving certain messages. A typical example of content gratification is media use to orient oneself in a complex situation or to find a topic to discuss with others later. A process gratification would occur, for example, when mass media are used as a means to do the same activity as others. Watching television in a group may be enjoyable, regardless of content.

McQuail (1984) elaborates on this theme, maintaining that uses and gratifications research should distinguish between cognitive and cultural types of contents and media use. This builds on the distinction made by Carey (1975) between transmission and ritual approaches to communication. The cognitive model suggests that media content is used for achieving gratifications beyond the text. In the ritual approach, media use is consummatory, an end in itself. McQuail presents the models as shown in Figures 14.2 and 14.3.

It is clear that the cognitive model is most similar to the dominant uses and gratifications model, where satisfactions (gratifications) usually are, in time and space, disconnected from the act of using or consuming media content. The cognitive model connects media use to such aspects of everyday life as knowing about the environment, getting help for making choices, etc. The cultural model, in contrast, stresses the immediate experiences and gratifications resulting from consuming. Those experiences are less dependent on elements outside the act of reading, listening, and viewing.

This distinction between cognitive and cultural use offers a number of lessons to communication planners. First, the planner should be aware that individuals attend to communication for a variety of reasons. As noted above, these reasons do not have to coincide with the sender's intentions.

Second, too often planners rely on the cognitive model, even though receiver behavior suggests using the cultural model. That the individual attends to the planner's communication does not necessarily imply a positive cognitive attitude. A person attending a political meeting may well do so just for the sake of being in the crowd and experiencing a feeling of belonging. For the planner, it is all too easy to interpret the person's presence as an indication of desire to attend to the political message being offered.

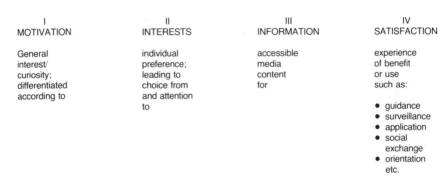

Figure 14.2 *A cognitive model of uses and gratifications (after McQuail 1984)*

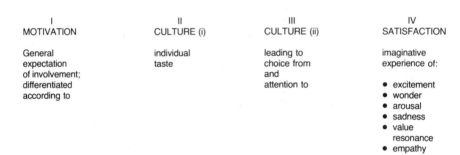

Figure 14.3 *A cultural model of uses and gratifications (after McQuail 1984)*

Third, there are interesting connections between the cognitive model and the content/distribution strategy (described in Chapter 5) on the one hand, and the cultural model and the processing strategy (see Chapter 5) on the other. The rationalistic approach underlies both the cognitive model and the content/distribution strategy. Likewise, just as the receiver's motives and gratifications within the cognitive model are to a large extent disconnected from the communication act itself, so too are the intended consequences of the content/distribution strategy separated from the act of consumption. The processing strategy, in contrast, is based largely on the idea that communication has a value in and of itself, for both the planner and the participants.

Fourth, planners often combine cognitive and cultural models in practice. It is quite common, for example, for planners to use a cultural model to make people attend to communication while having the ultimate goal of people learning or valuing something beyond the act and circumstances of communication. In other words, the communication planner may entice people to attend to communication by stressing rewards of the cultural type; once they are attending to the message, the planner tries to interest them in other messages reflecting the cognitive model.

Gratifications Sought and Obtained

The notion of gratifications sought and obtained (Greenberg 1974; Palmgreen and Rayburn 1984) provides a method to evaluate communication channels and contents. Researchers within the uses and gratifications tradition have found, not surprisingly, that there is a moderately strong correlation between gratifications sought and those the audience members obtain (Palmgreen and Rayburn 1985). The relationship, however, has proven to be quite complex with some rather unexpected research results.

Analysis based on this notion offers the communication planner a useful tool. Measuring the discrepancy between gratifications sought and obtained for a certain channel or content offers the following insight: the smaller the gap between the two, the more likely that the channel or content will be appreciated by the audience since people will not be frustrated by not getting what they are looking for. A large discrepancy, in contrast, may mean that people feel misled in one way or another.

Palmgreen and Rayburn (1985) warn against equating gratifications sought and obtained in theory and research. The same applies to the practical work of the communication planner. If people buy a book on health because they expect it to be useful, they still may not use it or not like it for several reasons. To conclude that a communication effort is successful because people say that something "looks interesting," or even because they purchase it, is presumptuous.

The Uses and Effects Model

Most uses and gratifications models include consequences or effects of media use. Little research, however, has been done into the use–effects relationship. This is due in part to the gratifications paradigm being seen as competing with the effects models, taking them one step further.

Windahl (1981) discusses the uses and effects relationship. His model, presented in Figure 14.4, indicates that different types of use tend to produce different outcomes. The type of content consumed, how much is used, and how it is consumed (the degree of involvement, etc.) are important factors of content use for predicting outcomes. The model also tries to shed some light on the origins of media use outcomes. It differentiates between outcomes that result mainly from the content of communication and outcomes that result from media use itself. When media researchers talk about effects, they are usually alluding to the relationship between message and outcome. Certain types of content tend to produce certain types of effect. The model labels these outcomes "effects."

Media researchers sometimes look at the results of the act of using media content. For example, several studies deal with the consequences of television viewing on other activities among young people. These *consequences* have less to do with media content than with watching television as such. Sometimes media use and content interact in certain ways to bring about what we call "conseffects." For example, people who watch

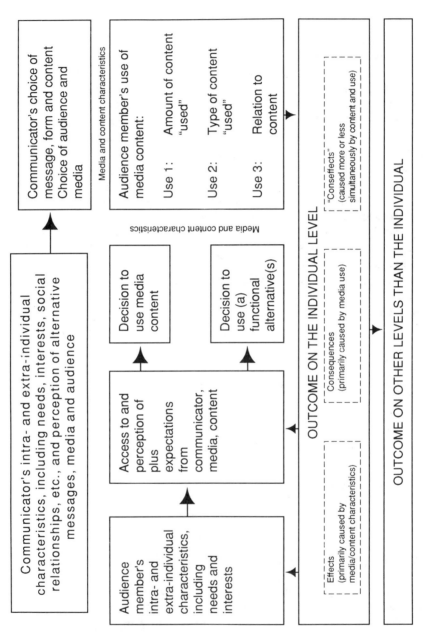

Figure 14.4 *A uses and effects model (after Windahl 1981)*

a lot of television define themselves as "TV viewers"; they also may regard TV content positively and are, therefore, keen to accept and be influenced by its messages. In this situation, both use and content are independent causal variables.

Consequences and Effects

The concept of consequences has some bearing on communication planning as well. The traditional content/distribution notion of communication is interested exclusively in getting the message through to the audience. Its aim is effects, to use Windahl's terminology. By contrast, the process approach regards the communication process (not primarily the content) as a means to reach certain goals. With the uses and effects model in mind, we would say that the goal is consequences, not effects, of communication. Hornik (1988) points out that communication programs may have intrinsic values beyond the goals of the program. For example, a study group on new farming practices in a Third World country may not lead to the adoption of agricultural innovations, but it may nevertheless foster a feeling of belonging and improve communication skills.

Uses and Gratifications: A Comment

It often has been said that uses and gratifications introduced the human being into communication theory. While this may be an overstatement, uses and gratifications does present a more positive image of the audience member than did any prior communication theory. For communication planning, uses and gratifications theory reminds us of the importance of competence, empathy, and quality in communicating. Audience members will not accept everything that is offered to them. Gratifications theory points out that sender and receiver may enter the communication process with different perspectives. What the sender means to be serious information may be used as light entertainment by the receiver – if it is used at all. The information may not relate in any way to the needs and interests of the receiver. An essential component of the gratifications approach – the notion of the active audience – will be discussed below.

Reception Theory

While uses and gratifications theory provides ideas of how the individual selects and uses communication contents, reception theory deals with what happens in the act of consumption, that is, how a certain content is approached and interpreted by the receiver. This analysis is valuable since in many cases correct and unbiased reception is taken for granted, often mistakenly.

Reception theory is a catch-all phrase for several directions of study that have the following characteristics in common (McQuail 1987):

Individuals form frames to interpret media contents; these frames may be more or less shared with others, and they are suggested by and learned from the media or result from the needs and experiences of the individual. The frames produce more or less different readings of the same content by different individuals.

Reception theory is especially useful in the planning phases of communication efforts. We view this theory as strongly stressing the notion of variations within the audience and supporting the use of pretests of messages and segmentation of audiences.

What is an Audience?

Up to this point, we've used the term "audience" as if there were only one meaning of the word. In fact, there are several definitions. Mass communication research tends to define audience in terms of people who have chosen voluntarily to attend to a certain content or medium. The communication planner talks about the audience in terms of an aggregate of people one intends to reach. When these two definitions are confused, problems arise.

Defined by the Sender

When senders have something to tell a certain category or group of people, they may refer to them as an audience. In many cases, this aggregate of people identified by the sender has no sense of having something in common. In fact, the sender's criterion for grouping individuals may be the only characteristic they do have in common. A health communication specialist may want to communicate with people who have too much salt in their diet. In that case the intended audience is sodium abusers. A closer look at this category shows that it includes people from all walks of life, with different social, geographical, and cultural backgrounds. The fact that they all eat too much salt may be of limited relevance because this behavior means very different things to the different subgroups in this target audience. The activity of eating salt may not provide its practitioners with any common language or frame of reference that the health communicator can tap into. To regard salt addicts as a monolithic audience undoubtedly will result in a failed communication campaign.

Here is another example: The local authorities of Northfield, a suburb in a large metropolitan area, want to increase political participation. In a series of communications, they urge Northfielders to take pride in making their community politically active. Nothing happens as a result of this campaign. An evaluation shows that people did not identify themselves as Northfielders, but rather as residents of the larger metropolis. Many homosexuals do not define themselves as such and will not believe that the messages apply to them (Windahl 1989).

Communication planners often err by assuming that targeting an audience guarantees that the audience will be motivated to attend to messages. One factor contributing to this misconception is mass communication's definition of an audience, i.e. one that is motivated enough to voluntarily use the mass media. Another, less abstract basis for this mistake is that the sender overestimates the intrinsic value of the message. The health communicator cannot understand why people do not find fiber-rich bread fascinating, and the public relations manager cannot comprehend why the media refuse to publish a press release about a new production facility. Communication planners tend to see their aims and issues as extremely important. For the citizen who is bombarded with demanding messages every day, however, there is little room for further information.

Several problems arise when the sender defines the audience without a proper analysis. The audience may be too heterogeneous to communicate with effectively, the sender may assume audience identification where none exists, and the intended audience may not share the sender's enthusiasm for the actual subject. The risk of trying to reach audiences that simply do not exist is great.

Defined by the Audience Members

As alluded to above, people may define themselves as part of an audience based solely on attending to a certain mass medium or a certain content, especially if they do it frequently. And while certain types of contents and media may bring about fan groups and devoted audiences (McQuail 1987), the content/medium-audience identification usually proves to be a weak bond. Readers of certain dailies and mass magazines traditionally do not feel strongly that they share a social or cultural identity with other readers. As the media of many societies move toward more diversification and monopolization, this lack of identification may change.

Quite a few media have launched advertising campaigns for themselves, stressing exactly this sense of shared identity among their audience members. Media also are communicating with their audience not only via content, but also via their corporate identity, e.g. newspapers that sponsor discussion forums on AIDS or donate large gifts to a local museum and publicize their own generosity. Witness, too, the growing number of broadcasting companies that periodically organize open houses, that is, tours of their facilities, and offer opportunities to meet on-camera talent. How successful these efforts are is difficult to assess, but the technique is something for communication planners to consider.

So although individuals in a mass medium or content category define themselves as members, they usually still represent a fairly heterogeneous and loosely connected aggregate of people. This should caution communication planners not to regard media or content audiences as natural groups that will react more or less uniformly to a message. Also, it is *normally* the case that media audiences cannot be motivated as a group. There are exceptions, such as groups that attend to certain prestige, religious, or minority media and contents.

The lesson for communication planners is the following: if they are looking for audiences with which to communicate effectively, they should try to find aggregates that define themselves as a group based on something stronger than just media content use. Grunig and Hunt (1984), in their definition of publics for public relations, maintain that publics are made up of people who face a similar problem (latent publics), recognize that the problem exists (aware publics), and organize themselves to do something about the problem (active publics).

Some sort of problem recognition is a basis for defining oneself as belonging to an audience. Sometimes the first goal of a communication planner is to make the people define themselves as part of a group and an audience. This is the strategy used by some gay associations that, in order to fight AIDS, need to reach several homosexual subgroups. "What we need to do," a gay communication planner argues, "is to give certain homosexuals a gay identity before we can make them receptive to AIDS information. Otherwise, by denying their identity, they also deny the relevance of the information. They do not feel it is directed toward them" (Windahl 1989). This goal also has been noted in organizational communication, which considers it important to create a corporate identity on which further communication may be built.

Defined by Media Use

Mass communication research often defines audiences by their media use. One category may be called "readers of youth magazines," others may be referred to as "science program listeners." Such categorizations are useful, for example, to marketing people, whose communication efforts often begin with looking at different channels and their publics and asking questions such as, "How many potential buyers will I reach and at what cost through this channel?"

Audiences defined by media use often are chosen as a point of departure for a communication effort constrained by availability of a limited number of channels to reach an audience. For example, if one local radio station has promised to carry a traffic campaign message for free, the communication planner must ask, "Whom will I reach, and how will I talk to that audience?" The medium and channel dictate the identification of the audience, which, in turn, will influence the content of the messages.

While communication planners may use this type of audience categorization, they should be aware of the problems tied to it. First, mass media audiences range from fairly homogeneous to very heterogeneous. The more heterogeneous the audience, the more difficult it is to effectively communicate with its members as a group. Thus, attempting to reach all the readers of a specific newspaper may prove futile since the readership comprises so many different types of people. Only certain subsets of the audience will be reached. In other cases, though, the audience for a medium is more homogeneous; it is, therefore, easier to define and to communicate with effectively, e.g. the audience of special interest magazines or specific types of radio programs (say, for homemakers).

Second, the public being targeted may not correspond to the audience of a certain medium. Choosing a youth magazine as a channel does not ensure that the young smokers who are the message's target will be reached.

A common problem in planned communication is that the choice of medium is made too early in the process. Many planners have stories about situations where an employer says, "Look, we have a problem here. Let's come up with a brochure and send it to all households in the community." The audience has been defined – prematurely – as "brochure-readers," making the chances of reaching the relevant audience marginal, at best. Obviously, this is beginning communication planning at the wrong end. The "whom-to-reach" question should precede the "what-channel" question.

Functions of Audiences

There are other dimensions that can be considered in relation to the audience. Audiences may have different functions. We will deal here with the following functions: the audience as a market, as clients, as dialogue partners, and as communicators.

As a Market

McQuail defines the audience as market as "an aggregate of potential customers with a known social-economic profile at which a medium or message is directed" (1987: 221). Important to note here is the dual character of the audience member: (a) a potential customer for the medium and (b) a target for the advertising message (and, consequently, a potential customer for the advertised product).

In the commercial media, the significance of this duality lies in the fact that advertising constitutes the principal source of revenue. Such a conceptualization of the audience undoubtedly will influence media content and the self-image of the sender. The communicator will, for better or worse, try to adapt to the perceived tastes and needs of the audience. At the same time, the market perspective empowers the audience. When audience members do not like what they are offered, or so the argument goes, the sender must try to please them by some other means.

The view of the audience as a market is prevalent in certain aspects of communication planning. This is the case, for example, in social marketing (Chapter 9). Solomon (1989) discusses how important it is for the planner to assess what "price" the audience members are prepared to pay. As in any market, individuals will deliberate about the price for getting certain information or taking part in certain communication. In social marketing one should also take all relevant markets into account, meaning that not only the ultimate consumers should be included in communication plans. In an anti-drug campaign directed to students, parents, school officials, and teachers are important complementary markets.

In the end, however, it should be the effects on the ultimate consumers that count: did they learn what they were supposed to, behave in the way advocated, etc.? Too often, the success of communication efforts is judged on factors such as how the planning staff members feel about the campaign. For the commercial marketer, sales figures are paramount. In communication planning as well, more attention should be focused on the ultimate consumer.

There are differences between commercial markets and social markets. In a commercial market, the most profitable segments are targeted. In social marketing, the reverse is often true – the hardest-to-reach segments that are the most in need of the information being offered are sought, often at considerable cost. Also, in social campaigns, the aim frequently is to discourage people from doing certain things (such as smoking) instead of promoting positive action, such as purchasing certain products.

As Dialogue Partners

Mass communication audiences are normally talked to or at, not with. The mass communication process is, in principle, one-way – a characteristic that poses restrictions on the use of the mass media as channels for communication planners. Planners may consider using models other than those of traditional mass communication to build a more dynamic process. In our discussion about the processual approach to communication planning (Chapter 5), and in the presentation of the two-way symmetric model (Chapter 8), as well as in other approaches, the audience is more active and contributive. In these models, it is difficult to regard the audience as just an aggregate of receivers. In the processual model, the audience normally consists of subgroups that communicate with each other (as well as with the communication planner); they should be regarded as communication or dialogue partners. The two-way symmetric model suggests that communication planners and their publics communicate on an equal footing. In these cases, the aim is one of mutual understanding, negotiating, and problem solving rather than one of informing. Communication using these models has greater potential to achieve creative goals.

As Clients

In many communication efforts, audience members are regarded as clients, the beneficiaries of the communication. Like clients in the commercial sense, they are, as noted above, the end-users of a service or product.

Occupational sociology also uses the concept of client, especially in connection with professions. Without forcing a non-communication interpretation onto the concept of audience, let us look at what client-related dimensions occupational sociology offers to communication planning for audience analysis.

The professionalization view of the client involves the claim that the interests of the client (e.g. the patient of a medical service) take precedence over the interests of both the employer (e.g. the hospital) and the professional (other than the planner – in our example, the physician). It is also the duty of the planner, at times, to defend the true interests of clients against the clients' own false perceptions of their interests. While this client orientation may serve as an ideological device by which the professions secure monopoly and privilege, it is not without relevance for planners, who quite frequently must, in the interest of their audience (clients), fend off non-professional interferences that threaten planning autonomy. When it comes down to finally devising the specifics of a campaign, the planner should have the autonomy to perform in the interest of the client-audience.

The more commercial meaning of the client conceptualization (i.e. as a customer) encompasses aspects quite commonplace in marketing thinking. Some of those are:

- The planner should become as well-informed as possible about the audience/client prior to the communication. (See Chapter 2 for a discussion of feedforward.)
- The goal is not only to have gained new customers (clients), but also to maintain them (consolidation) and eventually to turn them into recommenders who will recruit other clients.
- The client often does pay for the product/service in planned communication, although payment usually is indirect (for example, through taxes that enable the National Science Foundation to provide grant money) or in the sense of spending time attending to the messages. The implication is that the client should be treated with the same amount of respect as someone engaged in a business deal or in some other professional/client relationship.

In terms of power relations in communication planning, the concept of audience as client comes close to two-way models of (public relations) communication. In asymmetric models (see Chapter 8), clients are approached and investigated only with a view to persuading them more efficiently and smoothly; the symmetric two-way model, in contrast, regards the client as a partner who, in a balanced relationship, should have as much influence on the content of the communication and how it is delivered as the sender/planner.

As Communicators

Few mass communication theories have recognized that members of an audience can assume roles as active senders and communicators. There is increasing recognition of this potential, however. The two-step flow of information hypothesis offers a rather dated, although in many respects still relevant, example. It suggests that certain members of the audience are more active than others: opinion leaders pass on mass communicated contents in face-to-face situations; followers are people who turn to the opinion leaders for advice. Another example is the uses and gratifications approach, which suggests that one motive for attending to the mass media is to acquire topics to talk about with others.

For the communication planner, picturing the audience as a communication tool offers problems as well as promises. A major problem is that it is usually difficult for the planner to control how audience members pass on a message; severe misunderstandings and misconceptions might arise.

To be spread, the messages must concern a subject that is topical and relevant for audience members. AIDS communication planners in Sweden, for example, discussed how people can be "provoked" through the mass media to talk about issues that are not the standard fare of everyday conversations. A communication planner who sees the audience as potential furtherers and mediators may build into campaign messages phrases such as "Tell a friend," "What does your neighbor think?"

Hornik (1988) describes the radio forum as an example of an active audience in a communication setting. In the Third World, radio forums involve a group of people who listen to educational programs about, let's say, agriculture. These groups then discuss the content among themselves and also may pass the content on to others.

Receiving Mass Communications: Activity or Passivity

The discussion of ways to look at the mass communication audience makes it obvious that the activity/passivity dimension is crucial. In this section we will examine this dimension since the communication planner needs to take it into account in order to create effective communication.

The Audience-as-Receivers

Several traditional accounts of audience behavior depict the audience member as a rather passive creature who receives and reacts to mass communication content rationally and predictably. In the sender–receiver relationship, the sender is active, the receiver passive. The sender defines the goal and designs and produces messages. It is left to the receiver to react, rather than act (McQuail 1984). These are, by and large, the characteristics of what Dervin (1981) calls the "consensual portrait" of the communication process. As we have seen, however, uses and gratifications theory and reception theory have modified this picture. (For recent critical discussions of the notion of audience activity, see, *inter alia*, Gunter 1988; Biocca 1988; and Lindlof 1988.)

Biocca (1988) points out that the mass communication audience is often thought of in terms of the traditional physical audience, like that found in a theater. This conceptualization produces an image of an obedient crowd, waiting to be pleased, informed, thrilled, or the like.

This consensual portrait creates a subjective sense of predictability and control. A communication planner will strive to find the right channels to convey the right message to cause the audience to obey. The audience will receive the information and react in the desired way. The planner is satisfied that the process is under control. This model of a passive, obedient audience member undoubtedly has produced unwarranted hopes for obtaining intended effects. Indeed the element of passivity on the part of the audience may also serve as an excuse or an explanation for an absence of effects. ("Those people are just too lazy to read what we have to say.")

The Audience-as-Creators

The audience-as-receiver orientation typically treats the audience as an aggregate of people. The individual as an active participant in the communication process does not really fit into this picture. The reverse of that view has the individual as a point of departure. It is represented by, among others, Dervin (1981), who, in line with the psychology of "becoming" (C. Rogers 1979), maintains that people create their own information in an effort to make sense of the world around them. In this conceptualization, individuals are active; the result of their sense-making activity tends to be unique since meaning/sense is specific to a certain individual at a certain point in time and space.

In describing this approach, Dervin (1984) has summarized the main points of sense-making. These points are especially relevant to communication planning.

- Sense-making starts with the receiver and looks at message use only in terms of how it intersects with the receiver's present, past, and expected future.
- Sense-making does not presuppose impacts of messages, but rather lets receivers define what impact messages have on them.
- Sense-making sees the characteristics of life contexts of receivers not as barriers to and mediators of messages, but rather as contexts within which receivers use messages to make sense of the world.
- Information is defined as that which informs from the receiver's point of view. It is seen as the sense the receiver makes to bridge gaps in his or her world.
- Sense-making is situational, predicted by situational conditions.

Anderson and Meyer similarly point out that sense-making of communication should be seen as having "its own ends in the *empowerment* of the sense-maker. . . . Empowerment describes the method by which the premises of action are created and maintained" (1988: 28). Thus, the receiver will use communication as part of social action, interpreting and forming messages to be usable tools in social action. This perspective is of the utmost importance in the planner's understanding of an audience. Also, it may be a guiding principle in structuring messages, which should be suitable for the empowerment function.

Other types of media research also rely on the notion of an active receiver. For example, in her studies about romance novel reading, Radway (1984a, 1984b) demonstrates how readers create their own stories when reading, ignoring parts of the text that do not fit their expectations of a romance novel and emphasizing other parts that do fit.

An actively creating, sense-making audience poses a challenge for the communication planner. Is it at all possible for the planner to communicate with an audience that creates its own information from what is offered? Schroeder's (1987, 1988) question whether different TV viewers really view the same program is crucial to planned communication. Sophisticated and emphatic planning can enable planners to overcome some of the obstacles to effective communication posed by an active audience; therein lies the challenge. But when that challenge is met, communication may reach the audience more forcefully than ever envisaged by conventional thinking.

There are several responses to the question of whether receivers who actively create information in idiosyncratic ways will nevertheless understand the content in such a way that meaningful communication will result. One answer is based on the concept of *intersubjectivity*. Members of the same culture and subculture tend, in spite of their uniqueness, to share meanings and understandings with each other to a degree that makes meaningful communication possible (see O'Sullivan et al. 1983).

Another approach to the question is *preferred reading* (Hall et al. 1980), which is a frequent focus of works originating with the Centre of Contemporary Cultural Studies at the University of Birmingham. Those researchers maintain that texts tend to mirror the ideological power structure in society. That means that a preferred interpretation of texts arises from groups with ideological dominance and is more or less accepted by the members of the audience. Alongside these preferred readings, however, exist oppositional readings, derived from alternative, oppositional meaning systems representing other ideologies, and negotiated readings that adapt to the consciousness of the reader (O'Sullivan et al. 1983).

A practical approach for communication planners to make reasonably certain that their communication will be understood lies in empathy and learning as much as possible about the situation of the audience and subaudiences. Dervin (1981), from her sense-making perspective, has formulated some questions to guide this process of finding out about the audience.

First, *when do people use messages?* Communication planners should determine when and under what circumstances people make use of their communication. As noted before, timing is often lacking in planned communication work, ensuring that the communication often reaches the audience at times when it is not needed and will be rejected. Planners should tailor the message to the situation where it is likely to be used, thereby increasing the chances that the audience will actively accept it.

Second, *what do people use messages for?* Communication may be used for a variety of reasons. Dervin points out that it is important to find out how a certain type of message will be used. The reception and interpretation is then adapted to this probable use or function. Uses and gratifications research has shown that media content is often used for other reasons than those intended by the sender.

Third, *what predicts message use?* In order to adapt the message to the audience members, Dervin suggests that instead of traditional predictors of media use such as age, education, etc., planners use people's perceptions of certain situations and the informational needs of those situations. If someone, for example, decides he or she is overweight, that person may look for information about how to get rid of the excess pounds.

The better our communication is adapted to specific situations in time and space where there is a need for it, the greater the chance that it will function effectively with receivers who create their own information according to situational needs.

The Levy-Windahl Model

In the audience-as-creator view, the activity of the audience largely concentrates on the act of receiving. The mass communication receiver is, however, active in other respects. Levy and Windahl (1985) have inventoried possible activities before, during, and after mass media exposure and consumption.

Before exposure, receivers may actively select what they want to consume to obtain certain gratifications. Communication planning can encourage this activity by offering information about information itself, thereby helping and motivating audience members to find what they want and need.

During exposure, audience members selectively perceive and interpret communication content as well as identify with elements of the message. It is the planner's task to craft the message in such a way that audience members can distinguish what is important and less important.

After exposure, receivers selectively recall information from what they received. They also may talk to others about the content to which they have been exposed. Getting people to retain and recall the content is a communication goal that is often overlooked. The communication planner has much to gain by getting people to talk about the message they hear, see, or read.

The Notion of Audience in Grunig's Situational Theory

Grunig and Hunt maintain that a public's communication behavior can be predicted and understood by analyzing its perceptions of a certain situation (Grunig and Hunt 1984; Grunig 1987a). The theory is built on five variables: problem recognition, constraint recognition, level of involvement, information-seeking, and information-processing. Once we know the nature of these variables for a certain public/audience, we also can predict whether it will become active or not.

Problem Recognition
For people to think or communicate about an issue, they must perceive that there is a problem about which something should be done. The higher the problem recognition, the greater the chance that the public will communicate about that issue.

Constraint Recognition
This variable represents to what extent people perceive obstacles and limitations to freely planning their own behavior. The more closely linked constraint recognition is to an issue, the less likely it is that audience members will engage in communication dealing with the issue and solve problems associated with it.

Level of Involvement
Involvement is the extent to which people relate or connect themselves with an issue or a situation. The more involved they are, the more likely they will become active.

Information-seeking
The three variables above will, among other things, determine the amount and nature of communication related to the issue. Information-seeking denotes an active communication behavior, what Clarke and Kline (1974) describe as the "planned scanning of the environment for messages about a specific topic." A public that identifies an issue as a problem, perceives little constraint recognition, and is strongly connected to the issue, i.e. highly involved, will probably also actively communicate about it, seeking information to solve the perceived problem.

Information-processing
Information-processing is a way to passively relate to communication. Clarke and Kline refer to it as "the unplanned discovery of a message." People who merely process information are not actively looking for it, but

they may deal with it when they come across it, even if the encounter is just by chance. For example, if a public does not regard a certain issue as a problem, it will process rather than seek information about the problem, if it deals with it at all.

Note that Grunig and Hunt's theory does not attempt to explain persuasion. "The theory predicts whether people have an attitude or engage in a behavior, but not whether that attitude or behavior supports or opposes the organization" (Grunig 1987a: 6).

The Grunig–Hunt model contains several concepts and notions important to the communication planner. To activate people, for example, it is important that problem recognition be established; obstacles and limits to action must be minimized; and the planner needs to make people identify with and feel affinity for the problem's solution.

An AIDS campaign provides an example: It is essential from the beginning that people believe that AIDS is a problem. This enables them to recognize its importance and makes them conscious of it. Many AIDS campaigners place high priority on getting the issue onto various agendas. Once high problem recognition exists, audience members actively seek more information. (Members with moderate problem recognition more likely will only process information about AIDS.) The planner's next step is to try to reduce constraint recognition by telling audience members that they themselves control whether they will get infected or not. "It is your choice" is the catch phrase of many campaigns. At the same time, it is important to make people aware that AIDS is not just someone else's problem. It is a problem for anyone engaging in risk behavior. That information involves the risk-takers in the issue.

In public relations, the model may be used to foresee problems in the form of hostile publics who should be prevented from actively involving themselves in the issue. One strategy, albeit of doubtful effectiveness, would be to discourage hostile publics' involvement by stressing factors limiting their options, thereby increasing their constraint recognition and making them less willing receivers.

The Emancipated Audience

This book may give the impression that planned communication is always an effort to exercise control and power, to make others act the way planners or their organizations want them to. But the planner may have quite another aim, namely to activate a public so that it becomes more powerful, liberated, and emancipated.

Such ideas have been put forward by critical theorists of the Frankfurt School. Democratic/participant thinking has been applied to communication and the media. An early and much-quoted statement of this view came from author/playwright Bertold Brecht who suggested that radio be converted from a means of distribution to one of communication. Radio,

Table 14.1 **Repressive versus emancipatory use of media**

Repressive	Emancipatory
Centrally controlled program	Decentralized program
Single transmitter and various receivers	Each receiver also is a potential transmitter
Immobilization of isolated individuals	Mobilization of the masses
Inactive behavior of consumers	Interaction from participants, feedback
Depolitization	Politization (a learning process)
Production by specialists	Collective production
Control by owners or bureaucrats	Societal control through self-organization

Source: Enzensberger 1985: 484

according to Brecht, could be "the most wonderful public communication system imaginable . . . if it were capable not only of transmitting but of receiving, of making the listener not only hear but also speak, not of isolating him but of connecting him" (Brecht 1983: 169).

In the 1970s, another writer, Hans Magnus Enzensberger, picked up Brecht's ideas and developed his well-known juxtaposition of repressive versus emancipatory use of media (see Table 14.1).

Apart from the talking-back concept in critical communication theory, what appears to be most interesting for the planner is the supposition that the audience members interact and are connected among themselves. Thus, the more pragmatic view of the audience as active is supplemented by an ideological dimension as well.

Communicative Competence

Following from the societal value that people *should* talk back to the media and interact among themselves is the question of whether people *can* do it, and how. Theorists such as Dieter Baacke (1980, 1982) speak optimistically of the characteristic of communicative competence, which, in principle, all humans have at their disposal. This competence must be set free. One way of accomplishing this is through participation.

Not only individuals possess and need to actualize their communicative competence; so do groups of people and organizations. This is crucial for more enlightened views of directed communication (and public relations), which heavily stress two-way communication and dialogue, to have any practical meaning at all.

Two-way communication has as a logical prerequisite communicative competence on both/all sides of the communication process. For communication planners, this competence must be accounted for when designing two-way communication settings. If not, the planners may be rightly accused of window-dressing or, worse, of using the two-way philosophy merely as a propagandistic device. German PR theoretician Barthenheier (1982) goes so far as to state that public relations without communicative competence on the part of *everyone* involved is logically inconceivable.

(He demands education in communicative competence in schools as a means of addressing this problem.)

Habermas on Communication

At a much more theoretical level, Habermas' theory of *communicative action* provides insights and arguments for communication planners who want to intellectually position themselves or others on a continuum of symmetrical–asymmetrical communication. Habermas (1981–82) distinguishes between two fundamentally different kinds of rationality that determine a strategy's position on this continuum: cognitive instrumental rationality on one end and communicative rationality on the other.

In cognitive instrumental rationality, "rational actions basically have the character of goal-directed, feedback-controlled interventions in the world of existing states of affairs." Its goal is instrumental mastery. Approaches to planned communication that stress environmental control have this as a goal. In Grunig and Hunt's public relations model, this is the asymmetrical type of communication. The aim of two-way communication can be to gain control of the environment, too.

The other end of the continuum, communicative rationality, carries with it "connotations based ultimately on the central experience of the unconstrained, unifying, consensus-bringing force of argumentative speech." For Habermas, the world is created through intersubjective, communicative action.

Pearson (1989) has applied Habermas' distinction to the tensions between the asymmetric and the symmetric approaches to communication planning. Emphasis on social scientific methodologies and "management by objectives" techniques suggests an instrumental rationality; in contrast, emphasis on symmetry, dialogue, conversation, and mutual understanding implies a communicative rationality.

Defining the Audience

As we have noted elsewhere (Chapter 11), mass media communicators often have a complicated relationship with their audience, depending in large degree on the distance and anonymity between the two. We have seen how mass communicators use individuals as representatives of the general public in order to facilitate communication. It is important to ask with whom the communicator really communicates; in this section we shall discuss possible audiences.

Miller (1986) discusses the basis on which communicators predict consequences of their messages to an audience. Such predictions can be founded on cultural, sociological, and psychological information. When cultural (knowledge about the audience's language, values, etc.) and sociological (knowledge about the audience's membership and reference groups) information is used for these predictions, "they are founded on a process of *stimulus generalization,* i.e. the communicator abstracts a set of characteristics common to most members of a group and then assumes that any given individual or individuals belonging to that group will manifest these characteristics" (1986: 134). Since a number of people deviate from the principal group in mass communication audiences, the predictions and resulting communication will never be 100 percent effective.

When the communicator's predictions are based on psychological information, such as knowledge about personal learning history, the process is characterized by *stimulus discrimination.* "The communicator seeks to determine how particular persons differ from others of common cultural and sociological lineage" (Miller 1986: 135).

We have seen, however, that mass communicators often circumvent stimulus generalization by choosing one person (inside or outside the actual group) to represent the audience.

Addressing a group, a large public, or audience while trying systematically to take into account as many characteristics of that group as possible is problematic. Because of this, most communicators and communication planners simply ignore this approach.

In planned communication, messages very often are structured as though directed to each member of the audience, which is regarded as an aggregate of individuals with similar characteristics. What is missed in such an approach are group dynamics and variations within the audience. One way to circumvent this problem is to identify key individuals as opinion leaders, as described in the section about two-step flow of information theory (see Chapter 6).

In some cases, it may be useful to regard the audience as composed of dyads, pairs. We could conceive of information campaigns for contraceptive use in which the dyad is targeted. Persuasive messages might use arguments such as taking care of each other, discussing the matter beforehand, taking responsibility for each other, etc.

In other instances, a group may be the audience unit. Using the family as an example, children will receive information about a health campaign at school, while their parents receive the campaign's messages at their workplaces. The expectation is that the communication through these two channels will be discussed further in the family setting, whereby some intra-family decisions about health-related activities will be reached.

Segmentation of Audiences

Several areas of mass communication research lead away from the notion of media that reach everyone to a differentiated media market. Witness, for example, the rise of special interest magazines in nearly every industrialized society. The catch phrase "from mass media to class media" illustrates this phenomenon as well. Rogers (1986: 7) speaks of the "individualized, demassified nature" of the new media that will be an integral part of the so-called information society, which is conceptualized as more individualistic with components such as mass production, mass media, and mass culture.

The notion of a differentiated audience is widely accepted by media scholars. De Fleur and Ball-Rokeach (1982) have labeled one media research perspective "the social categories perspective"; it deals with differentiated audiences and their differentiated responses to media stimuli. The assumption is that groups or collectives (social categories) will react more or less uniformly to a given set of stimuli.

A key concept in communication planning is segmentation. The concept relies on differentiated audiences with their subaudiences; an audience is divided into subgroupings that are internally homogeneous but differ from each other (Frank et al. 1972; Haley 1985; Kotler 1986). The subgroups receive different messages and/or are reached through different channels.

We talked earlier about the problems of communicating with heterogeneous audiences. The more homogeneous the receiver group, the easier it is for the communicator to communicate with its members. A mass communication sender typically has difficulties in adapting to an audience, and communication will be more or less blindly directed at a perceived "average" audience or to a secondary audience that a planner knows, for example, colleagues or superiors.

Segmentation research and practice has its strongest tradition in marketing. As early as the 1950s, Wendell Smith (1956) published "Product Differentiation and Market Segmentation as Alternative Product Strategies," a seminal in-depth review of the then existing literature. Interest in segmentation among American marketing people today can be traced to four trends. First, growth of world population to a projected 270 million by the year 2000 will result in ever more segments large enough to make segmentation efforts profitable. Second, there has been a tremendous brand proliferation among consumer products; the average supermarket stocks 12,000 to 14,000 items, making it necessary for individual brands to find market segments where they can dominate. Third, the rise of individualism to create what some observers call the "Age of Me" lends itself to segmentation. Fourth, specialized media are on the rise, with a trend from "broadcasting" to "narrowcasting" as a result of the decline of national audiences, but with increased possibilities of reaching smaller market segments with quite specific interests and needs (Haley 1985).

We believe that these trends will increase the need for segmentation in non-commercial areas of general communication planning as well.

The most obvious argument for not segmenting in planned communication is lack of resources. Segmentation always means more effort, at least in the initial stages, than non-segmentation. In an information campaign, it is always less expensive to present a uniform stimulus to one large audience than different stimuli to several smaller and different receiving groups. It is highly probable, however, that in most cases the latter strategy will be more effective.

It must be remembered that not all communication situations benefit from increased group homogeneity; therefore, segmentation should not be treated dogmatically, but situationally. Granovetter's (1973) notion of the importance of "weak ties" (new and different group members) in group communication serves to remind us that sometimes, especially in communication situations where creative solutions are sought, the communication planner could strive for heterogeneity as well. Segmentation is typically used in content/distribution types of communication strategies (see Chapter 5).

With regard to market segmentation, Percy and Rossiter (1980) maintain that almost any personal characteristic may be used for segmenting a market. While it is true that the theoretical possibilities for segmentation are many, the lack of resources (and creativity) will be a strong limiting factor. The selection of segmentation factors follows a contingency principle – every type of case tends to have its own preferred segmentation.

We have listed some of the more important dimensions of segmentation here, but there are many more.

Segmentation by Demographic Characteristics
This is a traditional and usually simple approach to segmentation. It involves characteristics such as age, gender, occupation, family size, position in the family life cycle, income, education, geographical location, religion, race, and nationality. These data tend to be reasonably precise in terms of definition and measurement. Goals for planned communication are often structured around this approach: to encourage more teenagers and retired people to use the library; to reach men aged 45–65 and women 55–70 with a health campaign; to convince college students to join in a lobbying effort in support of higher education; etc. Frequently, the communication planner will combine two or more of these variables (multivariable demographic segmentation).

An assumption of segmentation according to demographic variables is that one demographic category suggests certain other characteristics. An AIDS prevention program may use the subgroup "men 18–30 years" not because of the age and gender *per se* but because it is known that many high-risk individuals fall into this age group. A traffic campaign for pedestrian safety targets "men and women over 65" as a subgroup because this category includes many pedestrians. From a theoretical point of view, demographic segmentation may be a compromise approach, but since reaching the target subaudience in another way may prove technically impossible or too resource-demanding, it may be the only possible approach.

OWN PERCEPTION

	Belongs	Does not belong
Belongs	1	2
Does not belong	3	4

OBJECTIVE
STATUS

Figure 14.5 *Segments according to objective and subjective membership of a risk group*

By Beliefs

People perceive the world differently, depending on experiences, environmental influences, etc. The same phenomenon may mean very different things to different persons and groups. For example, a program for getting people to improve their eating habits talks about the importance of planning and preparing meals in certain ways. We need first to find out what people mean by "meal." For some, it is a way to stay alive; for some, it is a social event; and for others, it is a means to stay healthy (Palm and Windahl 1989). Communication efforts will benefit from subgrouping the audience according to these distinctions.

Take another example from a disease prevention campaign. Subjectively, a person may or may not believe that he or she belongs to a risk group; objectively, he or she may or may not. These two variables, objective and subjective risk, are related as shown in Figure 14.5.

Strategies directed to people in each of the different categories will be very different; segmentation could be carried out according to Figure 14.5. It is important to reach people in Category 1; they probably will be easily persuaded to see a doctor. For individuals in Category 2, two-step argumentation may be necessary: first, they must be convinced that they really are at risk; second, they must be convinced to see a doctor. For persons in Category 3, efforts are directed to make them redefine their health status. And for those people in Category 4, a planner should question the necessity of any efforts to reach them at all.

A classic and imaginative example of differentiation of people based on their perception of themselves and their environment is found in Merton's (1968) and Gouldner's (1957) research. Using the terms "cosmopolitans" and "locals" to describe different types of influential people in communities and organizations, they described the former group as having a broader view of reality, whereas the latter had the local community as their point of reference. A communication planner would have to deal quite differently with these two categories of people.

By Attitudes

It generally is believed that communication directed to segments of the audience that already agree with a proposed standpoint and those that do not should be different (Lumsdaine and Janis 1953). For the former, how-to information (Rogers 1983) in the form of one-sided argumentation is the most important; the latter needs what and why information given in a form that discusses counterarguments. Segments with attitudes that differ greatly from the one advocated have to be treated with care since their perception of messages may result in boomerang effects; such effects have been noted in anti-racist campaigns (Cooper and Jahoda 1947; Vidmar and Rokeach 1974).

Percy and Rossiter (1980) talk about segmenting a commercial market into different attitude segments in relation to a certain product. Among others, the following groups emerge:

- the unsophisticated, who think that many products are too sophisticated for them and that higher price does not equal better quality;
- nothing-but-the-best, who think that nothing is too sophisticated for them to buy;
- the novice, who thinks that, while there is no need for the best, you get what you pay for;
- the expert, who is certain of what he or she wants and believes you get what you pay for.

Another technique developed by marketing researchers for focusing on attitudes vis-à-vis a certain product distinguishes between the following segments: enthusiastic, positive, indifferent, negative, and hostile (Kotler 1986).

Chaffee (1981) notes that, in political campaigning, it is important to identify at least three categories: supporters, neutrals, and opponents of a certain candidate or cause. These categories, of course, are applicable to areas other than politics as well.

In health and traffic communication, it may be useful to segment people into groups according to whether they like to take risks or not. Young people who drive fast because they like the excitement and the risks may be unconvinced by arguments pointing out the risks of such behavior (McGuire 1989).

By Behavior

The inability to describe certain social groupings and intended publics by use of simple demographic classifications led social science researchers and marketers to look for other descriptors. Some work with lifestyle characteristics. A lifestyle may be defined as "the behavior in daily life that differentiates us as individuals one from another" (Strid 1988: 4). Examples of lifestyle research in sociology are found in Greenberg and Frank (1983) and Zablocki and Kanter (1976). Research about patterns of

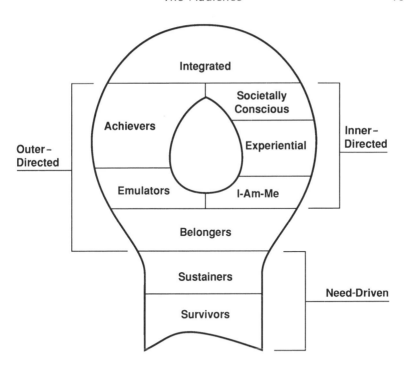

Figure 14.6 *The VALS typology (Mitchell 1983)*

behavior and lifestyles for aggregates of people was in vogue in the 1970s. Peterson (1983) notes that to a large extent it proved impossible to isolate clear lifestyle categories for most of the population. That does not mean, however, that behavior is not a meaningful segment indicator. A good example comes from anti-drug and anti-smoking campaigns among young people. Those who smoke or use drugs require different approaches from those who do not. In health education, an important behavioral segment is the high-risk group (Maccoby and Solomon 1981) that can be identified through health screening projects.

Marketing researchers also have developed elaborate lifestyle categories. Best known among them is "Values and Lifestyle" (VALS), which classifies American adults into various lifestyle typologies. Each represents a different approach to life that was derived by relating people's psychological needs to their behaviors (Mitchell 1983).

Figure 14.6 (known as the VALS Tulip because of its shape) groups the population into four general (consumer) categories which, in turn, are further subdivided.

- *Need-driven* (11 percent of the population): people whose lives are driven more by need than choice because of severe limitations in resources, especially financial. Subgroups include the Survivors (4 percent) and the Sustainers (7 percent).

- *Outer-directed* (67 percent of the population): representing the mainstream of society, people who respond to real or fancied signals from others in the conduct of their lives. The subgroupings are Belongers (35 percent), Emulators (10 percent), and Achievers (22 percent).
- *Inner-directed* (20 percent of the population): people who live according to inner needs and desires, rather than others' values. Their basic rewards in life are internal and emotional rather than external and materialistic. They are subdivided into I-Am-Me's (5 percent), the Experientials (7 percent), and the Societally Conscious (8 percent).
- *Integrated* (3 percent of the population): people who balance an inner-directed and other-directed approach to life.

There is a great deal of controversy in marketing circles about this type of segmentation technique, which is known as *psychographics*. VALS is only one of many such systems. While psychographics programs like VALS require sophisticated marketing approaches, other techniques such as *geodemographics* may be more directly applicable to communication planning. This refers to a segmentation system that divides a nation into neighborhoods with similar characteristics. One such program, PRIZOM, divides the 250,000 neighborhoods in the United States into 40 distinct neighborhood types.

For the non-commercial communication planner, it may be useful to think along these (marketing) lines once in a while. Susan Maloney of the US Public Health Service puts it this way:

> Psychographics might prove to be an important tool . . . If, for example, we know that black males between 25 and 40 are at high risk for high blood pressure, this still does not tell us how to reach them or why some people take their medicine and others do not. We have lots of health behavior data, but not health attitudes. (Quoted in Winkelman 1987: 23)

It is obvious that segmentation does not enable us to isolate beliefs, attitudes, and behavior from each other. The best we can expect is that certain beliefs will imply certain attitudes which, in turn, will imply certain behaviors.

By the Principle of Access

Communication planners often divide their publics into subgroupings according to the cost in terms of resources necessary to reach them. Easily accessible categories are given priority, while others may be considered later, if at all. Using this criterion alone may be unwise, for example, in public communication campaigns. A mixed solution that considers accessibility in relation to importance of reaching the category in question is usually more meaningful.

Rogers (1983) states that, in many cases, those who need an innovation most are the last to accept it, as has occurred with family planning. This can be blamed in part on communication planners and change agents who use a segmentation strategy directed at the groups that offer the least resistance. They target audience members who are socioeconomic elites, easy to reach, and often most receptive to innovations like family planning, even though they could afford to provide for many children. As a remedy, Rogers suggests that communication planners follow a segmentation strategy of greatest resistance, in which special resources are devoted to reaching groups that are not easily accessible, either physically or psychologically. Such a segmentation technique also will be helpful in reducing information gaps that may result from planned communication efforts (Tichenor et al. 1970; Thunberg et al. 1982; Nowak 1977; see Chapter 15).

By Public's Resources
Commercial segmentation typically is based on potential customers' economic resources, such as annual income, which determine their purchasing power.

For public communication, other resources may be more important. But the underlying concept is the same – the receiver should be economically able to act according to the message. Trying to convince poor Third World farmers to buy modern Western farming equipment is usually quite meaningless. In the case of a health campaign, people living in large cities will have ready access to medical facilities that are instrumental in achieving the goals of a communication campaign. For people living in the countryside where these facilities are not available, different argumentation must be used.

Another type of resource is psychological. We see an example of this in our school systems: different instruction is given to students of different ages because their ability to understand varies. In planned communication, this basic consideration often is, not taken into account. Minorities who speak a different language frequently fall outside the sphere of information campaigns, and messages too frequently are designed to appeal only to a fairly well-educated public, the same public that the communicator belongs to (see Atkin 1981).

Process-related Segmentation
Diffusion theory suggests several segmentation principles. In the innovation acceptance process, for example, several phases or stages exist (Rogers 1983):

- *knowledge*, when the individual is informed about the innovation;
- *persuasion*, when the individual forms a positive or negative attitude toward the innovation;
- *decision*, when the individual actively decides whether to accept or reject the innovation;
- *implementation*, when the individual puts the innovation into use;
- *confirmation*, when the individual seeks reinforcement for the decision made.

As was pointed out in Chapter 6, the information needed in these distinct phases varies. Individuals in the knowledge stage have information needs quite different from those of the confirmation phase. Therefore, in communication programs where the adoption stages are discernible, segmentation can be based on those stages. Rogers (1983) offers categories based on an individual's readiness to accept innovations: innovator, early adopter, early majority, late majority, and laggard. As seen in Chapter 6, these groups tend to have different communication habits and different communication needs, and use different communication channels. Rogers' categorization is widely used; it provides a good basis for segmentation.

By Media Use

Sometimes the medium and not the public itself is the basis for segmentation. The communication planner may, for different reasons, be limited to using certain media. The first step in this situation is to analyze the structure of those media's publics and to deal with them as segments. A communication planner may end up with a local newspaper segment, a segment of 8–10 p.m. radio listeners, and a segment of active Red Cross members. This segmentation process is not uncommon, but being restricted from the beginning by a fixed media structure limits the possibilities for effective communication.

By Issues and Communication

Grunig, a public relations theorist, has developed a segmentation approach based on how a public communicates about problems or issues that result when organizations behave in ways that have consequences for people outside the organization. Using the variables "information-seeking" and "information-processing" on the one hand and "problem recognition," "constraint recognition," and "level of involvement" on the other, Grunig identifies four publics (Grunig 1987a: 8; see Chapter 8):

- *all-issue publics:* publics active on all relevant issues;
- *apathetic publics:* publics that communicate little about any of the issues;
- *single-issue publics:* publics active on a small subset of issues that usually concern a fairly small part of the population (e.g. the slaughter of whales);
- *involving-issue-only publics* (also called "hot-issue publics"): publics active only on an issue that affects nearly everyone in the population and that receives extensive media coverage (e.g. gasoline shortage).

Operationalization of Segmented Categories

A key problem in segmentation is moving from a theoretical, nominal definition of a segment to a practical, operational definition.

A typical segmentation process would be initiated with a theoretical, nominal conceptualization of the target publics. The question a planner must ask is, what characterizes those I want to reach? Depending on the focus of the campaign, answers could be:

- that they smoke;
- that they don't use seat belts;
- that they are shoplifters;
- that they are women battered by their husbands.

The next step is to operationalize the conceptualization, that is, in simplest terms, answer the question, who are these people and how can they be reached? In some cases, the process of operationalization will be more complex. For a public relations practitioner, the segment "employees" is not hard to identify in terms of individuals (even though, depending on the communication goal, a further breakdown of this category into, for example, older vs. younger employees, or new employees vs. long-time employees, may well prove beneficial). But the segment "interested members of the general public" is much harder to operationalize. Planners may resort to more or less homemade assumptions that often are expressed in rather crude demographic terms. For example, "shoplifters" may be operationalized as "mostly 8-to-15-year-old boys." "People who don't use seat belts" may be operationalized as "mostly very young male drivers without own family," etc. In this stage, the communication planner becomes an imaginative and creative social and cultural scientist. To operationalize "shoplifters," the planner may need to interview a number of people, including police officers, shop owners, teachers, criminologists, etc.

The next question is, through what medium can the operationalized category be reached? The communication planner has to find media that give an optimal fit between the operationalized category and a medium's potential reach.

Channel and Message Segmentation

When a subaudience is defined as a segment, the communication planner must find channels and messages that fit it. But not all segments can be reached through matching channels, that is, through channels whose audience equals the planner's target group. In such cases, *message segmentation* may be the solution. Message segmentation is the construction of a message to fit an intended segment; the message, however, reaches a wider public than just the intended public. For example, an anti-smoking campaign may use a large circulation tabloid newspaper to reach smokers. Its message is directed exclusively to the target group since there is no purpose in reaching other readers. This newspaper may be the only way to reach the people the planner wants to communicate with. And what may be considered a waste of effort is often necessary. The perfect channel–segment fit may be difficult to find.

The process we have just described can be summarized as conceptualization (theoretical/nominal definition) → operationalization (operational definition) → assignment of media. Not all segments require elaborate operationalization; for example, "men over 50, living in Middlebury" may not be too problematic. The segment "seat belt non-users," however, poses a challenge of definition for the communication planner.

15 Effects

Of all aspects of the mass communication process, effects seem to be the most studied and discussed. There are several reasons for that. The purpose of a great deal of research has been to study how to use the media to influence people to do what they might not do otherwise.

Another sizable share of the research and debate about mass media effects has its roots in fear of what the media may cause in terms of, for example, violence, apathy, and aggression. The voluminous study of mass media effects on children is but one case in point. Also, studies into effects have served to assess the importance and consequences of media in society.

As we will see in this chapter, a systematic analysis of different types and aspects of communication effects opens up a range of possibilities for their use in communication planning.

A basic definition of "communication effect" is given by Piätilä: "a communication effect has occurred if, as a consequence of a communication process, there is/is not in the individual mind something that would not be/would be there without it" (1977: 125). Anderson and Meyer define effect as "some circumstance that would not have occurred without the presence of some other circumstance. An effect, then, requires an agent and a reactant in a relationship" (1988: 161).

A Short History of Media Effects Research

It is a striking observation that histories of communication research many times are histories of effects research, a reflection of the importance of effects in communication study. Conceptualization of effects has changed considerably through the years. Three more or less distinctive phases in this development are commonly identified:

- In the initial phase, mass communication was assumed to have very strong effects. This view dominated the period between the two World Wars. Terms such as "the magic bullet theory" or the "hypodermic needle theory" are used to describe this early conceptualization of the effects of mass communication.
- The second phase occurred when researchers started doubting these effects, finding no evidence of them. Many used expressions like "limited effects theories" to designate the main thrust of this phase, which lasted from the end of World War II until the beginning of the 1970s.
- Since then, several scholars have advocated a return to the concept of the powerful mass media.

Asp (1986) describes the assumptions underlying *the first phase*: (1) stimuli factors (media content) occupy the central role of the effects process; (2) people exposed to the media content are assumed to react in a uniform way – there is little room for individual psychological differences; (3) influence occurs instantly and directly. Since the individual is seen as isolated, contextual factors are not taken into account. Asp concludes that this conceptualization equates media effects with media content.

Today's communication researchers view this period of research as one of naïveté and simplicity. But were the scholars of that time so naïve? Chaffee and Hochheimer maintain that the accepted version of the field's history does not correspond to the published record (1985: 93). They conclude that the hypodermic needle notion is a "non-tradition" and that it exists, in the simplistic form described, only in histories of communication research.

Despite the fact that the bullet theory largely has been rejected by communication researchers, versions of this naive/mechanistic view are subscribed to today by non-scholars. Communication planners often find that their employers and other lay persons maintain the notion of mass communication as a sort of "magic bullet." This typically results in over-confidence in the media's power to influence. These people tend to become frustrated if large expected effects are not attained; it is often quite difficult to convince them that the effects process is more complex than they believe.

The second phase is characterized by increased doubt about the strength and immediacy of mass communication effects. Asp (1986) points to two bases for this doubt. First, a research group at Yale University, led by Carl I. Hovland, found a number of factors contributing to the effects process. A model typical of those drawn from the Yale group's work is what De Fleur and Ball-Rokeach (1982) call the "psychodynamic model": (a) persuasive messages (b) alter or activate latent psychological processes, (c) whereby desired overt actions are achieved. Through this reasoning, the importance of the message gets smaller – other factors, such as receiver characteristics, play a decisive role, intervening in the process between stimuli and responses.

The second basis for doubt arose from the studies of a group of Columbia University researchers, directed by Paul F. Lazarsfeld. Their studies of voting behavior found that the ability of mass communication to change people's party preferences seemed to be much lower than expected. At least two factors came into play: the public seemed to be selective in its media use, and interpersonal communication was more effective than mass communication in changing beliefs and attitudes. These findings converge in the two-step flow of information hypothesis (see Chapter 6). Lazarsfeld brought a more sociological orientation to the study of effects.

Klapper, the author of one of the most influential reviews of mass communication effects (1960), summarized the thinking of the second phase by saying that mass communication does not usually function as a necessary and sufficient cause of audience effects. Instead it functions as part of a nexus of mediating factors.

The second phase teaches communication planners at least two lessons:

- Never expect strong effects. Too many factors other than the message are pushing and pulling in different directions for the outcome to be predictable and clear-cut.
- Use a contingency approach that accounts for as many of the relevant factors as possible.

The third phase has witnessed a shift back to the notion of potent mass media. A number of reasons for scholars to abandon the notion of limited effects, at least in part, can be mentioned. The widespread use of television has caused a resurgence of the belief in powerful effects. Also, Marxist researchers contend that mass communication plays a great role in legitimating capitalist and bureaucratic societies. New types of effects have been detected, for example, cultivation and agenda-setting effects (see below). The increased scope of media effects reminds the planner that the concept of "effect" is not one-dimensional and that effects can be of many types, with some easier to produce than others.

Asp (1986) maintains that the change in perspectives on effects occurred for several reasons, including alterations in the perception of the influence process, especially with regard to which effects are important to study. In the first phase, content factors were paramount to generate effects; in the second, individual characteristics were considered more important. The third phase, according to Asp, synthesizes content and individual factors. Phase I views the media as "omnipotent," Phase II regards the media as "powerless," and Phase III sees them as "powerful."

Another trend in effects research distinguishes between "person-centered" and "situation-centered" approaches. The former focuses on the influence of a particular content on changes in knowledge, attitudes, and behaviors in individuals. The latter places additional emphasis on indirect influences and effects (Merten 1987). Person-centered effects research corresponds with Phase I described above, situation-centered with Phases II and III.

The focus on different types of effects in each of the three stages of effects research makes it difficult to compare them and judge which assessment of the degree of power of the mass media is right.

For the planner, again, it is important to remain open-minded and situationally oriented. Despite the nearly universal abandonment of the person-centered approach by communication researchers, the planner may encounter cases, admittedly rare, in which there are no influences other than the message content; the approach discarded by the researchers may continue to play a useful role for the communication planner. In addition, budget and time restrictions and "organizational plausibility" may force the planner to follow approaches that are known to be out of date – and make the best of them.

Effects and the Time Dimension

We have noted elsewhere (Chapter 3) that the time dimension is very important for understanding and planning communication. This is especially true when studying effects. In this section, we will look at the impact of time on effects.

It is obvious that the time an individual can devote to each mass media message is limited. Waldahl (1989) discusses the evasiveness of mass communication contents, a factor that diminishes the chances for obtaining effects. He points out that new information is continuously fed into the stream of content. "Old" information is followed continuously by new information that will in a short time be considered old and irrelevant.

Not taking this phenomenon into account in communication planning may be devastating. Many planners stick to a sort of wishful thinking, envisioning people taking their time to attend to a certain message, their message, memorizing it, being ready to recall it long afterward. Even if it is observed, a message in the stream of communication is followed by thousands of others and thus stands a limited chance of being retained by a not-so-motivated receiver.

Short-term versus Long-term Effects

A major shift in the focus of effects research during the second phase as compared to the third phase (see discussion above) is from short-term effects to long-term effects. Lang and Lang (1986) attribute this partly to the development of research methods. The methods of the 1940s and 1950s tended to favor the study of short-term effects. In communication planning, short- versus long-term effects is an extremely important question that is often ignored, as we shall discuss later. First, however, let us define short-term and long-term effects.

While confusion exists among both researchers and practitioners as to what these concepts mean, most definitions incorporate one or both of these variables:

● how long it takes for an effect to occur, and
● how long an effect endures.

Let us examine a typology based on these variables as shown in Figure 15.1.

Cell I shows the common notion of a long-term effect – it takes a long time to build up and lasts a long time. Examples of this type of effect are knowledge gaps, value climates, socialization, and the like.

Cell II represents a fairly dramatic process dependent on strong stimuli. This type of effect might be caused by crises or remarkable events. In

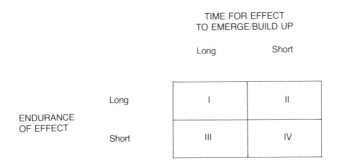

Figure 15.1 *A typology of short- and long-term effects*

health communication, Rock Hudson's known status as an AIDS victim, an event of short duration, has had long-range effects in terms of knowledge and attitudes. Another example from communication planning is the actions taken to earthquake-proof freeways following the 1989 San Francisco disaster. In planned communication, this cell represents the planner's dream: a short-lived communication effort resulting in a lasting effect.

An example from Cell III is a political campaign that has gone on for, let's say, one year. The desired effect is to have votes cast for a candidate. Even an effect with short duration (the action of voting) may take a long time to produce.

Cell IV is illustrated by the main stimulus–response experiments of the 1940s and 1950s where the aim was to assess the short-term effects of a movie or written text. Planned communication efforts often fall into this category – short interventions expected to produce effects of short duration, and, too often, accompanied by an unrealistic hope of effects of long duration.

Let us look at these four types using a communication planning example: AIDS information.

- *Long build-up, long-term effect.* The State Board of Public Health decides to educate young people about sexuality built on the values of love, responsibility, and openness. Getting that message through takes several years, but one might well expect the effect to last.
- *Short build-up, long-term effect.* The State Board of Public Health sends out an AIDS-infected person to motivate people at discotheques to practice safe sex. The strategy is that the stimulus is so strong that the effects will last a long time.
- *Long build-up, short-term effect.* This is hard to exemplify with an AIDS information case. Perhaps a campaign directed at young girls to be especially careful at their sexual debut – when they may be particularly vulnerable to contamination – would serve as a relevant example.

- *Short build-up, short-term effect.* An example of this is a three-day TV ad blitz during a gay rights convention. The hoped-for results are restricted to immediate compliance with the message, which might be as limited as, "Use a condom tonight!"

These illustrations should suffice to make apparent to the communication planner the importance of a clear definition of long- and short-term effects, to escape the fallacy that effects that need a long time to build up automatically have a long duration.

The Cumulativity of Effects

An interesting question is whether long-term effects are possible without short-term changes. The Rock Hudson example (short build-up, long-term effect) leads us to answer "yes." For many, Rock Hudson's illness changed their perceptions of AIDS immediately and for a lasting period.

Lang and Lang (1986), Asp (1986), and Schulz (1987) advance a concept that is interesting in this context, the *cumulativity* of effects. Cumulativity on one dimension leads to changes at a different level of analysis, that is, a certain number of changes at the individual level are required to obtain macro-level changes. But cumulative effects also may emerge from several different dimensions. Individuals who receive a series of messages about different aspects of their lives may step-by-step arrive at long-lasting behavioral or attitudinal changes. This is sometimes called a "strategy of small steps." For the communication planner aiming at long-term effects, the soundest strategy in many cases may be not to try to achieve a long-lasting effect all at once, but to accomplish it through a cumulative series of more limited effects.

A Model of Unplanned Long-term Effects

McQuail (1987) discusses how unplanned long-term effects of great significance to the communication planner may emerge. Much of the communication that yields effects is, in one way or another, unplanned. It is both important and problematic for the communication planner to determine what results from both planned and unplanned communication. This has, for example, been significant for AIDS campaigners, who have great difficulties sorting out what are the consequences of their own campaigns and what is the result of unplanned media coverage (Windahl 1989).

McQuail's model depicts a three-step process. The first of these steps is represented in Figure 15.2, showing how multiple media act as sources in society, distributing messages that form a more or less systematic structure. This leads to the first effect: an available stock of knowledge, values, and opinions.

The next step is the encounter between what is available and what the public selects, plus its reactions to the content chosen. This step generates the second effect: actions on and reactions to content that depend on

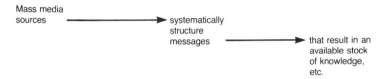

Figure 15.2 **A model of unplanned, long-term effects, Part I**
(McQuail 1987)

FIRST EFFECT	SECOND EFFECT	THIRD EFFECT
Available stock of knowledge, etc.	differential selection, and response, which lead to	differential behavior, socialization, knowledge, etc.

Figure 15.3 **A model of unplanned, long-term effects, Part II**
(McQuail 1987)

people's backgrounds and frames of reference. These behaviors lead to the final step and the third effect – creation of real long-term effects such as socialization, different definitions of reality, social control, knowledge gaps, and differential behavior. These steps are shown in Figure 15.3.

The communication planner can intervene in this process by feeding information via the media or by educating the public about the system or structure encompassing the flow of messages. Public relations people often do this, for example, by suggesting that a certain media content or medium should be interpreted in a certain way. The planner may intervene as well by directing the audience to search for certain types of information that are available "out there" or by referring positively or negatively to information. These practices point to several aspects of planning in this process of "unplanned" communication.

An interesting aspect of McQuail's model is the systematically structured messages from the media. While that may indicate the use of standard formats and language, it also may imply that there is a repertoire of stories or "lessons" that are told repeatedly. This set of stories becomes part of a common culture available to draw from. Critics of media have pointed at dominant themes that may, through the multi-step process described above, bring about long-term effects. Thomas (1986) mentions several themes that permeate the US media and help maintain societal order:

● There's room at the top.
● Anyone can reach the top.
● It's not so great at the top.

It is important to note that "effect" does not necessarily need to mean "change"; it can also result in maintenance, stability, and order. Societies must have mechanisms by which change does not occur too rapidly (Thomas 1986); the stories, tales, and myths found in the mass media serve as one of those mechanisms.

It is essential for the communication planner to have a feeling for what the lessons or stories of a society are during a given time period. Sometimes it is of value to know them in order to argue against them; sometimes they may be used as support for one's own argumentation.

Other Considerations about Time and Effects

Agenda-setting is an important effect of the media. In agenda-setting research, time has always been crucial. The following quotation about agenda-setting research considerations, taken from McCombs and Gilbert, explains several time-related factors that have an impact on effects:

> One of the most critical aspects in the concept of an agenda-setting role of mass communication is the time frame for this phenomenon. In analyzing this concept, we must examine what determines the time frame. Among the facets to be considered are: (a) the overall time frame, which is the total period of time under consideration; (b) the time lag, which is the elapsed time between the appearance of an item on the media agenda (the independent variable) and its appearance on the public agenda (the dependent variable); (c) the duration of the media agenda; (d) the duration of the public agenda measure; and (e) the optimal effect span, which is the peak association between media emphasis and public emphasis of an issue. (1986: 8)

This passage suggests several important questions for the communication planner to consider.

What is the Overall Time Frame of my Communication Effort?

It is important to determine the time span for the whole period between the first stimulus and the last point in time for expected or hoped-for effects. This analysis brings to the fore the question about which time frames you work within. The answer to this question serves as an indicator of the long-term or short-term nature of the overall time frame for the health communication agency, the PR department, or those responsible for external communications in the environmental group. A simple but useful device to arrive at the time frame consists of two time lines, one for the stimuli (the communication efforts) and the other for expected and/or desired effects. This is shown in Figure 15.4. It may be useful to draw two effects lines – one representing sought or hoped-for effects; the other, more realistic, for expected effects.

When can I Expect the Effects to Show?

Communication planners often find themselves in circumstances similar to those of communication researchers as described by Lang and Lang (1985). Because of institutional pressures to observe effects (too) soon, the scholar turns to research methods that produce quick results, such as

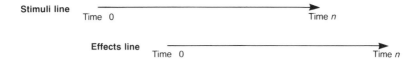

Figure 15.4 ***Determining the overall time frame of a communication effort***

laboratory experimental studies. Planners may be forced to adhere to strategies aimed at producing immediate effects, or they may start looking for effects too soon. This second tendency arises from the notion of immediacy found in the variations on the "magic bullet" metaphor that many planners and lay people carry in the back of their minds. Some types of effect take a long time to appear; trying to establish whether a communication effort is a success or not by searching for immediate effects may be unwise and unproductive (McGuire 1989).

How Long should the Communication Phase Be?
One decisive factor in the emergence of effects is the duration of the stimuli. In some situations, only a stimulus of short duration is required; in others, a message or a system of messages needs to be communicated for years to produce effects. A common mistake is to make the communication phase too short. We have pointed out that communicative support often ceases too soon, thereby preventing a process from consolidating. This is a common failing in the process of diffusion of innovation.

How Long can I Expect Effects to Last?
We have said that it may be a mistake to look for effects of communication too soon after the stimulus stage. On the other hand, as Lang and Lang (1985) point out, immediate effects often disappear quite quickly. People tend to forget, and new communications soon catch their interest. It is important that communication planners, if they want long-lasting effects, incorporate ongoing communication efforts into their strategies.

When will Effects Reach their Peak?
Most planned communication takes place in relatively open systems, where the possibility of controlling the extent and timing of effects is limited. It is difficult to anticipate the influence of other messages on the topic of a campaign. For example, AIDS campaigns take place in an environment of extensive media coverage of the disease (Windahl 1989). The strongest effects may then emerge from the mass media coverage which, in turn, has been initiated by the interest generated by the campaign.

We do have some knowledge to guide us in answering this question. Persuasion research suggests that knowledge effects usually occur faster than attitude and behavioral effects (Windahl 1975, 1981, 1989). Research about the so-called "sleeper effect" suggests that effects may occur long after message exposure because, after a while, audience members dissociate the source from the message. Thus, a low-credibility source will be forgotten, but the message will be recalled later (Devito 1986).

Direct and Indirect Effects

Most people have the notion that communication effects are direct. Even communication planners may be reluctant to conceive of or plan for indirect effects processes. Such a process may leave the planner perceiving a lack of control over what happens. This has some truth to it – the more stages in a communication process, the smaller the chance that the communication really is delivered. Nevertheless, indirect strategies that involve interpersonal communication may imply that the ultimate receivers are more willing to accept the message. And while we may assume that there is a tendency in indirect processes for the message to be distorted, the process of selection may ensure that it is more relevant for the receiver and more likely to cause effects.

An indirect effects strategy may prove more effective than a direct one. In the case of the two-step flow of information model, feeding the communication content through motivated intermediaries may prove worthwhile. In his ethnomethodological studies, Lull (1986) explains how members of a television audience use the medium to demonstrate their personal competence, using arguments from programs to support their positions. Thus, mass communication may furnish people with the "right" arguments, thereby having an indirect but nonetheless powerful effect.

Levels of Effects

Effects can occur at different levels: individual, group, or organizational, social institutional, societal, and cultural (McQuail 1987; see also Berger and Chaffee 1987). We can say a certain effect can be found at the group level. In addition, however, the individual in any of the above levels (group, social institution, etc.) is affected. This appears complicated, so let's give an example.

In an anti-drug campaign, the communication planner chooses to focus communication efforts on the school-class level. One of the following goals is set:

(a) to produce effects in as many class members as possible; or
(b) to produce effects in as many classes qua system as possible.

For the first goal, one indicator of success is how many students follow the messages' suggestions. The effects may be expressed in terms of amount of change within classes, but we are still talking about aggregates of individuals.

For the second goal, communication planners view the school class, not the students in the classes, as the entity to be changed. The planners regard the class as a social or communicative system, not as an aggregate of individuals.

The question "What happens if a pot-smoker joins the class?" in the first case elicits an answer such as, "The majority of students are now against smoking pot. The newcomer will find the majority of students hold negative attitudes toward drugs and will either turn to members of the minority, who have positive attitudes toward drugs, or quit." In the second case, the conclusion might be, "This school class as a system provides a total negative environment for the pot-smoker." The newcomer will comply with the system's rules or leave the system.

The first case exemplifies a sort of "false" group effect, the second a "true" group effect. The true group effect implies that a group norm of some kind has emerged through communication and interaction among the group members. This group norm can be seen as a synergy effect – the whole is greater than the sum of its parts.

Distinguishing between *micro* and *macro* effects is complicated as well. Asp states that

> Effects on systems or any other collective level implies theoretically that there exist effects on the individual level. To study the political effects of the mass media must, then, be a . . . "round trip" between "micro and macro." But we should add that the trip always shall start with short-term effects on the individual level. (1986: 17)

This reasoning is correct. If the individual does not change, there will be no change on a higher level. Effects on higher levels are, in this framework, cumulative. This is important for the communication planner to bear in mind. But as we saw above, we also have to be clear about what we mean by an effect on a "higher" level – are we dealing only with aggregate effects on a certain level or "true level effects"? A true level effect is an effect that has impact on the social system as an entity.

This distinction is quite important for the planner. A PR practitioner, for example, may try to motivate a company's employees by using one of two methods: he or she may reach each employee individually with persuasive messages or bring the employees and managers together to discuss a problem in order to arrive at some sort of consensus as to how to approach the issue. In the first case, we find aggregate effects; in the second case, there are organizational effects.

McLeod and Reeves note, "Societal consequences cannot be inferred solely from estimates of the number of changes. The social location (i.e. social class) must be considered in assessing system consequences" (1981:

246). In other words, the communication planner may need more information about a change than sheer numbers.

An interesting example of how the problem of social location is *not* addressed is how AIDS information effects are handled. For example, national surveys show that in Sweden, during a one-year period, 11 percent of the adult population changed its sexual behavior. This is an aggregate effect on the societal level. But nothing is known about whether the changes have occurred in the relevant risk categories (a behavioral category level) (Windahl 1989). If the changes are found within non-risk categories, they are, of course, less valuable.

Level, Time, and the Sources of Effects: A Model

A good part of this chapter is intended to demonstrate the many aspects that characterize "effects." The communication planner must be sensitive to these aspects. The following illustrates several perspectives.

In a study of political opinion formation, Asp (1986) has proposed an inventory of different effect types based on three variables: level, time frame, and source of effects.

- Level is dichotomized into "individual" or "system."
- Time frame may be short- or long-term.
- Source may be "content" or "institution" (e.g. the mass media or other communication organization).

Figure 15.5 shows the combination of these variables. The following are examples of effects from each of Figure 15.5's cells:

1 The effects on individuals in a political campaign using information leaflets. The aim is to influence the voters to behave in a certain way at a specific moment.
2 The changes in nutrition habits among individuals during a five-year health information campaign. The content is known, the time span is relatively long, and the effects are found at the individual level.
3 Reactions to a presentation of AIDS information in schools. It is not the content itself that creates the effect; it is the institution's decision to communicate about a delicate and taboo issue.
4 The effects on Third World peasants of mass-media-communicated information from the authorities. We are interested in a long-term effect created by the emergence of new sources of knowledge.
5 The effects of a series of motivational speeches on the communication climate in the workplace. Change in the communication climate is a social system effect. The problem is, however, that we do not know whether the speeches themselves or their content are causing the change.
6 The effects of TV portrayals of immigrants over a long period of time on job opportunities for that group.
7 The immediate effects on the quality of patient care of a new communication technology introduced in a hospital.

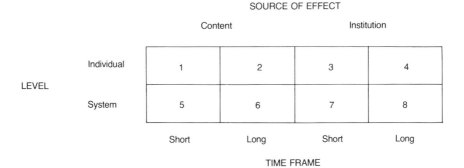

Figure 15.5 **A typology of effects (after Asp 1986)**

8 The long-term effects of an alumni-oriented university administration on curriculum reform.

Effects and Change

For many practitioners, "effect" always seems to imply change, in knowledge and beliefs, attitudes, or behaviors. This notion obscures the fact that a great deal of communication fosters and/or is planned to support and reinforce the status quo. While this function of communication has been recognized by several communication researchers for a long time, the narrow focus on change in communication planning practice often has caused the planner to overlook it.

Piätilä (1977) has addressed the question of alternative outcomes of communication. In the typology presented in Figure 15.6, Piätilä uses a certain mass communication content as a point of departure. This information conveys Opinion A about an issue. The receiver initially may be "non-A-minded," "opinionless," or "A-minded." We may use the same attributes to characterize the same individual after media exposure.

- For the initially non-A-minded, the expected effect would be *conversion*, since the content is antagonistic to held beliefs and attitudes of the individual (see also Schenk 1987).
- The Opinion A message also may *extinguish* the initially held opinion of the non-A-minded without substituting another. An individual then becomes *opinionless*. It is well known from communication theory literature that cross-pressure may lead to disinterest and lack of opinion.
- Those who are initially non-A-minded and end up non-A-minded are *"no-effect"* cases. Piätilä states, however, that the new information also may have helped to reinforce the initially held opinion. Therefore, paradoxically, the effect can be of a maintaining type.
- Those opinionless from the beginning may, after exposure, have become A-minded, experiencing an *awakening effect*.

AFTER EXPOSURE TO STIMULUS

		Non-A-minded	Opinionless	A-minded
BEFORE EXPOSURE TO STIMULUS	Non-A-minded	No effect or maintaining effect	Extinguishing effect	Conversion effect
	Opinion-less	Awakening effect	No effect or repressing effect	Awakening effect
	A-minded	No effect	No effect	Maintaining effect

Stimulus = Opinion A through mass media messages

Figure 15.6 *A directional typology of effects (Piätilä 1977)*

- Those who remain opinionless may be cases of *no effects*, but may also, because of the information, have decided to stay opinionless (*repressing effects*). The new information may have been seen as uninteresting or too complicated to process.
- Some who originally are opinionless may be interested in the issue, but may draw other conclusions from the message and become non-A-minded (*awakening effect*).
- Among those who from the beginning held an A-minded opinion, most probably will stay that way after exposure. The initial opinion is *maintained*.
- The originally A-minded who, after exposure, end up opinionless or with a non-A-minded opinion have probably been influenced from other sources, according to Piätilä; therefore, the effects are labeled *no effects*.

Piätilä's scheme may be criticized from several points of view, but it brings to the fore the fact that there are several interesting alternatives to conversion effects. It is important that the communication planner realize that the effect of communication efforts may be passivity and absence of opinion, as noted above (extinguishing effects). Also significant are repressing effects. Planners often fail to produce conversion or maintaining effects because they kill the existing interest and opinions with dull and irrelevant information that makes people define the issue as dull, complicated, and/or irrelevant.

Also, Piätilä's conceptualization reminds us that maintaining the effects, often taken for granted by planners, is relevant. It is not true that, once convinced, a person will remain convinced forever. Opinions usually have to be maintained to stay alive.

The conversion effects of mass communication – that individuals change their beliefs, attitudes, and values from positive to negative or vice versa – usually are assumed to be small. This assumption is, to some extent, based on the work of Lazarsfeld et al. (1944) in their political studies. That research group noted that mass communication seems more suited to reinforce existing beliefs and attitudes.

Another type of effects activates the receiver. For example, political campaigns increase interest in political information and communication. De Fleur and Ball-Rokeach (1982) mention as activation effects issue formation and issue resolution. Through mass communication, individuals learn about and become interested in issues that were unknown or uninteresting. Communication, according to De Fleur and Ball-Rokeach, often creates a feeling of frustration and ambiguity in the individual who is unclear as to what the media are talking about. In order to resolve the ambiguity, the individual may look for more information that ultimately may stimulate activity in relation to the issue. The same authors also point to de-activation as an effect. The receiver may react with, for example, boredom and apathy to a message. This corresponds to Piätilä's "no effects."

"Enlargement Effects"

De Fleur and Ball-Rokeach (1982) also point out that mass communication may expand people's systems of beliefs (enlargement) by conveying information about new categories of beliefs. Some decades ago, "environment" was a not-so-common category of beliefs. Today most people have an environment category of beliefs produced by the use of the media.

Enlargement means that the number of beliefs within each category increases through communication. In communication planning, it is essential not to communicate about issues not included in the receivers' belief systems. Therefore, an early step in planning a communication strategy is to make sure that the members of the audience recognize as relevant the category dealt with. This is important, for example, in a diffusion of innovations context. When AIDS was a new phenomenon, a good share of communication efforts had to be devoted to describing and defining the issue for a public that was not familiar with the category "incurable contagious diseases."

Cognitive Complexity Effects

"Cognitive complexity refers to the number and type of cognitive constructs and schemata people have available for interpreting aspects of their environment" (Reardon 1987: 80; see also Delia and Clark 1977).

DISEASE	Heart disease
RISK FACTOR	High blood pressure
CAUSE	Heredity

Figure 15.7 **Simple cognitive scheme before campaign (Pavlik 1987a: 104)**

DISEASE	Heart disease		
RISK FACTOR	High blood pressure	Smoking	Over weight
CAUSE	High sodium diet	Heredity	Diet high in cholesterol	Lack of exercise

Figure 15.8 **More complex cognitive scheme after campaign (Pavlik 1987a: 104)**

Cognitive constructs are "mental structures by which people interpret the meaning of objects, people, and events" (Reardon 1987). The individual may use few or many constructs for interpreting a certain subject (the degree of differentiation). The constructs are built on other constructs (the degree of abstraction) and may be more or less strongly interrelated (the degree of integration).

Increased cognitive complexity as a result of communication has become a focus of effects research in recent years. The schemata referred to vary in complexity and are subject to constant change through communication and other experiences. Pavlik (1987a) gives an example of how the complexity of the cognitive structure concerning the subject "heart disease" changes after exposure to a health campaign. His before and after models can be seen in Figures 15.7 and 15.8.

Pavlik concludes that communication planners should map the cognitive complexity status of an audience before addressing it. By doing so, the planner can tailor communication to diverse subgroups according to their cognitive sophistication. Grunig and Ipes (1983) maintain that, in the same way knowledge gaps exist and shape communication efforts, there are also gaps of cognitive complexity.

Reciprocal, Boomerang, Spill-over, and Third Person Effects

Lang and Lang have dealt with the nature of effects and discussed less common notions of effects. One of these is the *reciprocal effect*. They describe this as what commonly occurs when a phenomenon changes its characteristics just because it is communicated. A sports event is regarded as more significant for the competitors because it is televised. Press conferences of political leaders, since they have been televised, change from informal background briefings for journalists to high-visibility platforms for the politician. A local election receives unexpected attention because the media detect appeal and newsworthiness in one of the candidates for mayor (Lang and Lang 1986).

Communication planning should take reciprocal effects into account. The mere fact that a certain issue becomes the subject of a communication campaign may change people's perception of it, and those operating within the issue's realm may change their behaviors to fit the communication situation. For example, a company launches a campaign to reduce costs in everyday work. The employees start wondering about the state of the firm's economy, leading those responsible for the financial health of the company to act defensively, and so on. The cost-saving campaign, if not properly explained, may prove devastating. Another example is health communication directed to a large audience that portrays a certain image of doctors and nurses. Health care professionals may find these images positive since they have been publicly demonstrated in the campaign, and start acting according to them.

Related types of *boomerang effects* can be identified. One deals with people's perceptions of a communicated issue. The effect on the audience becomes the opposite of the intended one: anti-drug information in a high school leads students to try marijuana instead of discouraging use.

Another boomerang effect finds communication affecting the senders negatively. This has led the mass media in some countries to avoid explicit AIDS information, fearing negative reactions from segments of the audience. A company's public relations department may lose its credibility among employees after distributing half-truths from the management. A local soccer club may be distrusted if it describes itself as broke and needing financial support by means of a flashy, four-color leaflet.

A third type of boomerang effect may occur through repetition of exposure to messages, even if they are consistent with the audience's attitudes. Such exposure may sometimes lead to reduced commitment to these attitudes (Devito 1986; Paletz et al. 1972).

Spill-over effects emerge when people outside the intended or expected target population are affected by communication. Lang and Lang (1986) point to cases in mass communication, such as the Watergate scandal of the 1970s, when virtually everybody was aware of the issue – heavy and light media users, people directly exposed to the media message as well as those only indirectly involved, politically interested and disinterested alike. For the communication planner, signs of such effects must be interpreted carefully. They may indicate that the planner's targeting has not been accurate. But it may as well be a sign that the planner has reached potential audiences that may prove profitable. If a campaign to persuade women students to choose non-traditional careers generates a great interest among their parents, this may indicate that the planner should try to communicate with the parents as well. Spill-over effects, further, may serve to decrease information and knowledge gaps (see p. 211).

The *third-person effect* of communication was developed by Davison and proposes that media effects may be due to the actions of those "who anticipate, or think they perceive, some reaction on the part of others" (1983: 3) and *not* to the actual reactions of the message's intended audience. This hypothesis predicts that people overestimate the influence media communication will have on others; people think communications will not have their strongest impact "on 'me' or 'you,' but on 'them' – the third person" (1983: 3). In evaluations of AIDS information, for example, individuals commonly rate the effects of mass communication on sexual behavior of others as great, while saying that the information has not changed their own behavior.

A common mistake of communication planners is to overreact to others' communication, especially in the mass media, thereby interesting audience members in what the other argument is. Perloff found that "under highly involving conditions, individuals overestimate the directional influence, as well as the magnitude, of media effects on third persons" (1989: 256). His experiment showed that both pro-Israeli and pro-Palestinian partisans thought that TV news would render neutral observers more positive toward their antagonists. The effect of the news on non-partisans, that is, people with no ego-involvement, was *not* significant in terms of influencing their attitudes vis-à-vis Israel or the PLO, nor did the news coverage influence opinions about Jews or Arabs.

This third person effect/involvement hypothesis suggests that planners, on the one hand, should not be blinded by their own position, and, on the other, should try to exploit this effect by enhancing it. Thus, as part of an anti-smoking campaign, a planner might publish the results of a public opinion survey demonstrating the effects the campaign is already having on the population (see also Glynn and Ostman 1988).

The Agenda-Setting Effect of Communication

Our tracing of the development of effects research shows that in recent years several mass communication scholars have suggested that the media have strong effects after all. It is only, they say, that research has looked for the wrong types of effects. Among the effects used to prove that mass media effects do exist is agenda-setting.

A study by McCombs and Shaw in 1972 is viewed as the germinal study in agenda-setting research, although the idea of the media determining the public's agenda was not totally new when that study was done (see, for example, Trenaman and McQuail 1961; see also Schenk 1987; Schönbach 1981; Weiss 1982).

The agenda-setting function of the media is described as a tendency of the media to affect what people will think about, what they perceive as

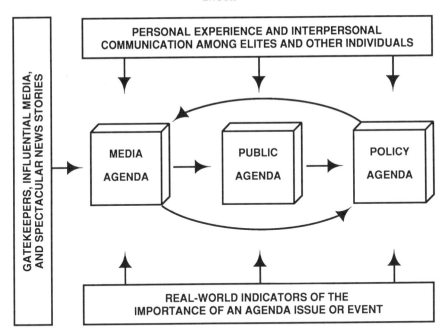

Figure 15.9 *The main components of the agenda-setting process*
(Rogers and Dearing 1988)

important. Earlier research was preoccupied with the effects of what to think, for example, in terms of attitudes. Rogers and Dearing define agenda-setting as "a process through which the mass media communicate the relative importance of various issues and effects to the public" (1988: 556).

An agenda is "a list of issues and events that are viewed at a point in time as ranked in a hierarchy of importance" (Rogers and Dearing 1988: 565). "Events" are defined as discrete happenings that are limited by space and time; "issues" are a series of related events (Shaw 1977).

McQuail (1987) points out that the agenda-setting process deals with not one, but three different agendas. One agenda resides with political or other interest groups. Another is the media agenda, which is affected and structured by news values and perceived audience preferences. The third agenda is the public agenda, supposedly affected by that of the media. Rogers and Dearing (1988) have constructed a diagrammatic model of the relationship between these three agendas, as seen in Figure 15.9.

The media agenda supposedly is affected by a number of factors, including events reported in the media that become "issues." Reports about one event may trigger reports about other, similar events, leading to identification as an important question in the media. Knowing the media agenda enables communication planners to set communication strategies, so, for example, a planner for an environmental organization makes use of a debate on nuclear power in the media. As we have noted before (Chapter 8), public relations practitioners work with "issue management." The same environmental organization and PR practitioners may want to *act on* the media agenda, rather than limiting themselves to *reacting to* it. This type of activity is represented by the arrow from "policy agenda" to the "media agenda" in Figure 15.9.

This proactivity is problematic for many in the media who regard communication planners as intruders trying to get "free rides." This issue has been the subject of a great deal of discussion within the field of public relations (Grunig and Hunt 1984). In such a context, the question becomes, who sets the media agenda (Pavlik 1987a)? Research indicates that the media agenda often mirrors the agendas of organizations that have established a strong public relations function. Daniel Boorstin's (1961) notion of the "pseudo-event," conceived more than two decades ago, still highlights today's situation. Boorstin wrote that power to make a reportable event is the power to make experience. Organizations create events that are reported by the media as news (Pavlik 1987a). A great deal of public relations research has been devoted to finding out how, to what extent, and under what circumstances organizational agendas can influence media agendas (Baerns 1987; Turk 1985; Reichmann 1988; Stocking 1985; Newsom 1983; Weaver and Elliott 1985).

To a greater extent, however, research has dealt with the relationship between the media agenda and the public agenda. Simply stated, the agenda-setting hypothesis maintains that the more importance the media give to an issue or event (the media agenda), the more importance the public will attach to it (the public agenda). Several contingency factors have been discussed, such as the time factor. How long does it take for the media agenda to influence the public agenda? What is the time lag that produces the highest correlation between the two agendas? Also, the nature of the event or issue is important. Some issues, such as dramatic ones that affect the everyday lives of audience members, are recognized by the audience as important rather quickly. Others that develop very slowly climb onto the agenda at a similarly slow pace.

Slow-paced developments, though, may get on the agenda by special efforts on the part of the media. Rogers and Dearing (1988) describe the Ethiopian drought and famine that burst on Western agendas mainly through a TV film report from a refugee camp in 1985 and the famous Band-Aid concert.

Another contingency factor is which public you're referring to. Seldom does an entire audience put an issue on the agenda. In research a significant variable is the degree of *need for orientation*. A certain subaudience may have a great need for orientation about a specific issue and easily puts it on its agenda. For another there is no such need and, thus, little chance for the issue to end up on its agenda.

An interesting question is how different agendas tend to influence each other. Figure 15.9 suggests that the media agenda influences both the public and policy agendas, that the public agenda influences the policy agenda, and that the policy agenda affects the media agenda. It seems plausible, however, that the media–public agenda relationship is reciprocal, too.

Studies about communication campaigns commonly point out that the first step for the communication planner may be to get the issue in question on the agenda. Once that is done, it becomes much easier to put the message across since the audience is aware of the issue and its importance.

In this context, the related concept of *priming* is of interest. Priming refers to enhancing the effects of the media by offering the audience a prior context – a context that will be used to interpret subsequent communication (Fiske and Taylor 1984; Iyengar et al. 1982). The media serve to provide the audience with standards and frames of reference. Agenda-setting refers mainly to the importance of an issue; priming tells us whether something is good or bad, whether it is communicated effectively, etc. The media have primed the audience about what a news program looks like, what a credible person looks like, etc. Communication planners as a rule must be careful not to violate the results of priming. Such violations may sometimes result in undesired effects. For example, if a doctor in a health campaign interview behaves in an unexpected way, the audience's interest may be piqued, but at the same time credibility may suffer.

Knowledge/Information Gap Theories

A communication effect that has created considerable interest among both researchers and practitioners is described in the knowledge (or information) gap hypothesis, introduced by Tichenor, Donohue, and Olien. Its originators define the concept as follows: "As the infusion of mass media information into a social system increases, segments of the population with higher socioeconomic status tend to acquire this information at a faster rate than the lower status segments, so that the gap in knowledge between these segments tends to increase rather than decrease" (Tichenor et al. 1970: 159–60).

The problem is not unique. There are several such variations on the have/have-not theme. Thunberg et al. (1982) describe it as a problem of general subsidies. When all are offered about the same amount of information, those who have the best initial knowledge (and other resources) will gain the most. Mass communication, then, functions like many other social institutions – it reinforces or increases existing inequities. The process is illustrated in Figure 15.10.

Three variables are involved: degree of knowledge or information about an issue, an event, etc.; the amount of resources the individual or the group possesses; and time. We see that the knowledge/information curves diverge. Those with a better start will gain knowledge faster than those with fewer resources. Note, however, that the gap is increasing in relative

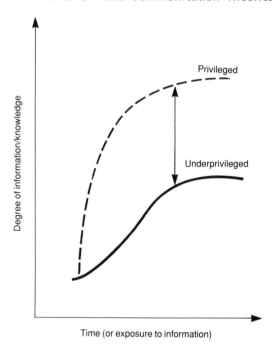

Figure 15.10   *A non-closing knowledge gap (Thunberg et al. 1982)*

terms, that is, even the underprivileged group acquires some information or knowledge.

We will see below that this basic model can be made far more complex. Several other variables can be added to the three originals. The model presents the information gap phenomenon as a process. We may also assume that, at a given point in time, there is a "higher correlation between acquisition of knowledge and education for topics highly publicized in the media than for topics less highly publicized" (Tichenor et al. 1970: 163). One of the reasons for these gaps is the pattern of media use. For example, higher education and socioeconomic status individuals tend to use more information-rich media, such as print media.

The problem described here is extremely important to information planning. A principal dilemma of planning is how to reach those lacking resources to receive, understand, and act. Among the first to discuss this theme in mass communication and public opinion research were Hyman and Sheatsley (1947), who coined the term "chronic know-nothings" to denote those who do not let themselves be informed. For many planners, increasing the knowledge gap between haves and have-nots is seen as a failure. For others, the hypothesis that additional information creates further inequality instead of reducing differences in social status and education presents a paradox that is hard to accept.

It is important to note that research results on knowledge gaps are inconclusive. Research points to several variables that must be taken into account when studying knowledge gaps as a communication effect. The causal variables of education or socioeconomic status should be supplemented with variables such as degree of motivation (Ettema et al. 1983), degree of interest (Gaziano 1983), access to information, and organizational involvement and activity (Nowak 1977). Also, the perceived utility of the actual type of knowledge and information may be decisive. Nowak (1977) concludes that gaps in knowledge and information about everyday issues seem to be smaller. Donohue et al. (1975) emphasize that when conflict characterizes the reporting of an issue, the gaps tend to narrow.

Through the years, several criticisms of the knowledge gap concept have arisen. One criticism is based on the nature of knowledge and information that produce gaps. Nowak (1977) questions whether it is meaningful to worry about knowledge gaps *per se* instead of defining what is *relevant and useful* knowledge for a certain group or category of people. While much of the concern about knowledge gaps may be seen as well-meant, middle-class uneasiness about the circumstances of the underprivileged, the concept is built on middle-class perceptions of what is good and useful. Nowak maintains: "The information gap implies that a more egalitarian society should result if low-resource groups were more able to handle the instruments for influence which are used by the high-resource groups. Maybe more fruitful is to facilitate for low-resource groups the development of their own instruments" (1977: 246). Similar ideas characterize the spiral of interaction model presented in Figure 7.3 (p. 80).

Several scholars have discussed "ceiling effects" that diminish or prevent gaps. Dervin (1981) identifies two types of ceiling. In a saturation process, the resource-rich stop acquiring information once they have all they want from a message. This gives the resource-poor the chance to catch up. The other type is interventionist – the communication planner creates information strategies that increase motivation and potential among the resource-poor to expose themselves to the actual information. We shall discuss some of these strategies below.

Dervin (1981) criticizes the knowledge gap model for being inadequately receiver-oriented. Based on a notion of absolute or objective information as a standard, it ignores the fact that people create their own meanings and their own information. Gaps in knowledge are relevant to researchers, but may not necessarily be so to audience members. They tend to look for information they need in their actual circumstances of time and space and do not consider issues held as important by researchers and other observers to be relevant. Dervin identifies another gap that she finds more interesting and pertinent, namely the gap "seen by receivers between the pictures in their heads and the sense they require to design movements for their lives" (1981: 105).

This, then, is a key criticism of the knowledge gap hypothesis: people seek information they perceive as important; knowledge gaps as discussed in research are but observers' constructs. A response to this criticism is that it is still problematic that some people, characterized by scarce resources, obtain less of the information that is valuable in terms of economics, career, health, etc. Therefore, for many communication planners, the notion that mass communicated information entering a social system may cause greater inequalities in some respects deserves attention. In the health area, for example, a society may consider it a norm that everyone should have the same opportunities to stay healthy. If some strata can make more use of health information than others because they have more initial resources, the norm is frustrated. This relativistic type of criticism should not lead to passivity, but rather to the formulation of new information strategies. Dervin's discussion provides a point of departure for structuring such strategies.

Diffusion of innovations theory, too, suggests that adoption of an innovation usually results in the widening of the socioeconomic gap between earlier and later adopters (Rogers 1983). When faced with such gaps, as well as the accompanying knowledge and information gaps, what can the communication planner do? Rogers (1983) suggests strategies for narrowing gaps, which fall into three categories:

1 When the resourceful have greater access to information:
   (a) Make the information appropriate and interesting to the lower socioeconomic status (SES) subaudience, even if it becomes less interesting or even redundant to the higher SES subaudience in the process.
   (b) Use communication channels that specifically target the under-privileged. In Third World countries, this means choosing traditional, accessible channels rather than channels that reach only the elites.
   (c) Form small groups of the resource-poor to discuss the innovations or other information matters.
   (d) Concentrate the change agents' efforts on the late majority and laggards instead of on innovators and early adopters (see Chapter 6). The former usually have a lower SES than do the latter.
2 When the privileged have greater access to information from peers than do the underprivileged:
   (a) Identify the opinion leaders of the lower SES groups and feed them information.
   (b) Use homophilic change agents in the lower SES groups.
3 When the privileged have more slack resources available for complying with the message to innovate than do the underprivileged:
   (a) Recommend innovations and behaviors that are appropriate to the lower SES groups.
   (b) Let the lower SES groups take part in the planning and execution of the programs.

The planner needs to develop a notion of why knowledge gaps exist. Severin (1988) cites studies (Ettema and Kline 1977; Lovrich and Pierce

1984) that advance and test two explanations. One line of thinking explains knowledge gaps in terms of transmissional factors (level of basic communication skills as a result of socioeconomic status); the other uses situation-specific factors (motivation to acquire information).

A Theory of Cultivation Effects

It has been argued that mass communication research does not capture the most important effects – there are some that may be difficult to demonstrate but that, nevertheless, are significant. During the last two decades, a group of researchers at the Annenberg School of Communication at the University of Pennsylvania has suggested that the cultivation effects of mass media are ubiquitous in modern society. The Annenberg group argues (see, for example, Gerbner et al. 1980) that in the United States, television transmits a set of stable messages that reflect mainstream US culture. Traditional effects research, they say, "misses the main point of television: the absorption of divergent currents into a stable and common mainstream" (Gerbner et al. 1980: 20).

According to cultivation theory, television in its storytelling function tends to deliver message systems that present the same lessons over and over again. Television creates and reflects opinions, images, and beliefs that are influenced by the institutional needs of the surrounding society. It also motivates people to give continued attention to its contents, which are likely to confirm the beliefs, images, etc. presented previously. Gerbner et al. maintain:

> The point is that cultivation is not conceived as a unidirectional process but rather more like a gravitational process. . . . Each group [of viewers] may strain in a different direction, but all groups are affected by the same central current. Cultivation is thus part of a continual, dynamic, ongoing process of interaction among messages and contexts. (1980: 24)

The effects of the cultivation process are manifold. One major effect that has been the subject of much study is the image of the surrounding world. Gerbner et al. have found that heavy TV users tend to view the world as more insecure and mean than do those who watch less television. US television shows us living in a violent world; heavy users of television tend, or so goes the argument, to regard the real world in the same way. (The results of the Annenberg group have been contested on various grounds, e.g. for not adequately controlling other variables. See, for example, Hirsch 1980.)

For communication planning, cultivation theory reminds us that communication takes place in "symbolic universes," which the mass media probably shape to a certain extent. For example, a campaign to employ immigrant workers benefits by considering findings about the degree of trust held by heavy and light TV viewers. The question, "Can people be trusted?" more likely would be answered, "You can't be too careful" by heavy viewers than by light viewers (Severin 1988).

Communication as Communication Effects

In communication planning, the goal often is to generate other communication. The health communicator realizes that chances for obtaining success are greater if a campaign causes people to discuss cancer among themselves. That behavior might lead to greater interest in campaign messages. Health projects building on social learning theory (Bandura 1977) emphasize communication among people as a means to influence. Communication within a public may increase creativity (Rogers and Rogers 1976), simplify assimilation processes (Jablin 1982), and create greater understanding and foster activity (Thunberg et al. 1979). What, then, does mass communication research say about communication as an effect of communication?

Let's first consider a case where communication results in noncommunication. German opinion scholar Noelle-Neumann (1973) has suggested with her spiral of silence model that dominant mass communication may impede communication between people instead of encouraging it. The model is constructed on the following assumptions:

1 People talk about their opinions with others if they feel that their opinions are shared. If they perceive that they are alone in holding a certain opinion, they will not express it openly.
2 An individual may use the mass media as a standard to find out how prevalent a certain opinion is. If the opinion is not expressed in the media, the individual infers that the opinion is not commonly accepted.
3 All media tend to express the same opinions in a more or less monopolistic way, leaving people with an often false picture of the opinion climate in society.
4 Therefore, many people with a certain opinion do not advocate it for fear of isolation. The more people remain quiet, the less prevalent the actual opinion seems to be, causing the build-up of a spiral of silence. People with deviant opinions will be increasingly less willing to speak out, and the media's opinion increasingly will be perceived as dominant and self-evident.

The spiral of silence works on several levels. In many social systems, communication planners are instruments used to feed the spiral. In an organization, it often occurs that a certain opinion is presented by management and communication planners as dominant. Those holding counteropinions come to believe they are "wrong" and do not express their views. This may eventually prove damaging to the organization because management and planners may convince themselves that the official opinion really is as dominant and accepted as they present it. As a rule, a communication planner should strive to form a realistic picture of the publics being dealt with and not try to suppress the existence of differing opinions.

Post-exposure Communication

Uses and gratifications research (see Chapter 14) frequently mentions obtaining topics for interpersonal communications as a motive for using mass communications. For example, Levy and Windahl (1985) emphasize the post-exposure activity of discussing what has been presented in the media. Lull states:

> Audience members talk about television in dozens of ways at home. They often use television examples to explain feelings or to clarify situations. By referring to television's stories and characters, for instance, it is possible to disambiguate confusion. . . . Television becomes the ultimate standard by which private situations are compared and evaluated. (1986: 609)

Television content, then, is communicable, which perhaps explains why its messages are so pervasive. We can expect spill-over effects from such a dominant medium. Viewers and non-viewers alike are familiar with much of its content. Again, the communication planner should recognize the importance of making messages topical so they will be transferred via mechanical media to interpersonal communication.

A Contingency Approach to Effects

We have found several reasons in this chapter not to be very optimistic about producing communication effects. Adding to the foregoing discussion, we again offer our contingency perspective. A communication planner has to carefully review the conditions at hand, some of which we will examine in this section. We begin with a series of contingency questions derived from a discussion about the knowledge–behavior gap in information campaigns by Hornik (1989a). He discusses reasons why behavioral effects appear in some cases but not in others. His examples originate in planned communication work in the Third World and demonstrate a difference between two ways of looking at communication problems. The first, common in industrialized countries, is to look for analysis variables within the individual/psychological realm. The other, commonly used in development communication in the Third World, is systemic/structural. This latter type of contingency is too often overlooked in the effects literature.

The five types of contingency derived from Hornik's approach are (a) structural characteristics of communities, (b) structural characteristics of individuals, (c) community social influences, (d) learned characteristics of individuals, and (e) enduring characteristics of individuals.

Structural Characteristics of Communities
This contingency is exemplified by the difference it makes in a health communication campaign in a Third World village if the village has a health center or school, in other words, institutions that carry out complementary development activities. Another example would be the inability to rely on disseminating certain AIDS information through interpersonal communication networks in small communities. The structural characteristics of such communities may demand that homosexuals conceal their identities and not form clubs or organizations that would serve as information channels.

Structural Characteristics of Individuals
Farm size in a campaign about innovations in farming offers a Third World example of this type. Owners of small farms may have no interest in, or opportunity to, transform knowledge into practice. The actual innovations may not be appropriate for small farms at all. A study of the national Swedish AIDS campaign directed to young people showed that working-class youth had not noticed or reacted to the campaign. The messages used in the campaign appealed to the middle class, in both text and pictures (Jarlbro et al. 1988).

Community Social Influences
In discussing the different levels of communication effects, we noted that individual change is necessary for obtaining group or system change. It is also important to note that influence goes the other way, too. Hornik maintains that "a social view of the process of behavior change says that behavior does not belong only to individuals but also belongs to social groupings" (1989b: 125). Many individuals do not change their behavior before others in the community, group, system, etc. have done it. Hornik refers to a study on the use of anti-diarrhea medicine in Ecuador. Women who found themselves in networks where a large proportion of the members used the medicine (a supportive environment) were much more likely to use the medicine than were others.

Learned Characteristics of Individuals
Here, prior knowledge, experience with the actual channel, and learned skills, etc. are predictors of effects. These types of condition were discussed above in connection with the knowledge gap effects. In Third World countries it is important to assess the audience members' degree of literacy and ability to comprehend campaign messages.

Enduring Characteristics of Individuals
Early reasoning about effects often included variables dealing with personality traits, e.g. could people be described as fatalistic, creative, entrepreneurial, susceptible, etc.? Eventually scholars became less prone to use these traits as independent variables. This does not mean they are

not possible contingency factors, however. The trait approach has been used to predict the receiver's responsiveness to a message, that is, if he or she can be persuaded. The traits employed would be, for example, self-esteem, dogmatism, cognitive differentiation, and self-awareness (Hewes and Planalp 1987).

What we would add to Hornik's scheme is *temporary characteristics of an individual*. For example, it matters whether an individual is temporarily motivated to behave in a certain way. It is also important if this person is lifted from fatalism by communication. A person who has even temporarily become ill from smoking may be easily persuaded to quit.

Effects literature offers several other contingency factors, such as media dependency, the value climate, and the audience's perception of reality, as well as the effects of socialization.

De Fleur and Ball-Rokeach (1982) maintain in their model of *media dependency* that an important condition for the emergence of effects is the degree of dependency on certain communication media. A channel that people feel dependent on for obtaining important information has a greater chance to bring about effects than a channel perceived as just one among many providing information that is insignificant. Also, the degree of dependency on certain media increases as the environment is characterized by change, conflict, and instability. Hence, the more unique and important functions a medium performs, the greater the possibility that its content can produce effects. The communication planner who provides information perceived as valuable at the right point in time via the right medium has the greatest chance of affecting the individual to whom the information is addressed.

Several scholars have emphasized the importance of the *value climate* in society. To be able to use values that are widely accepted in the actual social or cultural system in persuasive communication is a great advantage.

An often forgotten contingency factor is *reality* as perceived by the audience. Nordenstreng (1974) has written about what he calls "the principle of the pressure of facts". Individuals can observe phenomena in the environment; those observations may be contrary to information they are receiving. An auto factory worker who is informed by management that the company has to save money because of hard economic times will distrust this information if managers are observed getting large pay raises, driving expensive cars, etc. A problem for AIDS communication planners in some countries after 1987 was that the number of new HIV cases did not increase more than it did. That led many people to conclude that the risk of infection with AIDS was minimal, and they continued or reverted to high-risk behavior.

A typology of *effects of socialization* by Rosengren (1985) suggests two other contingency factors: (a) the individual's resources, and (b) the control exercised by the socializing agent. In a traditional socialization

CONTROL EXERCISED BY
SOCIALIZATION AGENT

		High	Low
	Rich	Consensual socialization	Pluralistic socialization
INDIVIDUAL'S RESOURCES			
	Poor	Protective socialization	Laissez-faire socialization

Figure 15.11   *Four types of socialization (Rosengren 1985)*

situation, Rosengren suggests the following typology (illustrated in Figure 15.11):

● *Consensual socialization* is typical of strivers, overachievers, careerists, and early adopters.
● *Pluralistic socialization* fosters rebels, bohemians, and innovators.
● *Protective socialization* results in loners, petty officials, and late adopters.
● *Laissez-faire socialization* brings about losers, drop-outs, and laggards.

With this socialization perspective, the outcome (or effect) is a personality type. If we change the socialization setting from a traditional one, such as the family, to, for example, an organization, we may speculate about the outcomes.

In a highly controlled organizational setting, we might expect communication to be used differently by people with high resources and people with low resources. The former (corresponding to a consensual socialization situation) may use their talents and the communication to get ahead, to find new solutions, etc., within the frame of the organization. The latter (corresponding to a protective socialization) may use communication to protect themselves in the present situation and to justify their behavior as being correct.

The low-resource people in a low-control organization (laissez-faire socialization) may act upon communication with confusion and disinterest, whereas their high-resource counterparts (pluralistic socialization) may use it in a more creative, although unpredictable way.

Rosengren's model may serve as a reminder for the planner of the danger of expecting uniform effects. Different people tend to use communication differently under different conditions which, in turn, leads to different effects.

Glossary

This glossary does not aim to give scientific definitions but simply to provide a handy reference explaining key terms as they are used in this book.

agenda-setting A process by which the mass media communicate the relative importance of various issues to the public. The more importance the media give to an issue or event, the more importance the public will attach to it. "The media don't tell people what to think, but they tell them what to think *about*" sums up the thrust of this theory.

change agent An individual who influences clients' innovation decisions in a direction deemed desirable by a change agency (Rogers 1983: 312). A change agent serves as a liaison between the client (the person or group that will change) and the change agency (the person or group promoting the change), allowing information to flow back and forth between the parties.

channel The physical means of carrying a signal (O'Sullivan et al. 1983). Often used interchangeably with "medium," channel has little to do with the meaning of messages.

commonsense theory Theory based in everyday experience. It is on this type of knowledge that the majority of the lay population relies for its understanding of complex social and scientific phenomena. Often, commonsense theories are tested and validated by scientific method, adding them to the body of social scientific theories.

communication The exchange and sharing of information, attitudes, ideas, or emotions. While early definitions of communication stressed a linear movement from a source to a receiver, current conceptualizations of communication stress mutuality and shared perceptions. Instead of "sending" or "receiving," people participate in the communication process.

communication network A group of interconnected individuals or organizations linked by patterned communication flows (Rogers 1986). Networks are a pervasive aspect of communication because virtually everyone in society belongs to one or more such networks.

communication planning A systematic and creative activity in which information, attitudes, emotions, and ideas are managed, to be exchanged and transmitted via specific messages through specific channels. Objectives and goals are established for communication efforts; efforts to shape and disseminate messages in order to accomplish those goals are the elements of communication planning.

communicationism The misguided tendency to conceive of and treat something as a communication problem when it is not.

consequences The results of the act of using media content which have less to do with the content itself than with the actual act. For example, the mere activity of watching television may affect other activities of the viewer.

convergence model of communication A model that describes the process of arriving at mutual understanding. Parties to communication initially share information; then, bringing their own backgrounds, personalities, etc., into the process, they arrive at a mutually acceptable understanding of the information. Whether that understanding is correct or not is immaterial; the point of the model is the process by which mutual understanding is achieved.

diffusion of innovations A research area that seeks to explain how innovations are introduced into society and whether and how people adopt or reject them. Rogers' (1987) theory of the diffusion of innovations is perhaps the most developed of such theories. Like other diffusion of innovation theories, it involves an interplay between mass and interpersonal communication.

effects The outcomes of communication. These may be planned, unplanned, long-term, and short-term. The goal of communication planning is to control communication in order to produce desired effects.

empathy A psychological term describing the capacity to understand how other people perceive and interpret reality, including communication, without giving up one's own view of this reality.

feedback A reaction on the part of the receiver to a sender's communication fed back to the sender. It may be spontaneous, when receivers communicate their reactions to a sender, or inferred, when a sender deduces from other indicators what receivers' reactions to a message were. Feedback is useful to the communication planner in refining messages to make them more effective.

feedforward Information about receivers and their possible reactions that is gathered by a sender prior to initiating communication with them. It is an essential element in planning effective communication.

format The way the media appear, their essential form, which includes the "rules and logic that transform and mold information (content) into the recognizable shape and form of a specific medium" (Altheide and Snow 1988).

general systems theory Based on synergism, this theory looks at wholes, the interdependent parts that make up the wholes, the relationships among the parts, and the relationships between the wholes and their environments. Communication under this theory is transactional, characterized by mutual causality, or interdependency, among the parts of a system.

information "A difference in matter-energy which affects uncertainty in a situation where a choice exists among a set of alternatives" (Rogers and Kincaid 1981: 48).

information overload The result of so many messages cluttering an individual's environment that he or she cannot adequately attend to all of them.

infusion An elicited response about a felt need. It is information sought by the communication planner that will enable the formulation of a comprehensive background upon which to design a communication strategy. The concept of infusion is closely related to feedforward.

knowledge gap model A theory that holds that the mere introduction of more information into a social system will not equalize segments of society. Additional information will cause a greater difference between the higher socioeconomic status segments, who acquire the information at a higher rate due to higher levels of income, education, etc., and lower socioeconomic status segments.

mediation theory See "mediatization."

mediatization A theory that emphasizes the effects of media logic and format on the communication process, calling for the study of how something is communicated as well as what is communicated. Communication planners can use mediatization to study how best to use available formats through manipulating them and being aware of how formats influence content.

medium An intermediate agency that enables communication to take place (O'Sullivan et al. 1983). While it is often used synonymously with "mass media," human beings may also play the role of a medium.

message That which is transmitted through the communication process. It exists at three levels: a set of words or images expressed somewhere, somehow; the meaning of communication content as perceived or intended by the individual expressing it; and the meaning attributed to it by those receiving it.

normative theory Theory that, based on values and ideological positions, dictates how communication should be formed and function.

priming Enhancing the effects of a message by offering the audience a prior context that will be used to interpret subsequent communication.

receiver group A group for which a certain message is intended. (See "target population.") A receiver group may be different from a target population, depending on the communication strategy being used.

social marketing The use of marketing principles and techniques to advance a social cause, idea, or behavior (Kotler 1982). Other names for the approach are social cause marketing, idea marketing, and public issue marketing.

social perspective taking The ability to understand the options available to others. (See "empathy.")

social scientific theory Theory derived from work done according to scientific rules and methods and characterized by reliance on abstract concepts.

synergism The combining of elements, resulting in increased effectiveness due to their very combination. "The whole is greater than the sum of its parts."

target population Those individuals whose behavior, attitudes, or knowledge a communicator wants to influence, directly or indirectly. (See "receiver group.") Depending on the communication strategy being used, a target population may not be the same as the receiver group in a given communication setting.

uses and gratifications A theory whose basic assumption is that audience members more or less actively seek the content that seems to be the most gratifying. Uses are driven by needs and motives; gratifications are assessed based on expectancy and evaluation.

working theory Combining practical and normative theories, working theory instructs the practitioner on how to do communication planning, based on formalized communication theory.

Bibliography

Abelson, R. (1976) "Script Processing in Attitude Formation and Decision-Making" in J. Carroll and J. Payne (eds.), *Cognition and Social Behavior*. Hillsdale: Lawrence Erlbaum Assoc.

Abrahamsson, K. (1972) *Samhällskommunikation*. Lund: Studentlitteratur.

Abrahamsson, U.B. (1987) "Det Populära Dramat" in U. Carlsson (ed.), *Forskning om Populärkultur*. Göteborg: NORDICOM.

Ajzen, I. and Fishbein, M. (1980) *Understanding Attitudes and Predicting Social Behavior*. Englewood Cliffs: Prentice Hall.

Albrecht, T.L. and Adelman, M.B. et al. (1987) *Communicating Social Support*. Newbury Park: Sage.

Altheide, D.L. (1974) *Creating Reality*. Newbury Park: Sage.

Altheide, D.L. (1985) *Media Power*. Newbury Park: Sage.

Altheide, D.L. and Snow, R.P. (1979) *Media Logic*. Newbury Park: Sage.

Altheide, D.L. and Snow, R.P. (1988) "Toward a Theory of Mediation" in J.A. Anderson (ed.), *Communication Yearbook*, Vol. 11. Newbury Park: Sage.

Anderson, J.A. and Meyer, T.P. (1988) *Mediated Communication: A Social Action Perspective*. Newbury Park: Sage.

Arbeitsgemeinschaft für Kommunikationsforschung (ed.) (1980) *Mediennutzung/Medienwirkungen*. Berlin: Spiess.

Asp, K. (1986) *Mäktiga Massmedier*. Stockholm: Akademilitteratur.

Atkin, C.K. (1979) "Research Evidence on Mass Mediated Health Communication Campaigns" in D. Nimmo (ed.), *Communication Yearbook*, Vol. 3. New Brunswick: Transaction.

Atkin, C.K. (1981) "Mass Media Information Campaign Effectiveness" in R.E. Rice and W.J. Paisley (eds.), *Public Information Campaigns*. Newbury Park: Sage.

Autischer, A. and Maier-Rabler, U. (1987) *Kommunikationsatlas Salzburg Stadt*. Salzburg: Institut für Publizistik.

Baacke, D. (1980) *Kommunikation und Kompetenz. Grundlegung einer Didaktik der Kommunikation und ihrer Medien*, 3rd ed. Munich: Juventa.

Baacke, D. (1982) "Partizipation und Massenmedien" in H.J. Kagelmann and G. Wenninger (eds.), *Medienpsychologie. Ein Handbuch in Schlüsselbegriffen*. Munich: Urban & Schwarzenberg.

Babrow, A.S. (1989) "An Expectancy-Value Analysis of the Student Soap Opera Audience," *Communication Research* 16: 155–78.

Baerns, B. (1985) *Öffentlichkeitsarbeit oder Journalismus? Zum Einfluss im Mediensystem*. Cologne: Verlag für Wissenschaft und Politik.

Baerns, B. (1987) "Journalism versus Public Relations: Determination of Latent Interaction through Analysis of Patterns of Influence" in D.L. Paletz (ed.), *Political Communication Research*. Norwood: Ablex.

Ball-Rokeach, S.J. and Cantor, M.G. (eds.) (1986) *Media, Audience, and Social Structure*. Newbury Park: Sage.

Bandura, A. (1977) *Social Learning Theory*. Englewood Cliffs: Prentice Hall.

Bandura, A. (1986) *Social Foundations of Thought and Action*. Englewood Cliffs: Prentice Hall.

Bang, J. (1988) "Perception Research and Studies of Culture," *Nordicom Review* 1: 14–20.

Barnes, J.A. (1954) "Class and Committees in the Norwegian Island Parish," *Human Relations* 7: 39–58.

Barnlund, D.C. (1968) *Interpersonal Communication*. New York: Houghton Mifflin.

Barthenheier, G. (1982) "Zur Notwendigkeit von Öffentlichkeitsarbeit" in G. Haedrich et al.

(eds.), *Öffentlichkeitsarbeit. Dialog zwischen Institutionen und Gesellschaft.* Berlin: De Gruyter.

Baskin, O.W. and Aranoff, C.E. (1988) *Public Relations: The Profession and the Practice*, 2nd ed. Dubuque: Brown.

Bauer, R. (1964) "The Obstinate Audience: The Influence Process from the Point of Social Communication," *American Psychologist* 19: 319–28.

Beck, U. (1986) *Risikogesellschaft. Auf dem Weg in eine andere Moderne.* Frankfurt: Suhrkamp.

Beniger, J.R. (1988) "Information and Communication: The New Convergence," *Communication Research* 15: 198–218.

Bentele, G. (1984) "Kommunikationswissenschaft, Kommunikation und Massenkommunikation" in Freie Universität Berlin (ed.), *Modellversuch Journalisten-Weiterbildung.* Munich: Ölschläger.

Berelson, B. (1949) "What 'Missing' the Newspaper Means" in P.F. Lazarsfeld and F.N. Stanton (eds.), *Communication Research 1948–1949.* New York: Harper & Row.

Berger, C.R. and Chaffee, S.H. (eds.) (1987) *Handbook of Communication Science.* Newbury Park: Sage.

Berger, C.R. and Chaffee, S.H. (1988) "On Bridging the Communication Gap," *Human Communication Research* 15: 311–18.

Berger, P. and Luckman, T. (1967) *The Social Construction of Reality.* New York: Doubleday.

Bernstein, B. (1973) *Class, Codes, and Control.* London: Routledge and Kegan Paul.

Biocca, F.A. (1988) "Opposing Conceptions of the Audience: The Active and Passive Hemispheres of Mass Communication Theory" in J.A. Anderson (ed.), *Communication Yearbook*, Vol. 11. Newbury Park: Sage.

Blackburn, H.B., Luepker, R.V., Kline, F.G., Bracht, N. and Carlaw, R. (1984) "The Minnesota Heart Health Program" in J. Matarazzo, C. Weiss, J.A. Herd, N. Miller and S. Weiss (eds.), *Settings for Health Promotion in Behavioral Health: A Handbook for Health Enhancement and Disease Prevention.* New York: John Wiley.

Blumler, J.G. and Katz, E. (eds.) (1974) *The Uses of Mass Communications: Current Perspectives on Uses and Gratifications Research.* Newbury Park: Sage.

Blyskol, J. and Blyskol, M. (1985) *How the Public Relations Industry Writes the News.* New York: Morrow.

Bonfadelli, H. (1987a) "Öffentliche Informationskampagnen: Was weiss die Medienwissenschaft?" *À jour . . . Magazine für Werbekommunikation* 27: 10–11.

Bonfadelli, H. (1987b) "Die Wissenskluftforschung" in M. Schenk (ed.), *Medienwirkungsforschung.* Tübingen: Mohr.

Bonfadelli, H. (1988) "Gesundheitskampagnen in den Massenmedien: Kommunikationstheorie für Kommunikationspraxis," *Sozial- und Präventivmedizin* 33: 86–92.

Boorstin, D.J. (1961) *The Image, or What Happened to the American Dream.* New York: Atheneum.

Bosshart, L. (1976) "Untersuchungen zur Verstehbarkeit von Radio- und Fernsehsendungen," *Rundfunk und Fernsehen* 24: 197–209.

Bostian, L.R. (1970) "The Two-Step Flow Theory: Cross-Cultural Implications," *Journalism Quarterly* 47: 109–17.

Boyd-Barrett, O. (1977) "Media Imperialism: Toward an International Framework for the Analysis of Media Systems" in J. Curran et al. (eds.), *Mass Communication and Society.* London: Arnold.

Bransford, J. and McCarrell, N. (1974) "A Sketch of a Cognitive Approach to Comprehension" in W.B. Weimar and D.S. Palermo (eds.), *Cognition and the Symbolic Processes.* Hillsdale: Lawrence Erlbaum Assoc.

Brecht, B. (1983) "Radio as a Means of Communication: A Talk on the Function of Radio" in A. Mattelart and S. Siegelaub (eds.), *Communication and Class Struggle: Liberation, Socialism.* New York: International General.

Breed, W. (1955) "Social Control in the Newsroom: A Functional Analysis," *Social Forces* 33: 326–55.

Broom, G.M. (1977) "Coorientational Measurement of Public Issues," *Public Relations Review* 3: 110–28.

Broom, G.M. and Smith, G.D. (1979) "Testing the Practitioner's Impact on Clients," *Public Relations Review* 5: 47–59.

Bryant, N.H., Stender, W., Frist, W. and Somers, A.R. (1976) "VD Hot Line: An Evaluation," *Public Health Reports* 91: 231–345.

Burkart, R. (1983) *Kommunikationswissenschaftliche Grundlagen und Problemfelder: Umrisse einer interdisziplinären Sozialwissenschaft.* Vienna: Böhlau.

Burkart, R. (1985) "Kommunikation 2000: Perspektive und Probleme: Über einige Schwerpunkte zukünftiger Kommunikationsforschung" in *Österreichisches Jahrbuch für Kommunikationswissenschaft 1985.* Vienna: Böhlau.

Burns, T. (1977) *The BBC: Public Institution and Private World.* London: Macmillan.

Burt, R.S. (1982) *Toward a Structural Theory of Action: Network Models of Stratification, Perception and Action.* New York: Academic Press.

Capella, J.N. (1987) "Interpersonal Communications: Definitions and Fundamental Questions" in C.R. Berger and S.H. Chaffee (eds.), *Handbook of Communication Science.* Newbury Park: Sage.

Caplan, N. and Nelson, S.D. (1973) "On Being Useful: The Nature and Consequences of Psychological Research on Social Problems," *American Sociologist* 28: 199–211.

Carey, J.W. (1969) "The Communication Revolution and the Professional Communicator" in P. Halmos (ed.), *The Sociology of Mass Media Communicators.* Kiel: University of Kiel.

Carey, J.W. (1975) "A Cultural Approach to Communication," *Communication* 2: 1–22.

Carlsen, J. (1984) *Det gode Fjernsyn.* Tönder: Dansklaerer foreningen.

Chaffee, S.H. (1981) "Mass Media in Political Campaigns: An Expanding Role" in R.E. Rice and W.J. Paisley (eds.), *Public Communication Campaigns.* Newbury Park: Sage.

Chaffee, S.H. (1986) "Mass Media and Interpersonal Channels: Competitive, Convergent, or Complementary?" in G. Gumpert and R. Cathcart (eds.), *Inter Media: Interpersonal Communication in a Media World,* 3rd ed. New York: Oxford University Press.

Chaffee, S.H. (1987) "Annual Report on 1985–86 Division Activities, Standing Committee on Research," *AEJMC News,* Nov. 15, pp. 6–8.

Chaffee, S.H. and Berger, C.R. (1988) "Levels of Analysis: An Introduction" in C.R. Berger and S.H. Chaffee (eds.), *Handbook of Communication Science.* Newbury Park: Sage.

Chaffee, S.H. and Hochheimer, J.L. (1985) "The Beginnings of Political Communication Research in the United States: Origins of the 'Limited Effects Model'" in M. Gurevitch and M.R. Levy (eds.), *Mass Communication Review Yearbook,* Vol. 5. Newbury Park: Sage.

Chaffee, S.H. and Wilson, D.G. (1977) "Media Rich, Media Poor: Two Studies of Diversity in Agenda-setting," *Journalism Quarterly* 54: 466–76.

Clarke, P.B. and Kline, F.G. (1974) "Mass Media Effects Reconsidered: Some New Strategies for Communication Research," *Communication Research* 1: 224–70.

Cooley, C.H. (1902) *Human Nature and the Social Order.* New York: Scribners.

Cooper, E. and Jahoda, M. (1947) "The Evasion of Propaganda," *Journal of Psychology* 23: 15–25.

Corner, J. (1979) "'Mass' in Communication Research," *Journal of Communication* 29: 26–32.

Crane, D. (1972) *Invisible Colleges: Diffusion of Knowledge in Scientific Communities.* Chicago: University of Chicago Press.

Dance, F.E. (1970) "The Concept of Communication," *Journal of Communication* 20: 201–10.

Daniels, T.D. and Spiker, B.K. (1987) *Perspectives on Organizational Communication.* Dubuque, Iowa: William C. Brown.

Davison, W.P. (1983) "The Third-Person Effect in Communication," *Public Opinion Quarterly* 47: 1–15.

De Fleur, M.L. (1962) "The Emergence and Functioning of Opinion Leadership: Some Conditions of Informal Influence Transmission" in N. Washbourne (ed.), *Decisions, Values, and Groups*. New York: Macmillan.

De Fleur, M.L. (1970) *Theories of Mass Communication*. New York: David McKay.

De Fleur, M.L. and Ball-Rokeach, S. (1982) *Theories of Mass Communication*, 4th ed. New York: Longman.

Deibel, T. and Roberts, W. (1976) *Culture and Information: Two Foreign Policy Functions*. Newbury Park: Sage.

Deisenberg, A.M. (1986) *Die Schweigerspirale – Die Rezeption des Modells im In- und Ausland*. Munich: Minerva.

Delia, J.G. (1987) "Communication Research: A History" in C.R. Berger and S.H. Chaffee (eds.), *Handbook of Communication Science*. Newbury Park: Sage.

Delia, J.G. and Clark, R.A. (1977) "Cognitive Complexity, Social Perception, and Listener-adopted Communication in Six-, Eight-, Ten-, and Twelve-year-old Boys," *Communication Monographs* 44: 326–45.

Dervin, B. (1981) "Mass Communicating: Changing Conceptions of the Audience" in R.E. Rice and W.J. Paisley (eds.), *Public Communication Campaigns*. Newbury Park: Sage.

Dervin, B. (1984) "A Theoretical Perspective and Research Approach for Generating Research Helpful to Communication Practice," *Public Relations Research and Education* 1: 30–45.

Dervin, B. (1989) "Audience as Listener and Learner, Teacher and Confidant: The Sense-making Approach" in R.E. Rice and C. Atkin (eds.), *Public Communication Campaigns*, 2nd ed. Newbury Park: Sage.

Deutsch, K.W. (1966) *Nationalism and Social Communication: An Inquiry into the Foundations of Nationality*. Cambridge, MA: MIT Press.

Deutsche Forschungsgemeinschaft (ed.) (1986) *Medienwirkungsforschung in der Bundesrepublik Deutschland*. Weinheim: VCH Verlagsgesellschaft.

Devito, J.A. (1986) *The Communication Handbook: A Dictionary*. Cambridge: Harper & Row.

Dewey, J. (1927) *The Public and Its Problems*. Chicago: Swallow.

Dominick, J.R. (1977) *The Dynamics of Mass Communication*, 2nd ed. New York: Random House.

Donohue, G.A., Olien, C. and Tichenor, P. (1975) "Mass Media and the Knowledge Gap: A Hypothesis Reconsidered," *Communication Research* 2: 3–23.

Duncan, W.J. (1978) *Essentials of Management*, 2nd ed. Hinsdale: Dryden.

Durell, J. and Bukoski, W. (1984) "Preventing Substance Abuse: The State of the Art," *Public Health Reports* 99: 23–31.

Dutton, W.H., Rogers, E.M. and Jun, S. (1987) "Diffusion and Social Impacts of Personal Computers," *Communication Research* 14: 219–50.

Ehlers, R. (1983) "Themenstrukturierung durch Massenmedien: Zum Stand der empirischen Agenda-Setting-Forschung," *Publizistik* 28: 167–86.

Ekecranz, J. (1978) *Makten och Informationen*. Lund: Studentlitteratur.

Elliott, P. (1972) *The Making of a Television Series – A Case Study in the Production of Culture*. London: Constable.

Enzensberger, H.M. (1985) "Baukasten zu einer Theorie der Medien" in D. Prokop (ed.), *Medienforschung*, Vol. 2. Frankfurt: Fischer.

Ettema, J.S. and Kline, F.G. (1977) "Deficits, Differences, and Ceilings: Contingent Conditions for Understanding the Knowledge Gap," *Communication Research* 4: 179–202.

Ettema, J.S., Brown, J.W. and Luepker, R.V. (1983) "Knowledge Gap Effects in a Health Information Campaign," *Public Opinion Quarterly* 47: 516–52.

Ettema, J.S. and Whitney, D.C. (1987) "Professional Mass Communicators" in C.R. Berger and S.H. Chaffee (eds.), *Handbook of Communication Science*. Newbury Park: Sage.

Etzioni, A. (ed.) (1969) *The Semi-professions and Their Organizations*. New York: Free Press.

Eurich, C. (1980) *Kommunikative Partizipation und partizipative Kommunikationsforschung*. Frankfurt: Fischer.

Evan, W.M. (ed.) (1976) *Interorganizational Relations*. New York: Penguin.

Evans, W.O. and Evans, M.E. (1970) "A Neutral Language for the Drug Scene" in J.R. Wittenborn et al. (eds.), *Communication and Drug Abuse*. Springfield: C.C. Thomas.

Fabris, H.H. (1979) "Der Mittelschicht-Bonus: Zum sozialen Herkunftsprivileg von Berufskommunikatoren," *Österreichische Zeitschrift für Soziologie* 4(1): 47–54.

Fabris, H.H. (1985) "Der Mythos der Massenkommunikation oder das Dilemma der Kommunikationswissenschaft" in *Österreichisches Jahrbuch für Kommunikationswissenschaft 1985*. Vienna: Böhlau.

Falcione, R.L., Sussman, L. and Herden, R.P. (1987) "Communication Climate in Organizations" in F.M. Jablin et al. (eds.), *Handbook of Organizational Communication*. Newbury Park: Sage.

Farace, R.V., Monge, P.R. and Russell, H.M. (1977) *Communicating and Organizing*. New York: Random House.

Farquhar, J.W., Maccoby, N. and Solomon, D. (1984) "Community Applications of Behavioral Medicine" in W.D. Gentry (ed.), *Handbook of Behavioral Medicine*. New York: Guilford Press.

Farquhar, J.W., Flora, J.A., Good, L.T. and Fortmann, S.P. (1985) *Integrated Comprehensive Health Promotions Programs*. Stanford: Stanford Center for Research in Disease Prevention.

Festinger, L.A. (1957) *A Theory of Cognitive Dissonance*. New York: Row Peterson.

Fett, J. (1974) "Gatekeepers in Agricultural Information Dissemination" in R.H. Crawford and W.B. Ward (eds.), *Communication Strategies for Rural Development: Proceedings of the Cornell-CIAT International Symposium*. Ithaca, NY: New York State College of Agriculture and Life Sciences.

Findahl, O. and Höijer, B. (1975) *Att Uppfatta Verkligheten genom Massmedia*. Stockholm: Sveriges Radio.

Findahl, O. and Höijer, B. (1984) *Begriplighetsanalys*. Lund: Studentlitteratur.

Fine, S.H. (1981) *The Marketing of Ideas and Social Issues*. New York: Praeger.

Fishbein, M. and Ajzen, I. (1975) *Belief, Attitude, Intention and Behavior*. Reading: Addison-Wesley.

Fiske, J. (1982) *Introduction to Communication Studies*. London: Methuen.

Fiske, S.T. and Taylor, S.E. (1984) *Social Cognition*. Reading: Addison-Wesley.

Flora, J.A., Maccoby, N. and Farquhar, J.W. (1989) "Communication Campaigns to Prevent Cardiovascular Disease: The Stanford Community Studies" in R.E. Rice and C. Atkin (eds.), *Public Communication Campaigns*, 2nd ed. Newbury Park: Sage.

Forsythe, S.A. (1950) "An Exploratory Study of Letters to the Editor," *Public Opinion Quarterly* 14: 143–4.

Frank, R.E., Massey, W.F. and Wind, Y. (1972) *Market Segmentation*. Englewood Cliffs: Prentice Hall.

Früh, W. (1980) *Lesen, Verstehen, Urteilen: Untersuchungen über den Zusammenhang von Textgestaltung*. Freiburg: Verlag Karl Alber.

Fry, D.L. and Fry, V.H. (1986) "A Semiotic Model for the Study of Mass Communication" in M. McLaughlin (ed.), *Mass Communication Yearbook*, Vol. 9. Newbury Park: Sage.

Galtung, J. and Ruge, M.H. (1965) "The Structure of Foreign News," *Journal of Peace Research* 2: 64–90.

Gandy, O. (1982) *Beyond Agenda-setting: Information, Subsidies and Public Policy*. Norwood, Ablex.

Gans, H.J. (1974) *Popular Culture and High Culture: An Analysis and Evaluation of Taste*. New York: Basic Books.

Gans, H.J. (1979) *Deciding What's News*. New York: Vantage Books.

Gaziano, C. (1983) "The 'Knowledge Gap': An Analytical Review of Media Effects," *Communication Research* 10: 447–86.

Gerbner, G. (1956) "Toward a General Model of Communication," *Audio-Visual Communication Review* 4: 171–99.

Gerbner, G. and Gross, L. (1976) "Living with Television: The Violence Profile," *Journal of Communication* 26: 173–99.

Gerbner, G., Gross, L., Morgan, M. and Signorielli, N. (1980) "The Mainstreaming of America: Violence Profile No. 11," *Journal of Communication* 30: 10–27.

Gerbner, G., Gross, L., Morgan, M. and Signorielli, N. (1984) "The Political Correlates of TV Viewing," *Public Opinion Quarterly* 48: 283–300.

Gieber, W. (1960) "How the Gate-keepers View Civil Liberty News," *Journalism Quarterly* 37: 199–205.

Gieber, W. and Johnson, W. (1961) "The City Hall Beat: A Study of Reporter and Source Roles," *Journalism Quarterly* 38: 289–97.

Gitlin, T. (1978) "Media Sociology: The Dominant Paradigm," *Theory and Society* 6: 205–53.

Glick, W.H. (1985) "Conceptualizing and Measuring Organizational and Psychological Climate: Pitfalls in Multilevel Research," *Academy of Management Review* 10: 601–16.

Glynn, C.J. and Ostman, R.E. (1988) "Public Opinion about Public Opinion," *Journalism Quarterly* 65: 299–306.

Goffman, E. (1959) *The Presentation of Self in Everyday Life*. New York: Doubleday.

Goldhaber, G.M. (1986) *Organizational Communication*, 4th ed. Dubuque: W.C. Brown.

Goldhaber, G.M. and Barnett, G.A. (eds.) (1988) *Handbook of Organizational Communication*. Norwood: Ablex.

Goodhardt, G., Ehrenberg, A.S.C. and Collins, M. (1975) *The Television Audience: Patterns of Viewing*. Aldershot: Saxon House.

Gouldner, A.W. (1957) "Cosmopolitans and Locals: Toward an Analysis of Latent Social Roles," *Administrative Science Quarterly* 2: 281–306.

Graber, D. (1976) *Verbal Behavior and Politics*. Urbana: University of Illinois Press.

Granovetter, M.S. (1973) "The Strength of the Weak Ties," *American Journal of Sociology* 73: 1361–80.

Greenberg, B.S. (1974) "Gratifications of Television Viewing and Their Correlates for British Children" in J.G. Blumler and E. Katz (eds.), *The Uses of Mass Communications*. Newbury Park: Sage.

Greenberg, M.G. and Frank, R.E. (1983) "Leisure Lifestyles: Segmentation by Interests, Needs, Demographics, and TV Viewing," *American Behavioral Scientist* 26: 493–508.

Grossenbacher, R. (1986) *Die Medienmacher: Eine empirische Untersuchung zur Beziehung zwischen Public Relations und Medien in der Schweiz*. Solothurn: Vogt-Schild.

Gruder, C.L. et al. (1978) "Empirical Tests of the Absolute Sleeper Effect Predicted from the Discounting Cue Hypothesis," *Journal of Personality and Social Psychology* 35: 1061–74.

Grunig, J.E. (1984) "Organizations, Environments, and Models of Public Relations," *Public Relations Research and Education* 1: 6–29.

Grunig, J.E. (1985) "A Structural Reconceptualization of the Organizational Communication Audit." Paper presented to the International Communication Association, Honolulu.

Grunig, J.E. (1987a) "When Active Publics Become Activists: Extending a Situational Theory of Publics." Paper presented to the International Communication Association, Montreal.

Grunig, J.E. (1987b) "Research in the Strategic Management of Public Relations," *International Public Relations Review* 11(2): 28–32.

Grunig, J.E. and Grunig, L.A. (eds.) (1989) *Public Relations Research Annual*, Vol. 1. Hillsdale: Lawrence Erlbaum Assoc.

Grunig, J.E. and Hunt, T.T. (1984) *Managing Public Relations*. New York: Holt, Rinehart and Winston.

Grunig, J.E. and Ipes, D.A. (1983) "The Anatomy of a Campaign Against Drunk Driving," *Public Relations Review* 9: 36–52.

Gudykunst, W.B. (1985) "Intercultural Communication: Current Status and Proposed Directions" in B. Dervin and M.J. Voigt (eds.), *Progress in Communication Sciences*, Vol. 6. Norwood: Ablex.

Gudykunst, W.B. (1987) "Cross-Cultural Comparisons" in C.R. Berger and S.H. Chaffee (eds.), *Handbook of Communication Science*. Newbury Park: Sage.

Gudykunst, W.B. and Kim, Y.Y. (1984) *Communication with Strangers*. Reading: Addison-Wesley.

Gudykunst, W.B., Ting-Toomey, S. with Chua, E.H. (1988) *Culture and Interpersonal Communication*. Newbury Park: Sage.

Gumpert, G. (1988) "Linguistic Character and a Theory of Mediation" in J.A. Anderson (ed.), *Mass Communication Review Yearbook*, Vol. 11. Newbury Park: Sage.

Gunter, B. (1988) "The Perspective Audience" in J.A. Anderson (ed.), *Mass Communication Review Yearbook*, Vol. 11. Newbury Park: Sage.

Habermas, J. (1981–82) *Theorie des kommunikativen Handelns*, Vols. 1 and 2. Frankfurt: Suhrkamp.

Habermas, J. (1984) *Vorstudien und Ergänzungen zur Theorie des kommunikativen Handelns*. Frankfurt: Suhrkamp.

Hadenius, S. and Weibull, L. (1973) *Press, Radio och TV*. Stockholm: Bonniers.

Hage, J. and Hull, F. (1981) "A Typology of Environmental Niches based on Knowledge Technology and Scale: The Implications for Innovation and Productivity," Working Paper 1, University of Maryland, Center for the Study of Innovation, Entrepreneurship and Organization Strategy.

Haley, R.I. (1985) *Developing Effective Communication Strategy: A Benefit Segmentation Approach*. New York: J. Wiley.

Hall, E.T. (1966) *The Hidden Dimension*. New York: Doubleday.

Hall, S. (1973) "Coding and Encoding in the Television Discourse" in S. Hall et al. (eds.), *Culture, Media, Language*. London: Hutchinson.

Hall, S. (1980) "Encoding/Decoding" in S. Hall et al. (eds.), *Culture, Media, Language: Working Papers in Cultural Studies, 1972–1979*. London: Hutchinson.

Hall, S., Hobson, D., Lowe, A. and Willis, P. (eds.) (1980) *Culture, Media, Language: Working Papers in Cultural Studies, 1972–1979*. London: Hutchinson.

Hallqvist, J. et al. (1983) *Nordkarelenprojektet*. Stockholm: Stockholms läns landsting.

Hamilton, C. and Parker, C. (1987) *Communicating for Results*, 2nd ed. Belmont: Wadsworth.

Harlow, R.G. (1976) "Building a Public Relations Definition," *Public Relations Review* 2: 34–42.

Haslett, B. (1987) *Communication: Strategic Action in Context*. Hillsdale: Lawrence Erlbaum Assoc.

Hawkins, R.P. (1987) "Researching Hard-to-Reach Populations: Interactive Computer Programs as Public Information Campaigns for Adolescents," *Journal of Communication* 37(2): 8–28.

Hawkins, R.P., Wieman, J.M. and Pingree, S. (eds.) (1988) *Advancing Communication Science: Merging Mass and Interpersonal Processes*. Newbury Park: Sage.

Heath, R.L. and Nelson, R.A. (1986) *Issue Management: Corporate Public Policymaking in an Information Society*. Newbury Park: Sage.

Heath, R.L. and Associates (1988) *Strategic Issues Management: How Organizations Influence and Respond to Public Interests and Policies*. San Francisco: Jossey Bass.

Heirich, M. (1964) "The Use of Time in the Study of Social Change," *American Sociological Review* 29: 386–97.

Hemanus, P. (1976) "Objectivity in News Transmission," *Journal of Communication* 26: 102–7.

Herzog, H. (1944) "What Do We Really Know About Daytime Serial Listeners?" in P.F. Lazarsfeld and F.N. Stanton (eds.), *Radio Research 1941*. New York: Duell, Sloan & Pearce.

Hewes, D.E. and Planalp, S. (1987) "The Individual's Place in Communication Science" in C.R. Berger and S.H. Chaffee (eds.), *Handbook of Communication Science*. Newbury Park: Sage.

Hirsch, P.M. (1977) "Occupational, Organizational, and Institutional Models in Mass Media

Research: Toward an Integrated Framework" in P.M. Hirsch et al. (eds.), *Strategies for Communication Research.* Newbury Park: Sage.

Hirsch, P.M. (1980) "The 'Scary World' of the Nonviewer and Other Anomalies: A Reanalysis of Gerbner et al.'s Findings on Cultivation Analysis," *Communication Research* 7: 403–56.

Höijer, G. and Findahl, O. (1984) *Nyheter, Förståelse och Minne.* Lund: Studentlitteratur.

Honneth, A. and Joas, H. (eds.) (1986) *Kommunikatives Handeln. Beiträge zu Jürgen Habermas' Theorie des kommunikativen Handelns.* Frankfurt: Suhrkamp.

Hornik, R.C. (1988) *Development Communication: Information, Agriculture, and Nutrition in the Third World.* New York: Longman.

Hornik, R.C. (1989a) "Channel Effectiveness in Development Communication Programs" in R.E. Rice and C. Atkin (eds.), *Public Communication Campaigns*, 2nd ed. Newbury Park: Sage.

Hornik, R.C. (1989b) "The Knowledge–Behavior Gap in Public Information Campaigns: A Development Communication View" in C.T. Salmon (ed.), *Information Campaigns.* Newbury Park: Sage.

Hovland, C.I., Lumsdain, A. and Sheffield, F. (1949) *Experiments on Mass Communication.* Princeton: Princeton University Press.

Hyman, H.H. and Sheatsley, P.B. (1947) "Some Reasons Why Information Campaigns Fail," *Public Opinion Quarterly* 11: 412–23.

International Public Relations Association (1982) "A Model for Public Relations Education for Professional Practice." Gold paper No. 4. Geneva: IPRA.

Iyengar, S., Peters, M.D. and Kinder, D.R. (1982) "Experimental Demonstrations of the 'Not-so-minimal' Consequences of Television News Programs," *American Political Science Review* 76: 848–58.

Jablin, F.M. (1982) "Organizational Communication: An Assimilation Approach" in M.E. Roloff and C.R. Berger (eds.), *Social Cognition and Communication.* Newbury Park: Sage.

Jablin, F.M., Putnam, L.L., Roberts, K.H. and Porter, L.W. (eds.) (1987) *Handbook of Organizational Communication.* Newbury Park: Sage.

Janowitz, M. (1952) *The Community Press in an Urban Setting.* Glencoe: Free Press.

Jarlbro, G. (1987) *Ungdomar och AIDS.* Stockholm: AIDS-Delegationen.

Jarlbro, G., Jönsson, A. and Windahl, S. (1988) "HIV och AIDS i Svensk Dagspress." Lund: mimeo.

Jarren, O. (1984) *Kommunale Kommunikation.* Munich: Minerva.

Jensen, K.B. (1988) "Answering the Question: What Is Reception Analysis?" *Nordicom Review* 1: 3–5.

Kagelman, H.J. and Wenninger, G. (eds.) (1982) *Medienpsychologie: Ein Handbuch in Schlüsselbegriffen.* Munich: Urban Schwarzenberg.

Karpf, A. (1988) *Doctoring the Media: The Reporting of Health and Medicine.* London: Routledge.

Katz, D. and Kahn, R.L. (1978) *The Social Psychology of Organizations*, 2nd ed. New York: Wiley & Sons.

Katz, E. (1957) "The Two-Step Flow of Communication: An Up-to-date Report on an Hypothesis," *Public Opinion Quarterly* 21: 61–78.

Katz, E. (1987) "Communication Research Since Lazarsfeld," *Public Opinion Quarterly* 51: S25–S45.

Katz, E. and Lazarsfeld, P.F. (1955) *Personal Influence.* Glencoe: Free Press.

Katz, E., Blumler, J.G. and Gurevitch, M. (1974) "Utilization of Mass Communication by the Individual" in J.G. Blumler and E. Katz (eds.), *The Uses of Mass Communications: Current Perspectives on Uses and Gratifications Research.* Newbury Park: Sage.

Kearl, B.E. (1976) "Communication for Agricultural Development" in W. Schramm and D. Lerner (eds.), *Communication and Change: The Last Ten Years and the Next.* Honolulu: The University Press of Hawaii.

Kepplinger, H.M. and Vohl, I. (1976) "Professionalisierung des Journalismus? Theoretische Probleme und empirische Befunde," *Rundfunk und Fernsehen* 24: 309–43.

Kim, Y.S. (1985) "Opinion Leadership in a Preventive Health Campaign." Unpublished doctoral dissertation. Palo Alto: Stanford University.

Kincaid, D.L. (1979) *The Convergence Model of Communication*. Honolulu: East–West Communication Institute.

Kingdon, J.W. (1970) "Opinion Leaders in the Electorate," *Public Opinion Quarterly* 34: 256–61.

Klapper, J.T. (1960) *The Effects of Mass Communication*. Glencoe, IL: Free Press.

Kline, F.G. (1977) "Time in Communication Research" in P.M. Hirsch et al. (eds.), *Strategies for Communication Research*. Newbury Park: Sage.

Klinzing, D. and Klinzing, D. (1985) *Communication for Allied Health Professionals*. Dubuque: Brown.

Kotler, P. (1972) "A Generic Concept of Marketing," *Journal of Marketing* 36: 46–54.

Kotler, P. (1982) *Marketing for Non-Profit Organizations*, 2nd ed. Englewood Cliffs: Prentice Hall.

Kotler, P. (1986) *Principles of Marketing*, 3rd ed. Englewood Cliffs: Prentice Hall.

Kotler, P. and Zaltman, G. (1971) "Social Marketing: An Approach to Planned Social Change," *Journal of Marketing* 35: 3–12.

Kreps, G.L. (1989) "Setting the Agenda for Health Communication Research and Development: Scholarship that Can Make a Difference," *Health Communication* 1: 11–15.

Kreutz, H. (1971) "Einfluss von Massenmedien, persönlicher Kontakt und formelle Organisation: Kritik und Weiterführung der These 'Two-step Flow of Communication'" in F. Ronneberger, *Sozialisation durch Massenkommunikation*. Stuttgart: Enke.

Kroeber-Riel, W. (1984) *Konsumentenverhalten*, 3rd ed. Munich: Vahlen.

Kroeber-Riel, W. (1986) "Wirkung von Werbungs- und Aufklärungskampagnen (Konsumentenforschung)" in Deutsche Forschungsgemeinschaft (ed.), *Medienwirkungforschung in der Bundesrepublik Deutschland*. Weinheim: VCH Verlagsgesellschaft.

Krugman, H. (1965) "The Impact of Television Advertising: Learning Without Involvement," *Public Opinion Quarterly* 29: 349–56.

Kuhn, T.S. (1970) *The Structure of Scientific Revolutions*. Chicago: University of Chicago Press.

Kurth, T. (1981) "Local Campaigns and Approaches by the Forest Community" in R.E. Rice and W.J. Paisley (eds.), *Public Communication Campaigns*. Newbury Park: Sage.

Lang, G.E. and Lang, K. (1986) "Some Observations on the Long-range Effects of Television" in S. Ball-Rokeach and M.G. Cantor (eds.), *Media, Audience, and Social Structure*. Newbury Park: Sage.

Lang, K. and Lang, G.E. (1985) "Method as Master, or Mastery over Method" in M. Gurevitch and M.R. Levy (eds.), *Mass Communication Review Yearbook*, Vol. 5. Newbury Park: Sage.

Langenbucher, W.R. (1974/75) "Kommunikation als Beruf: Ansätze und Konsequenzen kommunikationswissenschaftlicher Berufsforschung," *Publizistik*, 19/20: 256–77.

Lasswell, H.D. (1948) "The Structure and Function of Communication in Society" in L. Bryson (ed.), *The Communication of Ideas*. New York: Harper.

Lazarsfeld, P.F. and Merton, R.K. (1948) "Mass Communication, Popular Taste, and Organized Social Action" in L. Bryson (ed.), *The Communication of Ideas*. New York: Harper.

Lazarsfeld, P.F., Berelson, B. and Gaudet, H. (1944) *The People's Choice*. New York: Duell, Sloan and Pearce.

Levy, M. and Windahl, S. (1985) "The Concept of Audience Activity" in K.E. Rosengren, L.A. Werner and P. Palmgreen (eds.), *Media Gratifications Research: Current Perspectives*. Newbury Park: Sage.

Lewin, K. (1947) "Channels of Group Life," *Human Relations* 1: 143–53.

Lin, N. and Zaltman, G. (1973) "Dimensions of Innovations" in G. Zaltman (ed.), *Processes and Phenomena of Social Change*. New York: J. Wiley.

Lindlof, T.R. (1988) "Media Audiences as Interpretative Communities" in J.A. Anderson (ed.), *Mass Communication Review Yearbook*, Vol. 11. Newbury Park: Sage.

Locketz, L. (1976) "Health Education in Rural Surinam: Use of Videotape in a National Campaign Against Schistosomiasis," *Bulletin of the Panamerican Health Organization* 10: 219–26.

Long, L.W. and Hazelton, V. (1987) "Public Relations: A Theoretical and Practical Response," *Public Relations Review* 13: 3–13.

Lovrich, N.P. and Pierce, J.C. (1984) "'Knowledge Gap' Phenomena: Effects of Situation-specific and Transsituational Factors," *Communication Research* 11: 415–34.

Lull, J. (1986) "Ideology, Television, and Interpersonal Communications" in G. Gumpert and R. Cathcart (eds.), *Inter Media: Interpersonal Communication in a Media World*, 3rd ed. New York: Oxford University Press.

Lumsdaine, A.A. and Janis, I.L. (1953) "Resistance to Propaganda Produced by One-sided and Two-sided Communication," *Public Opinion Quarterly* 17: 311–18.

Maccoby, N. and Solomon, D.S. (1981) "Heart Disease Prevention: Community Studies" in R.E. Rice and W.J. Paisley (eds.), *Public Communication Campaigns*. Newbury Park: Sage.

Mahle, W.A. (ed.) (1986) *Langfristige Medienwirkungen*. Berlin: Spiess.

Maletzke, G. (1963) *Psychologie der Massenkommunikation*. Hamburg: Hans Bredow Institut.

Maletzke, G. (1976) *Ziele und Wirkungen der Massenkommunikation*. Hamburg: Hans Bredow Institut.

Maletzke, G. (1981) *Medienwirkungsforschung: Grundlagen, Möglichkeiten, Grenzen*. Tübingen: Niemeyer.

Maletzke, G. (1988) *Massenkommunikationstheorien*. Tübingen: Niemeyer.

Malone, G.D. (1988) *Political Advocacy and Cultivating Community: Organizing the Nation's Diplomacy*. Lanham, MD: University Press of America.

Manoff, R.K. (1985) *Social Marketing: New Imperative for Public Health*. New York: Praeger.

McAlister, A. (1981) "Antismoking Campaigns: Progress in Developing Effective Communications" in R.E. Rice and W.J. Paisley (eds.), *Public Communication Campaigns*. Newbury Park: Sage.

McAlister, A. (1987) "Social Learning Theory and Preventive Behavior" in N.D. Weinstein (ed.), *Taking Care, Understanding and Encouraging Self-protective Behavior*. Cambridge: Cambridge University Press.

McAlister, A., Puska, P., Salonen, J., Tuomilehto, J. and Koskela, K. (1982) "Theory and Action for Health Promotion: Illustrations from the North Karelia Project," *American Journal of Public Health* 72: 43–50.

McCarthy, E.J. (1975) *Basic Marketing: A Managerial Approach*. Homewood: Irwin.

McCombs, M.E. (1981) "Setting the Agenda for Agenda-setting Research" in G.C. Wilhoit and H. deBock (eds.), *Mass Communication Review Yearbook*, Vol. 2. Newbury Park: Sage.

McCombs, M.E. and Becker, L.B. (1979) *Using Mass Communication Theory*. Englewood Cliffs: Prentice Hall.

McCombs, M.E. and Gilbert, S. (1986) "News Influence on Our Pictures of the World" in J. Bryant and D. Zillman (eds.), *Perspectives on Media Effects*. Hillsdale: Lawrence Erlbaum Assoc.

McCombs, M.E. and Shaw, D.L. (1972) "The Agenda-setting Function of the Media," *Public Opinion Quarterly* 36: 176–87.

McGuire, W.J. (1969) "The Nature of Attitudes and Attitude Change" in G. Lindsay and E. Aronson (eds.), *Handbook of Social Psychology*, Vol. 3. Reading: Addison-Wesley.

McGuire, W.J. (1984) "Public Communication as a Strategy for Inducing Health-promoting Behavior Change," *Preventive Medicine* 13: 299–319.

McGuire, W.J. (1989) "Theoretical Foundations of Campaigns" in R.E. Rice and C. Atkin (eds.), *Public Communication Campaigns*, 2nd ed. Newbury Park: Sage.

McLeod, J.M. and Reeves, B. (1981) "On the Nature of Mass Media Effects" in G.C. Wilhoit and H. deBock (eds.), *Mass Communication Review Yearbook*, Vol. 2. Newbury Park: Sage.

McQuail, D. (1969) "Uncertainty About Audience" in P. Halmos (ed.), *The Sociology of Mass Media Communicators*. Kiel: University of Kiel.

McQuail, D. (1984) *Communication*, 2nd ed. London: Longman.

McQuail, D. (1987) *Mass Communication Theory: An Introduction*, 2nd ed. London: Sage.

McQuail, D. and Windahl, S. (1983) *Communication Models for the Study of Mass Communication*. London: Sage.

McQuail, D., Blumler, J.G. and Brown, J. (1972) "The Television Audience: A Revised Perspective" in D. McQuail (ed.), *Sociology of Mass Communications*. Harmondsworth: Penguin.

Mendelsohn, H. (1973) "Some Reasons Why Information Campaigns Can Succeed," *Public Opinion Quarterly* 37: 50–61.

Merten, K. (1977) *Kommunikation: Eine Begriffs- und Prozessanalyse*. Opladen: Westdeutscher Verlag.

Merten, K. (1982) "Wirkungen der Massenkommunikation. Ein theoretisch-methodischer Problemaufriss," *Publizistik* 27: 26–48.

Merten, K. (1987) "Methoden der Wirkungsforschung" in Deutsche Forschungsgemeinschaft (ed.), *Medienwirkungsforschung in der Bundesrepublik Deutschland*. Weinheim: VCH Verlagsgesellschaft.

Merton, R.K. (1968) *Social Theory and Social Structure*. New York: Free Press.

Meyer, A.J., Maccoby, N. and Farquhar, J.W. (1977) "The Role of Opinion Leadership in a Cardiovascular Health Education Campaign" in B.D. Ruben (ed.), *Communication Yearbook*, Vol. 1. New Brunswick: Transaction Books.

Meyer, M. (ed.) (1982) *Gesundheitserziehung in Fernsehen und Hörfunk*. Munich: Saur.

Meyer, T.P. (1988) "On Mediated Communication Theory: The Rise of Format" in J.A. Anderson (ed.), *Communication Yearbook*, Vol. 11. Newbury Park: Sage.

Meyrowitz, J. (1985) *No Sense of Place: The Impact of the Electronic Media on Social Behavior*. New York: Oxford University Press.

Middleton, J. (ed.) (1980) *Approaches to Communication Planning*. Paris: UNESCO.

Milio, N. (1985) "Health Education = Health Instruction + Health News" in E. Rubinstein and J. Brown (eds.), *The Media, Social Science, and Social Policy for Children*. Norwood: Ablex.

Miller, G.R. (1986) "A Neglected Connection: Mass Media Exposure and Interpersonal Communicative Competency" in G. Gumpert and R. Cathcart (eds.), *Inter Media: Interpersonal Communication in a Media World*, 3rd ed. New York: Oxford University Press.

Miller, G.R. (1987) "Persuasion" in C.R. Berger and S.H. Chaffee (eds.), *Handbook of Communication Science*. Newbury Park: Sage.

Miller, G.R. and Knapp, M.L. (1985) "Background and Current Trends in the Study of Interpersonal Communication" in M.L. Knapp and G.R. Miller (eds.), *Handbook of Interpersonal Communication*. Newbury Park: Sage.

Mitchell, A. (1983) *The Nine American Lifestyles*. New York: Warner.

Monge, P.R. (1987) "The Network Level of Analysis" in C.R. Berger and S.H. Chaffee (eds.), *Handbook of Communication Science*. Newbury Park: Sage.

Monge, P.R. and Eisenberg, E.M. (1987) "Emergent Communication Networks" in F.M. Jablin, L.L. Putnam, K.H. Roberts and L.W. Porter (eds.), *Handbook of Organizational Communication*. Newbury Park: Sage.

Montgomery, K.C. (1989) *Target: Prime Time. Advocacy Groups and the Struggle over Entertainment Television*. New York: Oxford University Press.

Moreno, J.L. (1934) *Who Shall Survive? A New Approach to the Problem of Human Inter-relations*. Washington, DC: Nervous and Mental Diseases Publishing.

Mucchielli, R. (1974) *Kommunikation und Kommunikationsnetze*. Salzburg: Otto Müller Verlag. (Translated from the French, *Communication et Réseaux de Communications*. Paris: Les Editions ESF (n.d.).)

Myers, M.T. and Myers, G.E. (1982) *Managing by Communication: An Organizational Approach*. New York: McGraw-Hill.

Nerman, B. (1973) *Massmedierstorik*. Stockholm: Alqvist & Wiksell.

Newcomb, T. (1953) "Approach to the Study of Communicative Acts," *Psychological Review* 60: 393–404.

Newsom, D.A. (1983) "Conflict: Who Gets Media Attention and Why?" *Public Relations Review* 9(3): 35–59.

Noelle-Neumann, E. (1973) "Return to the Concept of Powerful Mass Media," *Studies of Broadcasting* 9: 67–112.

Noelle-Neumann, E. (1982) *Die Schweigespirale: Öffentliche Meinung – Unsere soziale Haut*. Frankfurt: Ullstein.

Noelle-Neumann, E., Schulz, W. and Wilke, J. (eds.) (1989) *Fischer-Lexikon Publizistik-Massenkommunikation*. Frankfurt: R.G. Fischer Taschenbuch.

Norberg, L., Palm, L. and Windahl, S. (eds.) (1985) *Om Samhällskommunikation*. Stockholm: Liber.

Nordenstreng, K. (1974) *Informational Mass Communication*. Helsinki: Tammi.

Nordenstreng, K. (1977) *Kommunikationsteori*. Stockholm: AWE/Gebers.

Nowak, K. (1977) "From Information Gaps to Communication Potential" in M. Berg, P. Hemanus, J. Ekecrantz, F. Mortensen and P. Sepstrup (eds.), *Current Theories in Scandinavian Mass Communication*. Grenaa: GMT.

Nowak, K. and Wärneryd, K.E. (1968) *Kommunikation och Åsiktsförändring*. Stockholm: Prisma.

O'Keefe, G. (1985) "Taking a Bite Out of Crime: The Impact of a Public Information Campaign," *Communication Research* 12: 147–78.

Österreichisches Jahrbuch für Kommunikationswissenschaft 1985. Vienna: Böhlau.

Ostgaard, E. (1965) "Factors Influencing the Flow of the News," *Journal of Peace Research* 1: 39–63.

O'Sullivan, T., Harley, J., Saunders, D. and Fiske, J. (1983) *Key Concepts in Communication*. London: Methuen.

Paisley, W. (1984) "Communication in the Communication Sciences" in B. Dervin and M.J. Voigt (eds.), *Progress in Communication Sciences*, Vol. 5. Norwood: Ablex.

Paisley, W. (1989) "Public Communication Campaigns: The American Experience" in R.E. Rice and C. Atkin (eds.), *Public Communication Campaigns*, 2nd ed. Newbury Park: Sage.

Paletz, D. L., Koon, J., Whitehead, E. and Hagens, R.B. (1972) "Selective Exposure: The Potential Boomerang Effect," *Journal of Communication* 22: 48–53.

Palm, L. and Windahl, S. (1984) "Kommunikationsteorin in Informationspraktiken" in L. Norberg et al. (eds.), *Om Samhällskommunikation*. Stockholm: Liber.

Palm, L. and Windahl, S. (1988) "Focus Groups – Some Suggestions," *Scandinavian Journal of Primary Health Care* 1: 91–7.

Palm, L. and Windahl, S. (1989) *Kommunikation – Teorin i Praktiken*. Uppsala: Konsultförlaget.

Palmgreen, P. and Rayburn, J.D. (1984) "A Comparison of Gratification Models of Satisfaction." Paper presented at the Association of Education in Journalism and Mass Communication Annual Conference in Gainesville, Florida.

Palmgreen, P. and Rayburn, J.D. (1985) "An Expectancy-Value Approach to Media Gratifications" in K.E. Rosengren, L.A. Werner and P. Palmgreen (eds.), *Media Gratifications Research: Current Perspectives*. Newbury Park: Sage.

Pavlik, J.V. (1987a) *Public Relations: What Research Tells Us*. Newbury Park: Sage.

Pavlik, J.V. (1987b) "Campaign Planning in Public Relations: Learning from the Minnesota Heart Health Program." Paper presented to the Association of Education in Journalism and Mass Communication, San Antonio, Texas.

Pavlik, J.V. and Salmon, C.T. (1984) "Theoretical Approaches in Public Relations Research," *Public Relations Research and Education* 1(2): 39–49.

Pearson, R. (1989) "Beyond Ethical Relativism in Public Relations: Coorientation, Rules and the Idea of Communication Symmetry" in J.E. Grunig and L.A. Grunig (eds.), *Public Relations Research Annual*, Vol. 1. Hillsdale: Lawrence Erlbaum Assoc.

Percy, L. and Rossiter, J. (1980) *Advertising Strategy: A Communication Theory Approach.* New York: Praeger.

Perloff, R.M. (1989) "Ego-Involvement and the Third Person Effect of Televised News Coverage," *Communication Research* 16: 236–62.

Peterson, R.A. (1983) "Patterns of Cultural Choice: A Prolegomenon," *American Behavioral Scientist* 26: 422–38.

Pfaff, M., Kistler, E., Schulze, H. and Theis, A. (1982) "Methoden und Kriterien zur Überprüfung des Erfolgs von Aufklärungskampagnen" in *Handbuch zur Durchführung von Wirkungsanalysen.* Cologne: Bundesanstalt für Strassenwesen.

Piätilä, V. (1977) "On the Effects of Mass Media: Some Conceptual Viewpoints" in M. Berg, P. Hemanus, J. Ekecrantz, F. Mortensen and P. Sepstrup (eds.), *Current Theories in Scandinavian Mass Communication Research.* Grenaa: GMT.

Pool, I.S. and Shulman, J. (1964) "Newsmen's Fantasies, Audiences and Newswriting" in L.A. Dexter and D.M. Wright (eds.), *People, Society, and Mass Communications.* New York: Free Press.

Prott, J. (1976) *Bewusstsein von Journalisten.* Frankfurt: Europäische Verlagsanstalt.

Puska, P. et al. (1985) "The Community-based Strategy to Prevent Coronary Heart Disease," *Annual Review of Public Health* 6: 147–93.

Radway, J. (1983) "Women Read the Romance: The Interaction of Text and Context," *Feminist Studies* 9: 53–78.

Radway, J. (1984a) "Interpretative Communities and Variable Literacies: The Functions of Romance Reading," *Daedalus* 113(3): 49–73.

Radway, J. (1984b) *Reading the Romance.* Chapel Hill: University of North Carolina Press.

Ray, M. (1973) "Marketing Communication and the Hierarchy of Effects" in P. Clarke (ed.), *New Models for Communication Research.* Newbury Park: Sage.

Reardon, K.K. (1987) *Interpersonal Communication: Where Minds Meet.* Belmont: Wadsworth.

Reardon, K.K. (1989) "The Potential Role of Persuasion in Adolescent AIDS Prevention" in R.E. Rice and C. Atkin (eds.), *Public Communication Campaigns*, 2nd ed. Newbury Park: Sage.

Reardon, K.K. and Rogers, E.M. (1988) "Interpersonal Versus Mass Media Communication: A False Dichotomy," *Human Communication Research* 15: 284–303.

Reich, R.B. (1987) *Tales of a New America.* New York: Times Books.

Reichmann, H. (1988) "Wirtschaftsjournalismus und unternehmerische Public Relations in Österreich." PhD dissertation, Salzburg University.

Rencksdorf, K. (1970) "Zur Hypotese des 'Two-step-flow' der Massenkommunikation," *Rundfunk und Fernsehen* 18: 314–31.

Rice, R.E. and Atkin, C. (eds.) (1989) *Public Communication Campaigns*, 2nd ed. Newbury Park: Sage.

Rice, R.E. and Richards, W.D., Jr. (1985) "An Overview of Network Analysis Methods and Programs" in B. Dervin and M.J. Voigt (eds.), *Progress in Communication Sciences*, Vol. 6. Norwood: Ablex.

Riley, M.W. and Riley, J.W. (1951) "A Sociological Approach to Communications Research," *Public Opinion Quarterly* 15: 445–60.

Riley, M.W. and Riley, J.W. (1959) "Mass Communication and the Social System" in R.K. Merton, L. Broom and L.S. Cottrell (eds.), *Sociology Today: Problems and Prospects.* New York: Harper.

Robinson, J.P. (1976) "Interpersonal Influence in Election Campaigns: Two-step-flow Hypothesis," *Public Opinion Quarterly* 40: 304–19.

Roeh, I. and Ashley, S. (1986) "Criticizing Press Coverage of the War in Lebanon: Toward a Paradigm of News as Storytelling" in M.L. McLaughlin (ed.), *Communication Yearbook*, Vol. 9. Newbury Park: Sage.

Rogers, C. (1979) "The Foundation of the Person-centered Approach," *Education* 100: 98–107.

Rogers, E.M. (1973) *Communication Strategies for Family Planning.* New York: Free Press.

Rogers, E.M. (1976) "Communication and Development: The Passing of a Dominant Paradigm," *Communication Research* 3: 213–40.

Rogers, E.M. (1978) "The Rise and Fall of the Dominant Paradigm," *Journal of Communication* 28: 64–9.

Rogers, E.M. (1983) *Diffusion of Innovations.* New York: Free Press.

Rogers, E.M. (1986) *Communication Technology: The New Media in Society.* New York: Free Press.

Rogers, E.M. (1987) "The Diffusion of Innovation Perspective" in N.D. Weinstein (ed.), *Taking Care, Understanding and Encouraging Self-protective Behavior.* Cambridge: Cambridge University Press.

Rogers, E.M. (1988) "Information Technologies: How Organizations are Changing" in G.M. Goldhaber and G.A. Barnett (eds.), *Handbook of Organizational Communication.* Norwood: Ablex.

Rogers, E.M. and Balle, F. (1985) "Introduction to Communication Research in Europe and America" in E.M. Rogers and F. Balle (eds.), *The Media Revolution in America and Western Europe.* Norwood: Ablex.

Rogers, E.M. and Bhowmik, D.K. (1970) "Homophily–Heterophily: Relational Concepts for Communication Research," *Public Opinion Quarterly* 34: 523–38.

Rogers, E.M. and Dearing, J.W. (1988) "Agenda-setting Research: Where It Has Been, Where It Is Going" in J.A. Anderson (ed.), *Mass Communication Review Yearbook,* Vol. 11. Newbury Park: Sage.

Rogers, E.M. and Kincaid, D.L. (1981) *Communication Networks: Toward a Paradigm for Research.* New York: Free Press.

Rogers, E.M. and Rogers, R.A. (1976) *Communication in Organizations.* New York: Free Press.

Rogers, E.M. and Shoemaker, F. (1971) *Communication of Innovations,* 2nd ed. New York: Free Press.

Rogers, E.M. and Storey, J.D. (1987) "Communication Campaigns" in C.R. Berger and S.H. Chaffee (eds.), *Handbook of Communication Science.* Newbury Park: Sage.

Rogers, E.M., Aikat, S., Chang, S., Poppe, P. and Sopory, P. (1989) *Proceedings from the Conference on Entertainment–Education for Social Change.* Los Angeles, CA: Annenberg School of Communications, University of Southern California.

Rohner, R.P. (1984) "Toward a Conception of Culture for Cross-Cultural Psychology," *Journal of Cross-Cultural Psychology* 15: 111–38.

Rosengren, K.E. (1981a) "Mass Communications as Cultural Indicators: Sweden 1945–1975" in G.C. Wilhoit and H. deBock (eds.), *Mass Communication Review Yearbook,* Vol. 2. Newbury Park: Sage.

Rosengren, K.E. (1981b) *Advances in Content Analysis.* Newbury Park: Sage.

Rosengren, K.E. (1985) "Media Linkages between Culture and Other Societal Systems" in M. McLaughlin (ed.), *Communication Yearbook,* Vol. 9. Newbury Park: Sage.

Rosengren, K.E. and Windahl, S. (1972) "Mass Media Consumption as a Functional Alternative" in D. McQuail (ed.), *Sociology of Mass Communication.* Harmondsworth: Penguin.

Rühl, M. (1975) "Zum Problem der Popularisierung einer speziellen Thematik öffentlicher Kommunikation: Beispiel Arbeiterrentversicherung," *Geistliches Leben* 9.

Ryan, J. and Peterson, R.A. (1982) "The Product Image" in J.S. Ettema and D.C. Whitney (eds.), *Individuals in Mass Media Organizations.* Newbury Park: Sage.

Schenk, M.E. (1983) "Das Konzept des sozialen Netzwerke" in F. Neidhardt (ed.), "Gruppensoziologie," special issue of *Kölner Zeitschrift für Soziologie und Sozialpsychologie* 25: 88–104.

Schenk, M.E. (1984) *Soziale Netzwerke und Kommunikation.* Tübingen: Mohr.

Schenk, M.E. (1985) "Politische Meinungsführer: Kommunikationsverhalten und primäre Umwelt," *Publizistik* 30: 7–16.

Schenk, M.E. (1987) *Medienwirkungsforschung.* Tübingen: Mohr.

Schmidtchen, G. (1979) "Gesundheitsforschung und Öffentlichkeit," *Pharma Forum* 11: 5–18.

Schneider, L.A. (aka L. Grunig) (1985a) "The Role of Public Relations in Four Organizational Types," *Journalism Quarterly* 62: 567–76, 594.

Schneider, L.A. (1985b) "Public Relations and Environmental Niches: An Analysis of Organizational Communication and its Relationship to the Hage–Hull Typology of Organizational Structure." Paper presented to the International Communication Association, Honolulu, Hawaii.

Schnoor, P. and Tybjaerg-Hansen, A. (1976) "A Blood Pressure Information Campaign Including Mass Screening for Hypertension in Copenhagen Supermarkets," *Acta Medica Scandinavica* 199: 269–72.

Schönbach, K. (1981) "Agenda-setting im Europawahlkampf 1979: Die Funktion von Presse und Fernsehen," *Mediaperspektiven* 7: 537–47.

Schramm, W. (1954) *The Process and Effects of Mass Communication*. Urbana: University of Illinois Press.

Schramm, W. (1955) "Information Theory and Mass Communication," *Journalism Quarterly* 32: 131–46.

Schramm, W. (1964) *Mass Media and National Development: The Role of Information in Developing Countries*. Paris: UNESCO.

Schramm, W. (1977) *Little Media, Big Media: Tools and Technologies for Instruction*. Newbury Park: Sage.

Schroeder, K. (1987) "De Hellige Köers Krise" in E. Fabricius-Jensen and R. Pittelkow (eds.), *Det Ukente Publikum*. Copenhagen.

Schroeder, K. (1988) "Dynasty in Denmark: Toward a Social Semiotic of the Media Audience," *Nordicom Review* 1: 6–13.

Schulz, W. (1987) "Wirkungsmodelle der Medienwirkungsforschung" in Deutsche Forschungsgemeinschaft (ed.), *Medienwirkungsforschung in der Bundesrepublik Deutschland*. Weinheim: VCH Verlagsgesellschaft.

Schuurman, J. and de Haes, W. (1980) "Sexually Transmitted Diseases: Health Education by Telephone," *International Journal of Education* 23: 94–106.

Schweizerischer Nationalfonds (ed.) (1982) *Prophylaxe von Herz-Kreislauf-Krankheiten in der Schweiz*. Bern: Verlag Paul Haupt.

Scott, W.G. (1967) *Organizational Theory*. Homewood, IL: Irwin.

Severin, W.J. (with J.W. Tankred) (1988) *Communication Theories: Origin, Methods, Use*, 2nd ed. New York: Longman.

Shaw, D.L. (1977) "The Press Agenda in a Community Setting" in D.L. Shaw and M.E. McCombs (eds.), *The Emergence of American Public Issues: The Agenda-setting Function of the Press*. St Paul, MN: West.

Shelby, A.N. (1986) "Issues Management: A New Direction for Public Relations Professionals." Paper presented to the International Communication Association, Chicago.

Siegelman, L. (1973) "Reporting of the News: An Organizational Analysis," *American Journal of Sociology* 79: 132–51.

Signitzer, B (1988a) "Public Relations and Public Diplomacy: Some Theoretical Considerations on International PR from an Austrian Perspective." Paper presented to the International Communication Association, New Orleans.

Signitzer, B. (1988b) "Public Relations-Forschung im Überblick," *Publizistik* 33: 92–116.

Silbermann, A. and Krüger, U.M. (1973) *Soziologie der Massenkommunikation*. Stuttgart: Kohlhammer.

Singhal, A. (1990) "Entertainment–Education Communication Strategies for Development." PhD dissertation. Los Angeles: University of Southern California.

Singhal, A. and Rogers, E.M. (1989) "Prosocial Television for Development in India" in R.E. Rice and C. Atkin (eds.), *Public Communication Campaigns*, 2nd ed. Newbury Park: Sage.

Singletary, M.W. and Stone, G. (1988) *Communication Theory and Research Applications*. Ames: Iowa State University Press.

Smith, D.H. (1989) "Studying Health Communication: An Agenda for the Future," *Health Communication* 1: 17–27.

Smith, W.R. (1956) "Product Differentiation and Market Segmentation as Alternative Product Strategies," *Journal of Marketing* 21: 3–8.

Solomon, D.S. (1982) "Health Campaigns on Television" in D. Pearl, L. Bouthilet and J. Lazar (eds.), *Television and Behavior: Ten Years of Scientific Progress and Implications for the Eighties*, Vol. 2, Technical Reports. Rockville: National Institute of Mental Health.

Solomon, D.S. (1989) "A Social Marketing Perspective on Communication Campaigns" in R.E. Rice and C. Atkin (eds.), *Public Communication Campaigns*, 2nd ed. Newbury Park: Sage.

Solomon, D.S. and Cardillo, B. (1985) "The Elements and Process of Communication Campaigns" in T.A. van Dijk (ed.), *Discourse and Communication: New Approaches to the Analysis of Mass Media Discourse and Communication*. Berlin: De Gruyter.

Staehle, W. (1987) *Management: Eine verhaltenswissenschaftliche Einführung*, 3rd ed. Munich: Vahlen.

Stark, R. (1962) "Policy and the Pros: An Organizational Analysis of a Metropolitan Newspaper," *Berkeley Journal of Sociology* 1: 11–32.

Stempel, G.H. (1989) "Content Analysis" in G.H. Stempel and B.H. Westley (eds.), *Research Methods in Mass Communication*. 2nd ed. Englewood Cliffs: Prentice Hall.

Stocking, S.H. (1985) "Effects of Public Relations Efforts on Media Visibility of Organizations," *Journalism Quarterly* 62: 358–66.

Stockinger-Ehrnstorfer, K. (1980) *Der Leserbrief*. Salzburg: Landespressebüro.

Stotz, G. (1987) "Ist Massenkommunikation überhaupt Kommunikation?" *Sehen-Hören-Bilden* 25(146): 199–204.

Strid, I. (1988) *Svenska Folkets Intressen 1973–1982*. Göteborg: Avdelningen for Masskommunikation.

Suchman, E. (1967) *Evaluative Research*. New York: Russell Sage Foundation.

Thayer, L. (1986) "On the Mass Media and Mass Communication: Notes Toward a Theory" in G. Gumpert and R. Cathcart (eds.), *Inter Media: Interpersonal Communication in a Media World*, 3rd ed. New York: Oxford University Press.

Theodorson, S.A. and Theodorson, G.R. (1969) *A Modern Dictionary of Sociology*. New York: Crowell.

Thomas, W. (1986) "Mass Media and the Social Order" in G. Gumpert and R. Cathcart (eds.), *Inter Media: Interpersonal Communication in a Media World*, 3rd ed. New York: Oxford University Press.

Thompson, J.D. (1967) *Organizations in Action*. New York: McGraw-Hill.

Thunberg, A., Nowak, K., Rosengren, K.E. and Sigurd, B. (1982) *Communication and Equality: A Swedish Perspective*. Stockholm: Almquist & Wicksell.

Tichenor, P.J., Olien, C. and Donohue, G. (1970) "Mass Media and the Differential Growth in Knowledge," *Public Opinion Quarterly* 34: 158–70.

Trenaman, J.S.M. and McQuail, D. (1961) *Television and the Political Image*. London: Longman.

Troldahl, V.C. (1966) "A Field Test of Modified Two-step-flow of Communication Model," *Public Opinion Quarterly* 30: 609–23.

Tuchman, G. (1973) *Making News: A Study in the Construction of Reality*. New York: Free Press.

Tunstall, J. (1971) *Journalists at Work*. London: Constable.

Turk, J.V. (1985) "Information Subsidies and Influence," *Public Relations Review* 11(3): 10–25.

Turk, J.V. and Franklin, B. (1987) "Information Subsidies: Agenda-setting Traditions," *Public Relations Review* 13(4): 29–41.

Vacin, G.L. (1965) "A Study of Letter-writers," *Journalism Quarterly* 42: 464–65.

Van de Ven, A.H. and Rogers, E.M. (1988) "Innovations and Organizations: Critical Perspectives," *Communication Research* 15: 632–51.

VanLeuven, J.K. (1986) "A Planning Matrix for Message Design, Channel Selection and Scheduling." Paper presented to the Association for Education in Journalism and Mass Communication, Norman, Oklahoma.

Vidmar, N. and Rokeach, M. (1974) "Archie Bunker's Bigotry: A Study of Selective Perception and Exposure," *Journal of Communication* 24: 36–47.

von Bertalanffy, L. (1969) *General System Theory: Foundations, Development, Applications*, 2nd ed. New York: Braziller.

Wakefield, G. and Krider, D. (1988) "Theories, Models and Proficiencies for Public Relations Campaigns." Paper presented to the Speech Communication Association, New Orleans.

Waldahl, R. (1989) *Mediepåvirkning*. Oslo: ad Notam.

Wallack, L.M. (1981) "Mass Media Campaigns: The Odds Against Finding Behavior Change," *Health Education Quarterly* 8: 209–60.

Ward, S. (1987) "Consumer Behavior" in C.R. Berger and S.H. Chaffee (eds.), *Handbook of Communication Science*. Newbury Park: Sage.

Watzlawick,P., Beavin, J. and Jackson, D.D. (1967) *Pragmatics of Human Communication*. New York: Norton.

Weaver, D. and Elliott, S.N. (1985) "Who Sets the Agenda for the Media: A Study of Local Agenda-building," *Journalism Quarterly* 62: 87–94.

Weaver, D. and Wilhoit, C.G. (1986) *The American Journalist*. Bloomington: University of Indiana Press.

Webster, F. (1975) "Social Marketing: What Makes It Different?" *Management Decision* 13: 70–77.

Weiman, G. (1982) "On the Importance of Marginality: One More Step into the Two-step Flow of Communication," *American Sociological Review* 47: 764–73.

Weinstein, J.D. (ed.) (1987) *Taking Care, Understanding and Encouraging Self-protective Behavior*. Cambridge: Cambridge University Press.

Weiss, C. (1972) *Evaluating Research: Methods for Assessing Program Effectiveness*. Englewood Cliffs: Prentice Hall.

Weiss, H.-J. (1982) "Die Wahlkampfberichterstattung und Kommentierung von Fernsehen und Tagespresse zum Bundeswahlkampf 1980," *Media Perspektiven* 4: 263–75.

Wersig, G. (1974) *Information-Kommunikation-Dokumentation*. Darmstadt: Wissenschaftliche Buchgesellschaft.

Westley, B. (1971) "Communication and Social Change," *American Behavioral Scientist* 14: 719–42.

Westley, B. and MacLean, M. (1957) "A Conceptual Model for Mass Communication Research," *Journalism Quarterly* 34: 31–8.

White, D.M. (1950) "The Gate-keeper: A Case Study in the Selection of News," *Journalism Quarterly* 27: 383–90.

Whitney, D.C. (1982) "Mass Communicator Studies" in J.S. Ettema and D.C. Whitney (eds.), *Individuals in Mass Media Organizations*. Newbury Park: Sage.

Wiebe, G.D. (1951) "Merchandising Commodities and Citizenship on Television," *Public Opinion Quarterly* 15: 679–91.

Wiio, O.A. (1985) "The Basic Concepts of Communication and Information" in E.M. Rogers and F. Balle (eds.), *The Media Revolution in America and Western Europe*. Norwood: Ablex.

Wiio, O.A. (1988) "Organizational Communication: Contingent Views" in G.M. Goldhaber and G.A. Barnett (eds.), *Handbook of Organizational Communication*. Norwood: Ablex.

Wilensky, H.L. (1964) "The Professionalization of Everyone?" *American Journal of Sociology* 70: 137–58.

Wilson, G.L., Goodall, H.L. and Waagen, C.L. (1986) *Organizational Communication*. New York: Harper & Row.

Windahl, S. (1975) *Professionella Kommunikatörer*. Lund: Studentlitteratur.

Windahl, S. (1981) "Uses and Gratifications at the Crossroads" in G.C. Wilhoit and H. deBock (eds.), *Mass Communication Review Yearbook*, Vol. 2. Newbury Park: Sage.

Windahl, S. (1989) *Kommunikation och AIDS – Några Problemområden*. Stockholm: Socialdepartementet.

Winick, C. and Winick, M. (1976) "Drug Education and the Content of the Mass Media Dealing with 'Dangerous Drugs' and Alcohol" in R. Ostman (ed.), *Communication Research and Drug Education*. Newbury Park: Sage.

Winkelman, M. (1987) "Their Aim is True," *Public Relations Journal* 43(8): 18–23.

Wright, C.R. (1986) *Mass Communication: A Sociological Perspective*, 3rd ed. New York: Random House.

Zablocki, B.D. and Kanter, R.M. (1976) "The Differentiation of Lifestyles," *Annual Review of Sociology* 2: 269–97.

Index